The
Novel
as Faith

The
Novel
as Faith

Gambit
INCORPORATED
Boston
1973

THE GOSPEL ACCORDING TO JAMES,
HARDY, CONRAD, JOYCE, LAWRENCE
AND VIRGINIA WOOLF

by
John Paterson

First printing

Copyright © 1973 by John Paterson

All rights reserved including the right to reproduce
this book or parts thereof in any form

Library of Congress Catalogue Card Number: 74–137016

International Standard Book Number: 0–87645–075–3

Printed in the United States of America

For Susanna
and the Children

Contents

Introduction   ix

1 Henry James: The Romance of the Real 3

2 Thomas Hardy: The Faithful Imagination 40

3 Joseph Conrad: To Make You See 69

4 James Joyce: It's All Won 107

5 D. H. Lawrence: The One Bright Book of Life 143

6 Virginia Woolf: Fire in the Mist 184

7 Epilegomena: The Single Vision 230

Chapter Notes 295

Index 341

Introduction

The period from the first publications of James and Hardy to the last publications of Joyce and Mrs. Woolf surely represents the most conscious and self-conscious period in the history of English fiction. It measures the time when novels first became aware of themselves as major forms of literary expression, when novelists first felt free to take themselves seriously as artists on a par with poets and dramatists. Never before were they more articulate on the special nature of their common trade, never before more willing to make, in essay and preface, in memoir and letter, a fuller and more sophisticated statement of their feeling for the form they had elected.

Some, it's true, were less willing than others. Hardy was so indifferent to novels and novel-writing that he had very little to say about them and that very little he said with a disconcerting lack of enthusiasm. Joyce meditated on the mysteries of his craft or art as a very young man but he increasingly studied, as time went by, the secrecy, the reserve, that his own Stephen Dedalus had chosen. The sullen silence of a Hardy, the cunning silence of a Joyce, were hardly typical, however. In the more than fifty years of his exemplary life, James descanted long and lovingly on the fundamentals of his form and in the sadly shorter span of his, Lawrence descanted upon them with a passion and insight that matched the master's. Even more professionally the "scholar" of the novel than they were, Virginia Woolf left behind her a body of practical and theoretical criticism that defines, with extraordinary fullness, her idea of the art. The autocratic Conrad would doubtless have preferred, like Joyce, to keep his silence on the subject, but even he would deliver himself, however reluctantly, of a sufficiently coherent theory of fiction.

Hence this book. By reconstructing the assumptions of the six novelists who seem to have dominated their time and place, it hopes to reveal at once the various principles of form that separated them from each other and the essential principles of the form that united them and made them one.

Not that they provide us with a complete and systematic aesthetic of prose fiction. No one—not even a James or Virginia Woolf—offers us the convenience of a particular locus—a book, an essay, a preface—in which a theory of the novel is fully and elaborately expounded. No one, for that matter, offers us a theory of fiction entirely consistent with his practice of it. Conrad may have believed that a novel should derive from the author's own personal knowledge or experience, but this didn't prevent him from writing *Nostromo* and *The Secret Agent* and *Under Western Eyes*, novels on people and places that, by his own admission, he had no knowledge or experience of. Indeed no one—not James and Mrs. Woolf and not, certainly, Conrad and Lawrence—acts upon a consistent aesthetic of the novel, upon an aesthetic that doesn't change in time and contradict itself in time. It would even be hard to say that they conceive a theory that shows a logical development in time. This is doubtless because

they were artists first and aestheticians only second. But it
was also because the novel as they saw it was by its very
nature a community of contradictions. It was the special
form of fiction that it was, precisely for the reason that it
united the polarities that described both life itself and the
art that imitated it. As the representational form of forms,
it couldn't be this thing or that; it had to be everything. As
the representational artist of artists, the novelist couldn't
approach life this way or that, from one angle or another;
he had to approach it every way, from all angles at once.

Hence the complications, the contrarieties, in his notions of the novel. It had on the one hand to be written
dispassionately; it had on the other to be written passionately. It was the product on the one hand of a conscious
process; it was the product on the other of an unconscious
process. It had on the one hand to be written, not lived; it
had on the other to be lived, not written. Hardly any of
the novelists considered here failed to oscillate from time
to time between these and other polar positions. Was
Conrad the artist as Apollonian who believed that the
novel should be written with a conscious intention and a
steady mind? He was. But he was also the artist as
Dionysian who believed with Lawrence that it should also
be written from the deeps or darks of his unconscious life.
Was Lawrence the artist as Dionysian who believed that
the novel should be written in an ecstasy of unconscious
emotion? He was. But he was also the artist as Apollonian
who believed with Conrad that in ecstasy and ecstasy
alone there was no truth. Indeed, were they not all, Hardy
and Lawrence excepted, disciples of Flaubert and devotees
of the life of art? They were. But they were also, all of
them, James and Conrad, Joyce and Mrs. Woolf included,
as intensely skeptical as any Lawrence of the artist as
genius, seemed, like Lawrence, more interested in the art

of life than in the life of art, and made as little as he did of that mastery of craft and technique so dear to Flaubert and his men.

Accordingly, the book that follows is to some extent a purely manufactured article. In the first six chapters that define the theories of the individual novelists and in the final chapter that defines the relations (and disrelations) between them, it makes no attempt to organize the aesthetic ideas in terms of their relations to the novels themselves or in terms of their chronological development or in terms of some principle of coherence that applies to one author and not to another. The approach is almost wholly theoretical and abstract. In each chapter, the book explores first their sense of the novel as representation; next, its opposite or contradiction, their sense of the novel as something beyond representation; then, finally, their adjustment of the oppositions and contradictions, their sense of the unitary nature of the one and the other, of the representational and the nonrepresentational. The result is, inevitably and perhaps unhappily, repetition both in structure and in language. But insofar as it was inevitable, it was, I like to think, unavoidable. And if, in its rage for order, the book makes too much of the sameness of the many, it doesn't, I hope, neglect those differences and distinctions, without which no sameness is possible.

For their support and encouragement I am profoundly grateful to my good colleagues, James D. Hart, Josephine Miles and Mark Schorer.

JOHN PATERSON
Berkeley, California

The
Novel
as Faith

Henry James, 1843–1916. Portrait by E. O. Hopper, 1921. (*The Bettmann Archive*)

1 Henry James:
The Romance of the Real

It's not for nothing that James has been honored as the high priest of the novel, as the great custodian of its prestige and privilege. Few novelists in the history of the art could have practiced it longer and more lovingly, could have known and experienced it more intimately. No one, certainly, thought longer and more conscientiously about it or reflected more eloquently upon its reach and its range. This immense sympathy for his form was in part an aspect of his provincialism, of his intellectual innocence. Having only a poorly developed sense of history, feeling nothing of that veneration for the literature of antiquity that imposed itself on the most educated men of his time, he wasn't affected by the ancient prejudice against fiction in prose, wasn't deflected by the argument that poetry ruled supreme in the great republic of letters and that the novel was only a second-class citizen. For the same reason he wasn't oppressed by the sense that the novel had continuities with and obligations to the traditional literary forms, to tragedy and comedy, to epic and romance. Ignorant of or indifferent to the past and its monuments, he was free to see it as an entirely new thing in the world, as a unique and integral form without precedent in literary history.

I

The condition for James of the novel's originality was that it sought to compete with science and history, to register in literary form those empirical modes of knowing and thinking that had revolutionized man's sense of what was real and how to describe it. For the novelist as for the scientist and historian, reality eluded the *a priori* explanations of theological and metaphysical thinkers. For him as for them, reality was that which objectified itself in sensuous or sensible forms, in forms available alone to the human senses and sensations. For him as for them, the whole duty of life and art was to bear true and faithful witness to the world's substantial and objective reality, to know it and show it without the wilful prearrangements of traditional theologians and professional philosophers. "In proportion as . . . we see life *without* rearrangement," James said, "do we feel that we are touching the truth; in proportion as we see it *with* rearrangement do we feel that we are being put off with a substitute, a compromise and convention." The special mission of the novel was, precisely, to see and show life without rearrangement. It was to render "the real on the scale of the real," to be realistic or representational in a fashion hitherto unattempted in art and literature. "The most fundamental and general sign of the novel" was, James proposed, the "effort at *representation*," the "closeness of [its] relation [to life]."

It followed that the novelist had to be less the priest or the philosopher than the detached and disinterested observer of things. When reality was recorded from the standpoint of an *a priori* religious system or metaphysical theory, it was only the theory or the system that got recorded, not the reality. "Method and system . . . [had] spread so far from center to circumference," James complained of Zola, "that they ended by being almost the only thing we feel." In the work of Balzac, on the other hand, "religion, morals, politics, economics, esthetics . . . [were] as systematic matter . . . quite secondary and subservient." That novelist was most the novelist, James intimated, when he approached and described the world, as Hawthorne had, "with very few convictions or theories of any kind."

If the philosopher brought too much mind to bear upon the world as object, the poet brought too much passion or personality to bear upon it. The poet was a poet just because he expressed *himself*, felt the world as a form of his feeling or fancy; but the novelist was the novelist because he expressed the world rather than himself, refused to dissolve it in the fires of an excited or exasperated sensibility. "The Poet is most the Poet . . ." James put it, "when he speaks . . . most directly from his individual heart . . . It is not the *image* of life that he thus expresses . . . so much as his own intimate, essential states and feelings. By the time he has begun . . . to tell stories, to represent scenes . . . he is well on the way not to be the Poet pure and simple. . . . The lyrical element is not great . . . in Balzac, in Scott . . . nor in Thackeray, nor in Dickens—which is precisely why they are so essentially novelists . . . It *is* great . . . in such a writer as George Sand—which is doubtless why we take her for a novelist in a much looser sense than the others." The novelist was required, then, to be every bit as skeptical of the poet's imagination as the scientist and historian. For the realist of life and literature, it was obviously better to have too little imagination than too much. Dickens's misfortune was that he had too much, so that his characters became, as in *Our Mutual Friend*, "mere bundle[s] of eccentri-

cities, animated by no principle of nature whatever."
Trollope's good fortune, on the other hand, was that "his
imagination [had] no light of its own," so that he could
describe the life around him "without any of those artistic
perversions that come . . . from a powerful imagination."
As James conceived him, the novelist wasn't invited to
imagine what life and observation couldn't verify, wasn't
invited to invent or improvise in the promiscuous fashion
of the ancient poets and makers. His business was rather to
regard the world with the sanity and sobriety of the
scientist-historian. Not ordinarily an admirer of H. G.
Wells, James could nevertheless commend him for having
seen his lower class subject "in its *own* strong light," for
having "handled its vulgarity in so scientific and historic a
spirit."

For the novelist, in other words, the key to reality was
the particular, sensuous fact constituted by the world
itself. When life was really represented, what stood out
wasn't the philosopher's program or the poet's passion but
the concrete reality of things and objects, the reality
accessible alone to the human senses and sensations.
Particularizing, "solidity of specification," James accordingly celebrated as "the supreme virtue of a novel." Balzac
was so very much the master of his form because this
supreme virtue "it was his greatness to carry further and
apply more consistently than any member of the craft." In
more problematic novelists like Meredith and Stevenson,
on the other hand, this supreme virtue was absent: failing
to condense "either into audible or into visible reality,"
their work lacked "solidity of specification," didn't derive
from or appeal to the senses and sensations.

Reality wasn't all fact and no form, however. It wasn't
just the *sum* of the world's things. It was an effect of the
relations of these things to each other. To be a novelist, to
see one's subject "in the light of science," was accordingly

to see it "in the light of the bearing of all its parts on each other." It was, like scientist and historian, to define the causal and other connections between people, places, events, feelings, furniture, etc., and so define the infinite relatedness that expressed the character of life itself. If Balzac seemed to James the very prince of novelists, it wasn't only that he went in "for detail, circumstance and specification"; it was also that he "proposed to himself *all* the connections of every part of his matter and the full total of the parts."

For the novelist, then, reality was by definition comprehended by the categories of time and space. The world of epic and tragedy, romance and allegory, might be unaffected by temporal and spatial realities, might be subject to the miraculous interventions of the supernatural and the superhuman. But the world of the novel was the purely secular world of physical appearances, of time and space, where all things had their relations, their causes and effects, their reasons and explanations. The traditional makers of fiction could ignore the influence of time and history on human affairs; but the novelist could do so only at the risk of undermining the representational authority of his picture. Unless "the lapse of time, the duration of the subject," is accounted for, James insisted, "nothing else really is." *The Ambassadors* should be read at the rate of five pages a day, he suggested, because "all the drawing-out the reader can contribute helps a little perhaps the production of that spell." Life wasn't only the creature of time, however. It was also the creature of *the* time, of a *particular* time and place. In their passion for the universal, for a single and unchanging order of things, the ancient artificers of fiction had rendered life independently of its position in time and space. But for the novelist it was "absurd to say that there [was] . . . only one reality of things." For him there were as many realities as there were points in time and space. His proper study wasn't, therefore, like Homer's or Shakespeare's, the eternal, the immortal, "the hours and spots over the edge of time and space." It was, rather, like Turgenev's, "the world of the relations life throws up at every hour and on every spot." The measure of Meredith's failure was thus, said James, that his fiction was "incapable of precise location anywhere in space or time." But the measure of George Eliot's success was just that hers was a "great placed and timed prose fiction."

Not any intersection of time and space would do. Some intersections were more providential for the novelist than others. Where life failed to solidify itself in a rich and full social experience, where it failed to objectify itself in a complexity of social forms and customs, it couldn't provide the novelist with that precious fund of specific realities without which he could have no standing as scientist or historian. He could only represent life where life had already represented itself. He could only objectify life where life had already objectified itself. A writer like Stevenson, more romancer than novelist, more eager to imagine experience than to represent it, could wilfully reject the social world, "the shoddy sham world of cities, clubs and colleges;" but to do so, said James, was to miss life in its fullest and most objective form. It was, indeed, to miss life altogether. As James conceived it, social life was by definition life itself. It constituted all that man could really know, ascertain, prove. Men were what they were not by virtue of their invisible and unverifiable relations to God or Fate or the Universe but by virtue of their visible and verifiable relations to each other. "Experience, as I see it," James said, "is our apprehension and our measure of what happens to us as social creatures." The English novelists he accordingly preferred to their French

and continental cousins precisely because they chose to
deal with man "on his social and gregarious side."

The novelist had of course to be lucky. He had to be
lucky enough to be born at the right time and in the right
place, a time and place that offered him a rich supply of
social facts and forms. Balzac had been lucky. In the
"monarchical and hierarchal and ecclesiastical" France of
his time, he'd inherited a "mass of social phenomena the
most rounded and registered . . . and thereby most
exposed to systematic observation and portrayal, that the
world [had] seen." But Dickens hadn't been as lucky. If he
had imagined and invented more than he could observe
and verify, it may have been, James considered, because he
had to—because the social coherence of his English world
had begun to deteriorate, "the fatal fusions and uniformities inflicted on our newer generations" already destroying
"those inherent oppositions from type to type, in which
drama most naturally resides." The unluckiest novelist of
all, however, was the novelist in America, the novelist
whose "simple, democratic, thinly-composed society" was
poor in those objective correlatives so necessary to representational form. James's friend Howells could argue that
the social life wasn't everything, that the poverty of life in
America wasn't necessarily fatal to the future of its
novelists. But for Henry James such an argument was
unacceptable. "It is on manners, customs, usages, habits
. . . that a novelist lives . . ." he declared, "and in saying
that in the absence of those 'dreary and worn-out paraphernalia . . . we have simply the whole of human life
left,' you beg (to my sense) the question. I should say we
had just so much less of it as these same 'paraphernalia'
represent."

It wasn't enough, either, that the novelist address
himself to the reality of a specific time and place. He had

also to address himself to the reality of his *own* time and place. Such a reality comprised after all the only reality he knew or could know. James accordingly rejected the historical novel, the novel that groped for its material in a misty and mysterious past where facts and figures were hard to come by. "You may multiply the little facts that can be got from pictures and documents, relics and prints as much as you like," he reminded Sarah Orne Jewett after reading *The Tory Lover*, "*the* real thing is almost impossible to do." "Go back to the dear country of the Pointed Firs," he urged her, "*come* back to the palpable present *intimate*." It was also necessary to record the author's individual sense of the here and the now. Life had a habit of altering its shape from time to time and from place to place; but it also had a habit of altering its shape from witness to witness. The value of the novel was, accordingly, that having no dominating formal character of its own, enjoying "a luxurious independence of rules and restrictions," it made provision, as the traditional literary forms did not, for the individual artist's own unique appreciation of things. "Any form of the novel," James declared with Maupassant, "[was] simply a vision of the world from the standpoint of a person constituted after a certain fashion." It was just for this reason that James insisted so steadily on a total freedom as a fundamental condition of the novel's continuing prosperity. He had partly in mind the aggressive Victorian censorship that would rule out of bounds "whole categories of manners, whole corpuscular classes and provinces, museums of character and condition." But he had equally in mind the more subtle kind of censorship that would restrict this most experimental and adventuresome of forms to the duplication of past precedents and achievements. To say with a writer like Stevenson or a critic like Sir Walter Besant that novels were about stories and adventures, that they should have nothing to do with matters of motive and psychology, was to have them follow not life but literature. It was to condemn them to "the loose and thin material that keeps reappearing in forms at once ready-made and sadly the worse for wear." The novel couldn't imitate itself because life itself didn't. It must be free to change constantly because life itself changed constantly. It wasn't for nothing, then, that the novel was called the novel. Its status as the literary form of realism was utterly dependent on its news, its newness, its novel-ty. Like the science or history with which it would compete, it had to declare its independence of traditional values and verdicts. It had to declare its right to report life as it was seen and felt by some single individual who remained uncorrupted by literature and convention.

II

James's concept of the novel's form derived from his sense of its sheer representationalism. Whatever made for a simple schematization of things he accordingly denounced. The novelist had necessarily to select his facts, his particulars; but he couldn't afford to be *too* selective. Life wasn't one thing or another; it was all things acting together in all their infinite relations and ramifications. To register one particular phenomenon to the total exclusion of all other phenomena was to offend, therefore, against the representational, was to bring the novel down "from its large, free character of an immense and exquisite correspondence with life." Hence James's lively opposition not only to the Besants and Stevensons who would limit the novel to themes of love and war but also to the Stendhals and D'Annunzios who would limit it to themes of sexual passion. "The effect . . . of the undertaking to give *passione* its whole place," James reported gloomily, "is that . . . no place speedily appears to be left for anything else; and the effect of that in turn is greatly to modify . . . the truth of things."

James objected even more strenuously to the habit of allegory. Regarding the world not from the standpoint of empirical science but from that of moral or religious philosophy, allegory adjusted things to the shape of a pattern and so offered a theory instead of a representation of them. Balzac was archetypally the novelist, said James, because he wasn't tempted by allegory. Consulting "the palpable, provable world before him," he steadily refused to invent "a world of ideas, animated by figures representing these ideas." With his Dr. Pessimist Anticants and Mr. Sentiments, on the other hand, Trollope had proved himself less than the complete novelist: ". . . it would be better," James stated ominously, evoking the fearful phantom of the pre- or anti-novel, "to go back to Bunyan at once." James's contempt for "any conceit of a 'plot,' nefarious name," had the same foundations. Like allegory, it sacrificed the particular to the universal, presupposed a reality greater than and external to the merely phenomenal reality of men and things and so insisted on a design for which life itself could give no warrant. There were no plots in nature; nature declined to assume such symmetrical shapes as plots suggested. To manufacture them, therefore, was to make the novel "an artificial, ingenious thing," was to expose it to a foreshortening altogether fatal to the effort and effect of representation. Maupassant's *Une Vie* could suggest "the minimum of arrangement," could give "the uncomposed, unrounded look of life," only because, James said, "the necessity of a 'plot' [had] in no degree imposed itself."

Not plot, with its intimations of the universal, but character, with its intimations of the particular, was after all the only signature of the real. "There is no such thing

in the world," James wrote, flatly rebuking the assumptions of tragedy and comedy, epic and romance, "as an
adventure pure and simple; there is only mine and yours,
and his and hers." Balzac could *represent* the real, could
resist the temptation to rearrange it, just because he cared
"for nothing . . . so much as for the passions and
embroilments of men and women," for "the free-play of
character" which was, James said, "the natural food of
novelists." If character was to be somebody's and not
everybody's or nobody's, however, it had to be identified
in terms of its temporal conditions. When reality was
represented, what emerged wasn't character unchanging
and immutable in some void or vacuum, but character
struggling and evolving in the continuum of time. "A
character is interesting as it comes out," James said, "and
by the process and duration of that emergence." Character
had, too, to be defined in terms of its spatial conditions,
the conditions attaching to a particular locus in time and
space. "In the void, [characters] are not interesting . . ."
James declared. "Their situation takes hold of us because
it is theirs, not because it is somebody's, any one's, that of
creatures unidentified." The mark of the true novelist in
Balzac was that he labored to demonstrate "the *conditions*
of the creatures with whom he [was] concerned," was that
he felt them "as swimming in the vague and the void and
the abstract, unless . . . their generative and contributive
circumstances . . . [entered] into his representative attempt." The tragic and epic artist generalized character by
dissociating it from a particular point in time and space;
but the novelist individualized character by rendering it as
the product of just such a point in time and space.

If it was true that the closer the artist got to character,
the closer he got to life itself, then he couldn't get closer,
obviously, than by entering the precincts of the psyche.
Since life was no less a matter of feeling and thinking than

a matter of doing and acting, the wilful neglect of the purely subjective experience could only make for a failure of representation. Hence again James's refusal to believe that novels should only have to do with stories and adventures. "The moral consciousness of a child [was]," he was sure, "as much a part of life as the islands of the Spanish Main." Indeed, he would eventually insist that it was a great deal more: that *experience* was even more a part of life than *action*. "What a man thinks and what he feels are," he maintained, "the history and the character of what he does." He accordingly opposed Maupassant's position that "the analytic fashion of telling a story . . . [was] less profitable than the simple epic manner which 'avoids . . . all dissertations upon motives.' " He endorsed instead George Eliot's belief and behavior, her "effort to show [the] adventures and [the] history [of her characters] . . . as determined by their feelings and the nature of their minds." Hence once more the logic of his aversion for a plot-dominated fiction. If the history of what men thought included the history of what they did, then the plot could only suggest a wholly arbitrary simplification of things. The Turgenev who studied the psychology of his people showed a novelist's instinct for truth, James said, "much more strongly than by producing . . . a story of mysteries and surprises, excitements and escapes."

The same instinct for truth, for a representational rendering of life, inspired James's interest in the technique of point of view. The study of character and psychology produced a certain nearness to the surface of things. But it was possible, by the conscientious management of point of view, to bring the mirror closer still to that surface. The omniscient author's distance and detachment made for a foreshortened statement or report. Wanting something "better for the process and the effect of representation, my irrepressible ideal—than the mere muffled majesty of

irresponsible 'authorship,' " James called for some observer posted on the spot, for some concrete delegate or
deputy whose presence on or at the scene itself would
guarantee the fullness and fidelity of the report. Hence his
commitment "to the idea of the particular attaching case
plus some near individual view of it . . . an imagined
observer's . . . close and sensitive contact with it." Hence,
above all, his commitment to creatures sufficiently
equipped with sensibility to register that "immense and
exquisite correspondence with life." If Flaubert disappointed him, it was just because his reflectors weren't
sufficiently reflective, in both senses of the word, to receive
and return the maximum of life. "It was a mistake . . ."
James said of Frédéric, "to propose to register in so mean
a consciousness . . . so large and so mixed a quantity of
life as *L'Éducation* clearly intends."

At the same time the novelist was expected to record
the ordinary and the commonplace. By embracing not the
world of plot and action but, as in Turgenev, "the world of
character and feeling," the novelist expressed, said James,
his affection for "the usual, the inevitable, the intimate."
Indeed, by particularizing character, by identifying it as
the product of its social and psychological conditions, the
novelist defined life in the ordinary terms of what was
known or knowable. His business wasn't with the great
ones who populated the pages of the traditional forms of
fiction and triumphed over the conditions of time and
space and history. It was rather with those perfectly
ordinary agents, with that great majority of human beings,
who were the creations and the creatures of time and
space and history. Balzac's pictures of life could so closely
resemble life itself, said James, because they were peopled
by men and women "of the 'middling' sort," by men and
women who composed the central stuff of life: "the
vulgarity was . . . a force that simply got nearer than any

other could have done to the whole detail." James's own
affections, he made it very clear, were all with the common
and the ordinary. If he did cherish, for the sake of a close
and sensitive notation of reality, creatures of rare and
unusual perspicacity, he was perfectly aware of the risks he
was running. Reflectors exceptional enough to *reflect*, to
register fully and faithfully, "the surge and pressure of
life," he had of course to have. But they could be shown,
he recognized, "as knowing too much and feeling too
much . . . for their remaining 'natural' and typical, for
their having the needful communities with our own
precious liability to fall into traps and be bewildered." He
was confident, however, he'd run the risk successfully. For
all her bright intelligence and daring drama, Isabel Archer
was, he was sure, a perfectly average and normal agent. So,
too, was Fleda Vetch. Justifying her as the center of *The
Spoils of Poynton*—"Why a mere little flurried bundle of
petticoats, why not Hamlet or Milton's Satan at once, if
you're going in for a superior display of 'mind'?"—James
appealed to the logic of the ordinary: ". . . in pedestrian
prose . . . one is . . . no less on one's guard than on the
stretch," he said. ". . . The thing is to lodge somewhere
at the heart of one's complexity an irrepressible *appreciation*, but where a light lamp will carry all the flame I
incline to look askance at a heavy." Hence, surely, the
omnipresence in James's fictions of the female sensibili-
ties, of the Isabels and Fledas, the Maisies and Millies.
Even, one might add, the Newmans and Strethers who
seem, in spite of their wearing long pants, somewhat more
or less than masculine. They were such attestations of the
near and the familiar as the novel couldn't do without.

For James, accordingly, the novel was most itself when
its tone and terms were comic rather than tragic. In its
passion for the sublime, in its contempt for the ridiculous,
tragedy would heighten, exaggerate, falsify. More level

with life, more willing to accommodate the trivial and the vulgar, comedy acted to correct the tragic poet's extravagances. If James was skeptical of some continental novelists, it wasn't only because they made romantic love more important a factor in life than it really was. It was also because they treated it more gravely than it deserved and, like the Italian novelist, Matilde Serao, made what was intrinsically a comic theme a tragic one. "Is it . . . certain," James inquired, "that the effect most consonant . . . with truth is half as tragic as it is something else? Should not the moral be sought . . . where the muse of comedy rather would have the last word?"

In a very special sense, then, the art of the novelist was the art of the illusionist. An art that represented life, that studiously refrained from reshaping and rearranging it, could hardly be anything else. "The beginning and the end of the art of the novelist" was, as James put it, the cultivation of "the illusion of life," the reduction of the reader to "a state of hallucination by the images [he] has evoked." He accordingly protested Anthony Trollope's "suicidal satisfaction in reminding the reader that the story he was telling was only, after all, a make-believe . . . [and] that this novelist could direct the course of events according to his pleasure." To break the faith, as Trollope did, was to imply, James charged, that the novelist was "less occupied in looking for the truth . . . than the historian." It was to revive and justify the ancient suspicion of Platonists and Puritans and the more recent suspicion of scientists and historians that a "fiction" was a frivolity, an entertainment, a lie. If, said James, the novelist didn't regard his form as a form of history or science, then it had no standing whatsoever, could hardly claim to be, among literary forms, the realistic or representational form *par excellence.*

III

In the end, however, it wasn't enough for James that the novel be representational. It had to be abstractionist, too. It wasn't enough that the novelist be the scientist of things. He had, too, to be the poet and philosopher. The world he proposed to picture didn't after all make a sense of its own. It was, James said, "all inclusion and confusion"; it was "the unconscious, the agitated, the struggling, floundering cause." This being the case, the novelist couldn't be content to copy it. He had to measure it, too. He had to bring to bear upon its anarchic material the organizing resources of a personality, an intellect, an imagination. "The 'moral' sense of a work of art" was utterly dependent, James stated, on the quality and capacity of the artist's sensibility, on "the amount of felt life concerned in producing it."

Such a view required of course a reappraisal of the novel's positivist aesthetic, a revision of its commitment to the wholly physical realm of things and objects. To be too much the creature of such a realm was to be morally powerless to take its measure. The novel depended for its veracity on the availability of facts and figures; but it could have more facts and figures than it knew what to do with. It depended for its veracity on the availability of a palpable provable social reality; but that reality could be more overwhelmingly palpable and provable than was consistent with the power to appraise it. The densely constituted French world that was Balzac's great good fortune as scientist and historian was also, James observed, his great misfortune as poet and philosopher, was also, he said, the "dreadfully definite French world that built itself so solidly in and roofed itself so impenetrably over him." He called, accordingly, for less life and more meaning, less

science and more philosophy. "What in the last analysis is
his philosophy?" he asked of the novelist. ". . . Details
are interesting in proportion as they contribute to make it
clear." The weakness of the French novel was, he said, that
its details were more obvious than its philosophy: Balzac's
"generalizing . . . [was] markedly inferior to his particularizing," James declared. The value of George Eliot's
observation, on the other hand, was that there was visible
behind it "the constant presence of thought, of generalizing instinct." There could be, he said, "no authentic, and
no really interesting and no *beautiful*, report of things . . .
unless the great . . . interpreting mind . . . [had] inter-
vened and played its part."

If it behooved the novelist to be the philosopher, the
agent of truth, it also behooved him to be the poet, the
agent of beauty. To ask for poetry wasn't, James believed,
to undermine the novel's realism. Since the real did after
all include the ideal, a picture of life that was *less* beautiful
than life was just as unrepresentational as a picture that
was *more* beautiful than life. "Nothing tends more to
compromise it," James complained of the French concept
of realism, "than to represent it as necessarily allied to the
impure." In the end, however, he could even value that
beauty that didn't belong to life itself, that couldn't pass
the acid test of observation and experience. As he saw it,
the novelist's business wasn't just to create the record of
the probable; it was also to create the record of the
possible. "How can one consent," James asked, "to make a
picture of the preponderant futilities and vulgarities and
miseries of life without the impulse to exhibit as well . . .
some fine examples of the reaction, the opposition or the
escape?" For beauty's sake he would even cross the line
that separated novel from romance, would chronicle not
only "the things we cannot possibly *not* know, sooner or
later," but also the things "we never *can* directly know; the

things that can reach us only through the beautiful circuit and subterfuge of our thoughts and our desire." Called upon to justify his beautiful people, James replied with some complacency that "if the life about us for the last thirty years refuses warrant for these examples, then so much the worse for that life." To find its way into fiction, it wasn't necessary, it seemed, that a thing exist. It was enough that it was desired. It wasn't necessary that it be observed. It was enough that it be imagined.

If James regretted the rigorous realism that flourished in the France of Flaubert, then, it wasn't only because it was all observation and no thought. It was also because it was all observation and no imagination. It made no allowance, he said, for "the fine intuitions of a joyous and generous invention." The special virtue of Alphonse Daudet was thus that he hadn't been seduced by the joyless truthfulness of the Flauberts and Zolas, was that he could be the "passionate observer . . . of the whole realm of the immediate" and at the same time "the poet who sees all the finer relations of things." It was even that he could feel an affection for the oft-despised Dickens, "for oddities and exceptions . . . for situations slightly factitious, for characters surprisingly genial." James was indeed much more partial to the English novelists than has usually been granted. They might be inferior to the French "in the art of characterizing visible things," but they were surely superior in the art of characterizing invisible things. "They have been more at home in the moral world," James contended. The geniality of Trollope's sense of things seemed good to him, he confessed, when set beside "that narrow vision of humanity . . . lately offered us . . . by the votaries of art for art . . . in Parisian *quatrièmes*."

James rejected, therefore, the Flaubertian doctrine of impersonality. The novelist's possession of a powerful personality, of a powerful mind or imagination, was his only guarantee that he wouldn't be intimidated by a tyrannous external reality, that what he produced would be not just the "struggling, floundering cause" of life but the artist's moral assessment of it. Balzac's dilemma was, James said, that the dreadfully definite world he occupied struck dead the personality and so struck dead the moral sense: "to be solicited by the world from all quarters at once, what is that for the spirit but a denial of escape? We feel his doom to be his want of a private door." James made much, for the same reason, of the novelist's elucidation of human character. The world as object having no moral value of its own, the human creature as subject stood for all there was of value in the novel. If Zola was incapable of "projecting himself morally," it was, James decided, because his passion for masses of men and movements denied him access to "the world of the individual." And if the beauty of D'Annunzio's early novels wasn't "in any perceptible degree moral beauty," it was because they rested, James said, "so little on any picture of the personal character and the personal will." The English novelist *could* project himself morally, *could* register the real existence of moral beauty, precisely because he had a "more delicate perception of the play of character and the state of the soul."

• It was with the psychological in particular, however, that James identified the moral and the ideal. Consciousness and conscience, psychology and spirit, were for him nearly interchangeable terms. By excluding the record of psychology and motive, Maupassant had eliminated, as James saw it, "the moral nature of man." Turgenev's virtue, on the other hand, was that he could approach life "on the moral and psychological side." If continental novelists seldom allowed for ideal existences, then, it wasn't only because they were more interested in the material world of objects than in the immaterial world of characters. It was also because they were more interested in rude or rudimentary characters than in characters of developed sensibility, characters equipped to make sense or beauty of things. Balzac could make life less beautiful than it was, James believed, because he was more preoccupied with "middling" or "vulgar" human beings than with "the highest kinds of temper, the inward life of the mind, the *cultivated* consciousness." The same was true of D'Annunzio: like Balzac's, his heroes and heroines weren't given the psychological and moral energy to measure their situations, to make them either meaningful or beautiful. "What the participants do with their agitation . . . is never really interesting," James said, "save when something finely contributive in themselves makes it so." He accordingly opted in his own case for creatures liberally endowed with spirit and intellect, for creatures capable of weighing things as well as representing them. "Their being finely aware—as Hamlet and Lear, say, are finely aware . . . gives the maximum of sense," he said, "to what befalls them."

Hence the critical place in his theory of fiction of the technology of point of view. [To limit the report of life to that of a single observer placed at the scene of the action was to insure not only its closeness and fullness but also its beauty and significance.] When the point of view was *one*, was stringently single, it filtered the influx of facts and figures that threatened otherwise to overwhelm all sense and meaning. "The promiscuous shiftings of standpoint and center of Tolstoi and Balzac . . . are the inevitable result," James complained, "of the *quantity of presenting* their genius launches them in. With the complexity they pile up they *can* get no clearness without trying again and again for new centers." For beauty's sake, however, the point of view hadn't only to be single. It had also to be sensitive and aware. "A subject residing in somebody's excited and concentrated feeling about something . . . [had]," he chose to think, "more beauty to give out than under any other style of pressure."

James felt for this reason a special feeling for the genteel or aristocratic character. Entitled or enabled by his social experience to arrive at a high estate of consciousness or conscience, such a figure gave the novelist access to the ideal and the beautiful. Balzac's occasional interest in the aristocratic character reflected, James liked to think, a hunger for beauty, an eagerness to "escape from the walled and roofed structure into which he had built himself." The purely social reality appealed to James for the same reason. As an incidental or accidental form of censorship, it acted to refine and idealize human experience. The vulgarity of D'Annunzio's passionate lovers James could thus ascribe to the absence of those social forms and customs that would have regulated their romantic behavior. James was hardly opposed, therefore, to the official censorship he found in England. His evasion of all physical actualities, sexual and otherwise, may be explained by the prudence of his Victorian editors; but it must also be explained by the prudence of his own artistic values. "There are some things which should be sacred even to art," he wrote in an early review of the Goncourt brothers. ". . . when she begins to overhaul the baser forms of suffering and the meaner forms of vice . . . we think of her as one who has wasted her substance in riotous living." Nor was this malaise in the presence of sex and squalor a sometime thing with James. It was as characteristic of his later as of his earlier years. The erotic novels that came from the continent seemed to him, he wrote at the very end, to justify the English censorship, to establish a powerful argument against "any considerable lowering of the level of our precious fund of reserve." The tact and the taste should ideally of course be the author's, James

conceded; but, he went on to say, invoking the shade of
"dear old Jane Austen," "when we have not a very fine
sense the convention appears in a manner to have it on our
behalf. . . . Does not the dim religious light with which we
[in England] surround its shrine do more . . . for the
poetry of *passione* than the flood of flaring gas?"

In the last analysis, then, the art of the novelist meant
more for James than a rigorous representation of the real.
The real having no moral terms of its own to speak of, it
was the obligation of the artist in the novel to provide
them. Art was to life what the individual was to the world,
what human character was to nonhuman environment. It
incarnated the value, the truth or beauty, not inherent in
nature itself. James's aesthetic was thus designed to
increase the novelist's power to do with the world what he
would, to facilitate its conversion to value and beauty. His
business wasn't to surrender the work of art to life. It was
to liberate the work of art from life. It was to study reality
instead of merely copying it, was to create reality instead
of merely repeating it. The novelist had to be something
more than the mere observer of things. He had, too, to be
the thinker and the analyst of them. Like the abstractionist painter, he had to abandon the *plein air* of street and
field. He had to retire to the privacy of the study or the
studio. He had to get out of life.

James increasingly mistrusted, therefore, the actual or
historical sources of his fictions, was eager to destroy their
link with, their inspiration in, the matter of life itself. To
the extent that the artist could separate the germ of his
story from its circumstances in time and history, he freed
himself from the despotism of life, facts, observation,
assured himself the fullest, freest play of his inventive or
idealizing powers. Under the dominion of his densely
constituted French world, Balzac's fiction suggested "some
designedly beautiful thing but half-disengaged from the

clay or the marble." "The idea but half-hinted . . ."
James decided, "is apt to contain the germ of happier fruit
than the freight of the whole branch." He accordingly
celebrated the artist's freedom from the matter of life and
experience. He didn't want, he wrote of the Paris of *The
American*, "to write of places under too immediate an
impression—the impression that prevents standing off."
Its status as romance, as something "liberated and discon-
nected" from life, depended, he said, upon its conscientiously not being the product of observation and sensation: "I had indeed to exclude the outer air." At the very
last in fact, the novelist was advised to refuse altogether
such dangerous inspirations as life and nature had to offer.
He should consult instead the purity of his "idea" or
"conceit," should rejoice in his total independence of the
imperfect outer world and so make every possible provision for something of value and beauty. James's own point
of departure was increasingly the universal rather than the
particular, the idea responsible for things rather than the
things responsible for ideas. Having grasped the "idea,"
James exhorted himself, "one would invent and vivify the
particular circumstances—construct the illustrative action." If he was unhappy with the traditional English
novel, it was thus because, more life than art, more history
than philosophy, it was too little under the control of the
"idea." The novel of Arnold Bennett was, James complained, "a monument exactly not to an idea . . . but just
simply of the quarried and gathered material it happens to
contain."

James modified, then, the primarily objectivist assumptions of the novel. In its representational character, it may
have called for the resources of the scientist and observer;
but in its moral character it called for the resources of the
poet, the philosopher, the artist. Too much mind or art or
imagination confounded the one; but too little con-

founded the other. It was important, from the representational point of view, that the novelist see, observe; but it was just as important, from the moral point of view, that he think and feel, that he even invent and imagine. Since the world as object couldn't be trusted to give a coherent account of itself, it fell to the novelist as artist to supply the deficiency. He had to be the poet-philosopher as well as the scientist. He had to be the abstractionist as well as the representationalist.

IV

At the very last, however, representation and abstraction weren't for James incompatible categories. Life was a function neither of the poet's universal nor of the scientist's particular. It was a function of their unity, their interdependence. Under an older dispensation, reality was defined by the relations of things to some God or Fate outside the continuum of time and space, by their relation to some single theory advanced by a religious or metaphysical philosophy. But under a newer and wiser dispensation, reality was defined by the relations of things to each other, by their relations to other things inside the continuum of time and space. It wasn't something that had been created; it was something that was always creating itself. To say with the novelist, then, that life was a product of the particular wasn't to say that there was no universal at all. It was only to say that the universal was internal and immanental, not external and transcendental. It wasn't to insist there was no figure in the carpet of things. It was only to insist that the figure was an expression of the carpet itself, of its own internal relations, and not of some great weaver in the sky who had superimposed a design upon it from without. Consequently, just to represent life, just to record it fully and faithfully, was inevitably to reveal the meaning that lurked inside it. The novelist had only to study conscientiously the palpable provable world itself, James believed, and "ideas would inevitably find themselves thrown up."

If the principle of dramatic form occupied a central and even sacred place in his aesthetic, it was exactly because it declared the essential unity of the universal and the particular, the reality and the appearance. Since what life *meant* was inherent in what it *was*, the form of life itself was by definition dramatic. To be representational, therefore, the form of the novel must be no less so. It must not mean but be. It had to have a universal, a fable, a figure in its carpet; but in the novel as in life itself, the universal and the particular, the fable and the fiction, the figure and the carpet, had to be all one and indivisible. The novel's commitment to a rich and full particularization of things was in itself of course an aspect of its dramatic form. "To report at all closely and completely of what 'passes' on a given occasion is inevitably," James said, "to become more or less scenic." The novel's commitment to observable social phenomena had for him the same significance. To deal with man "on his social and gregarious side" was, he said, to deal with him "dramatically," "the free play of character and the sharp revelation of type" constituting, he proposed, "the real stuff of drama." To depict things as elements in a causal series was similarly, he believed, to approximate the condition of drama. Insofar as *The Spoils of Poynton* achieved "a close little march of cause and effect," it qualified, he said, as "unarrested drama."

In the end, however, James required still stronger assurances that the novel would match the dramatic form of life itself. He called, that is, for radical reforms in the management of point of view. To be the lyric or subjective author was to reduce the world to the terms of a theory or thesis. But to be the dramatic or objective author was to let the world be itself and explain itself. It was to maintain "that respect for the liberty of the subject" which James defined as "*the* great sign of the painter of the first order." If he deplored the first person singular conventions of *Jane Eyre* and *David Copperfield*, it was therefore because they invited the distortions of lyric form and so achieved the falsity of the romance instead of the truthfulness of the novel. "Save in the fantastic and the romantic," he wrote of the first person narrative, "it has no authority . . . its grasp of reality and truth isn't strong and disinterested. R. Crusoe, e.g., isn't a novel at all. There is . . . no authentic . . . report of things . . . unless a particular detachment has operated." The epic or omniscient novelist who brought too much mind to his subject was even less dramatic, was even less the detached reporter, than the lyric or autobiographic novelist who brought too much emotion to it. Thackeray's powerful presence had the effect, James charged, of frightening away his characters and drowning out "the general truthful hum of the human scene at large." "I see you 'behave' all along," James reproached Wells, "much more than I see [your characters] . . . your 'story' . . . says more to me than theirs." He accordingly opted for the reporter or reflector posted on the spot and, more specifically, for the highly sensitive and intensely aware reporter-reflector. To use for this purpose "the person capable of feeling in the given case more than another" was, he said, "to *record* it dramatically and objectively." The novelist who claimed the privilege of omniscience imitated in effect the transcendental deity who formalized the divorce between meaning and being, universal and particular. But the dramatic novelist, the novelist who disappeared into or behind his own handiwork, imitated, instead, that immanental deity who formalized the marriage of meaning and being, universal and particular. When the novelist practiced the aristocratic

self-effacement of the dramatist, when, like Turgenev, he
"cut the umbilical cord that bound the story to himself,"
he created an artistic form as self-explanatory and self-jus-
tifying and therefore as dramatic as the form of life itself.

Hence James's joy in felicities of structure, in the artful
arrangement of chapters and scenes that rendered super-
erogatory the author's presence or apology. Since things in
life derived their reality not from their invisible relations
to the supernatural but from their visible relations to the
natural, the novelist's proper study should be exactly the
form of their relations to each other. If James found good
the handiwork of *The Awkward Age*, it was just because
its form was "a form all dramatic and scenic . . . with
explanations reduced to the explanation of everything by
all the other things *in* the picture." Hence also James's joy
in felicities of style, in style as an expressional or dramatic
resource. The motive of the novel's style, like the motive
of its structure, was to dramatize, was to express, not the
author's self but the author's subject. Meredith's *Lord
Ormont* filled him "with a critical rage," James confessed,
because, for all its quantity "of airs and graces, of phrases
and attitudes," it could claim "not a figure presented, not
a scene constituted—not a dim shadow condensing once
either into audible or into visible reality." The miracle of
Flaubert was, said James, that he could be "so the devotee
of the phrase and yet never its victim"; was that "fine as he
inveterately desired it should be he still never lost sight of
the question Fine for what?"

· In effect, then, James endorsed the principle of organic
form. A universe that was dramatic, a universe in which
everything received its reality from everything else, was
also by definition an organic universe, a universe that had
its own internal unity, its own inherent reason and
explanation. The novel was most itself, therefore, when it
was "all one and continuous, like any other organism,"

when "the fusion of all [its] elements . . . [was] complete
. . . of all the parts of the drama with each other." To say
that the novelist couldn't rearrange life in the fixed and
formal fashion of the allegorist and the storyteller wasn't,
then, to say that he couldn't rearrange at all. It was only to
say that his arrangement of things had to match the
mystery and subtlety of life's own arrangement of them.
Because the universal he assumed was, like life's, immanental rather than transcendental, an aspect of things
themselves rather than of dogmas or doctrines, it had to be
smuggled into his picture without drawing attention to
itself. Like every other artist, the novelist was free to solicit
harmonies, but because he sought to compete with life, his
harmonies had necessarily to be those "secret harmonies"
that joined the universal and the particular, the philosopher's reality and the scientist's appearance.

If James was sure that the philosopher and the scientist
could co-exist in the novel, it wasn't only on the epistemological assumption that reality was at once universal and
particular. It was also on the epistemological assumption
that reality was at once subjective and objective. Life was
world; but it was also experience. It was what one
observed; but it was also what one thought and felt. It
derived first of all from the senses and sensations; but it
also projected itself from the imagination which was "just
as visible," James said, as "the actual." Life wasn't,
however, *either* object *or* subject. It wasn't even the *sum*
of object and subject. It was the product of their dynamic
reciprocal *relationship*. The unconscious world as object
had no reality in disconnection from the human consciousness as subject; the human consciousness as subject no
reality in disconnection from the unconscious world as
object. To this extent reality was coextensive neither with
what was measured nor with what did the measuring: it
was the act of measurement itself. There was no reality at

all that wasn't somehow an appraisal or appreciation. Life
and value, reality and morality, were in this sense one and
the same. The appraisal or appreciation wasn't just a
version of life; it was life itself. A representation that
wasn't also an evaluation was, in effect, no representation
at all. Like life itself, then, the novel could legitimize no
divorce between subject and object. Where it failed its
representational office, it wasn't in its failure to be, on the
one hand, science and history with their passion for world,
nor, on the other, poetry and philosophy with their
passion for mind and imagination. It was in its failure to
combine them. The beauty of Balzac was precisely that he
put the two together, the scientist and the philosopher,
the observer and the poet, the man who saw and the man
who felt. With "an imagination of the highest power,"
Balzac could still see his subject, James marveled, "in the
light of science as well."

Hence once again for James the supreme necessity of
dramatic form. In the same way that it rehearsed the
continuity of universal and particular, it also rehearsed the
continuity of subject and object. Since it was impossible in
life to distinguish the point where subject ceased and
object began, so it should be impossible in the novel to
distinguish the point where novelist ceased and novel
began. Thus the disappearance of the author into or
behind the work of his creation, and thus the perfect
correspondence of the literary form with the form of life
itself. To insist on the vision of some highly conscious
observer on the scene itself wasn't, James believed, to
advance a subjective over an objective reality. To account
for the one was, he was sure, to account for the other. He
could thus propose in *What Maisie Knew* to keep the
heroine's "limited consciousness the very field of my
picture while at the same time guarding with care the
integrity of the objects represented." The same epistemo-

logical assumptions made James dilate upon the vanity of
distinguishing between what belonged to the object, the
novel's substance, and what belonged to the subject, the
novelist's treatment of it. Since subject and object belonged in the same continuum, the matter of the novel
was its treatment and its treatment the matter. A character
in a novel was accordingly an aspect neither of the one nor
of the other but of both, the heroine of *The Golden Bowl*
appealing to James as "a compositional resource . . . as
well as a value intrinsic." He insisted for the same reason
on the interdependence of the novel's "subject" and the
novel's "idea," of the novel's particular and the novel's
universal. It didn't really matter whether the novelist
began with the "idea" or ended with it, whether the
"idea" was the cause or the effect of his fiction. It didn't
even matter *what* the idea was or *what* the subject was. It
only mattered that the *relation* between "subject" and
"idea" be as dramatic or organic as the relation in life
between the universal and the particular. Subject and
object being indistinguishable in life, the novel wasn't
representational if the idea and its incarnation, the fable
and its fiction, weren't similarly so.

It was just as impossible to dissociate the real and the
ideal. Like world and self, object and subject, the real and
the ideal defined one single and indestructible circuit. As
James bewilderingly put it in his essay on Browning, "the
real is his quest, the very ideal of the real, the real most
finely mixed with life, which *is* in the last analysis the
ideal." To record the ideal wasn't therefore to offend
against the cause of representation. Just as no picture of
life could be representational that didn't acknowledge the
action of the subject, so no picture could be representational that didn't acknowledge the action of the ideal. "Of
the men of largest responding imagination . . ." James
noted, with Scott and Balzac and Zola in mind, "the

deflexion toward either quarter has never taken place."
The trouble with Flaubert was just that it had. Appalled
by the impoverished life of *L'Éducation* and *Bouvard*,
Flaubert had sought relief, James said, in the other world
of erudition and imagination. The beauty of Turgenev, on
the other hand, was that he never doubted the novelist's
power to unite the life and the poetry of things, was that
he had worked to combine "the deepest reality of
substance . . . with the most imaginative, most poetic,
touches." The novel was most fully the novel, James
suggested, when it managed to achieve, as Howells had,
"the romance of the real."

If the novelist didn't have to choose between romance
and reality, neither had he to choose between ordinary
and extraordinary. To create "the romance of the real"
was in fact to make the commonplace interesting without
denying its aboriginal commonplaceness. It was in effect,
through the magic of mind or imagination, to convert the
ordinary into something rich and strange. The wonder of
Zola was thus for James that he could make his "deplora-
ble democratic malodorous Common so strange and so
interesting"; was that he could make it receive "the stuff of
the epic and still, in spite of that association with poetry,
never depart from its nature." Indeed, to the extent that it
was the application of consciousness to life and matter, art
itself performed the chemistry that made the ordinary
extraordinary, the pressure of style in Flaubert, for example, making the familiar take on character and importance.
"Where else shall we find," James asked, "in anything
proportionately so small such an air of dignity of size?
Flaubert *made* things big." It wasn't necessary that a thing
be large or great or important. It was enough that it was
within the power of the novelist's art to make it so.

James wasn't eventually interested, therefore, in any
hard and fast distinctions between novel and romance,

between the mode of the real and that of the ideal. When it was all one whether the actual was idealized or the ideal actualized, whether the ordinary was made extraordinary in Wordsworthian fashion or the extraordinary made ordinary in Coleridgean fashion, then for all practical purposes the line of demarcation between novel and romance disappeared altogether. James was hard put to decide whether the fantastic in Balzac's work was the product of vision or the product of observation. "It is *done*—we are always thrown back on that . . . all we can do is to say that the true itself can't be more than done and that if the false in this way equals it we must give up looking for the difference." What, in short, distinguished novel from romance wasn't subject as such but the treatment of it, romance allowing imagination more free play than experience and observation could give warrant for, romance disconnecting or liberating the life of the fiction from the life outside it. Since, however, the liberation or the disconnection had, James said, to be accomplished without the reader's being aware of it, the difference even here was in no degree considerable. In closing the gap that separated novel and romance, James asserted in effect that as the real and the ideal, the object and the subject, interpenetrated in life, so should they also in art.

To accommodate, then, the universal, to bring to the world the author's capacity to philosophize and poetize, was by no means to compromise the novel's representational authority. On the contrary, it was to place it on the broadest and deepest foundations. The novel was asked to evaluate as well as represent life, but since life was by definition life reflected, life appreciated, life appraised, to evaluate it wasn't really distinct from representing it. The registration of moral value and beauty didn't call after all for the repudiation of the novel's formal realism. It called, rather, for a revision, for a grand liberalization and extension, of that realism.

V

The novel had, finally, a moral resonance that originated neither in the self of the novelist nor in the world that surrounded him. It originated in the novel itself, in its representational form.* For James the novel's realism wasn't morally neutral or indifferent. It expressed, rather, a specific moral attitude in the presence of life and nature. To be nonrepresentational, to reduce the world to the terms of the philosopher's program or the poet's passion, was to reveal a profound dissatisfaction with and even detestation for its limitations. But to be representational, to render the world on its own terms and scale, was to reveal a profound sympathy and satisfaction with it. The novelist's fidelity-to-life had a moral as well as an aesthetic significance. Because he was faithful to it in the aesthetic sense, he was also faithful to it in the moral sense.

If James abominated allegory, it was accordingly because it didn't keep the faith. Invoking as it did the reality of the next or another world, it betrayed a churlish and ungenerous impatience with this one. It told a story, James noted reproachfully, "as if it were another and a very different story," as if there really did exist a reality other than this one. But for the novelist, for the artist as empirical scientist, there was only this reality, and it didn't have, for its dignity, for its significance, to connect with another. James mistrusted for the same reason the effects of a powerful Dickensian imagination. Insofar as it acted to heighten and distort reality, it betrayed an imperfect sympathy with it. It suggested that in itself and of itself life simply wasn't good enough, that it could only be *made* good through the magic transformations of humor and

sentiment. Dickens "reconciles us to what is commonplace, and he reconciles us to what is odd," but for the
truly great novelist, there were, James said, "no oddities,
for him there [was] nothing outside of humanity." It was,
he decided accordingly, "an offense against humanity to
place Mr. Dickens among the greatest novelists."

  The morality of the novel's realism had very much to
do, then, with its social value. Insofar as it *represented*
things, recorded them in the sober and disinterested spirit
of the scientist, the novel affirmed in the author and
inspired in the reader a sympathy and solidarity with life.
By supplying men and women with a fund of vicarious
experience, by increasing their knowledge and intensifying
their awareness of things outside the range of their
immediate experience and observation, the novel aroused
the flow of human sympathy, made real and concrete the
essential community of men and things, and so established
the foundations of a better and happier society. A novel
was, James said, "something more than a simple *jeu
d'esprit*." As a form of science or history, "as a composition that treats of life at large and helps us to *know*," it
made, he said, "for the extension of experience" and
enlarged "our knowledge of the world." It was thus
another sign of Dickens's failure to *represent* that he had
"added nothing to our understanding of human character," had added nothing to the saving knowledge that
created the human community. "Humanity," said James,
"is nearer home than the Boffins, and the Lammles, and
the Wilfers, and the Veneerings. It is in what men have in
common with each other, and not what they have in
distinction."

  To the extent that its morality was social, the novel's
realism reflected for James an optimistic estimate of
human life. Stendhal's "air of unredeemed corruption"
seemed to him "a quality which in the novel amounts to a

positive blight and dreariness." Zola and his followers he
denigrated because they were, among other things, "intense pessimists." Hence James's impatience with the
French conception of the novel, with its accent on things
instead of people, crowds instead of individuals, sensations
instead of motives. To enter with the English the realm of
character and psychology, of social form and custom,
wasn't only to be more fully representational. It was also
to register a more generous sense of the human chances; a
belief in the power of the human spirit to survive the
world and its conditions. James insisted for this same
reason that the novelist account for the influence of time
on the making of character. Unless the passage of time was
recorded, there could be, he claimed, no proof of the
human creature's moral progress and achievement. James's
quarrel with the obsessively impassioned lovers of D'Annunzio and Matilde Serao was that the brevity and poverty
of their relations made impossible what he called "luminous developments." Lacking both time and relationships,
they loved or lived, said James, "for nothing and in the
void, to no gain of experience." If he cherished, then, "the
small expanding consciousness" of the child in *What
Maisie Knew*, it was for the reason that it made provision
for "the chance of happiness and of an improved state."
The novel's preoccupation with character and consciousness and time was more than a representational requirement. It was a moral requirement, too.

The novel's interest in commonplace and even trivial
characters had the same genesis. It wasn't only that the
novelist recognized them as more numerous and hence
more level-with-life. It was also that, as novelist, he felt a
special moral affiliation with them. James indeed assumed
a special connection between a novelistic aesthetic and a
democratic ethic. "Like almost all people who possess in a
strong degree the storytelling faculty," he once observed,

"Hawthorne had a democratic strain in his composition and a relish for the commoner stuff of human nature." The novelist's affection for the ordinary human specimen also reflected, James recognized, the new humane and humanitarian sentiment of the age. The literature of epic and romance had honored the heroic virtues of love and war cherished by the old aristocratic community; but the literature of the novel was content to honor the less spectacular virtues cherished by the new middle class community. It was all very well, said James, for a romancer like Stevenson to prefer "wars and rumours of wars" to "decrepit peace in Middlesex," but, he protested, "there is no romantic life for which something amiable has not to be sweepingly sacrificed." The sweeping sacrifice of something amiable he regretted equally in the chroniclers of romantic love. The erotic life recorded in George Sand's *Elle et Lui* seemed "scarcely life at all," he complained, "as the civilised conscience understands life;" Matilde Serao's celebration of *passione* was at the cost, he charged, of "the common humanities and sociabilities." Indeed, if James identified the rise of the English novel at least with the rise of a female reading public, it wasn't only because its particularity, its pleasure in the minutiae of the human experience, appealed to the myopia of the female sensibility: "Women are delicate and patient observers; they hold their noses close, as it were, to the texture of life." It was also because its milder and more domestic values appealed to the moral tenderness of that female sensibility. The heroic world of epic and romance, a world made dangerous and unpredictable by the passions of love and war, was predominantly a man's world. But the un- or anti-heroic world of the novel, a world domesticated by the bourgeois instincts for peace and profit, was, more consolingly, a woman's world. It was the ladies, James gallantly observed, who had "done most to remind us of man's relations with himself . . . His relations with the pistol, the pirate, the police, the wild and the tame beast—are not these prevailingly what the gentlemen have given us?"

The novel's realism was something more for James, then, than a morally uncommitted medium of expression. As he conceived it, the medium itself was the message. It wasn't only a way of knowing and recording the form or forms of natural and human life. It was also a way of celebrating them. It was also a way of expressing and inspiring a fundamental feeling for their value, a fundamental belief and confidence in their virtue. To this extent the novel was the one bright book of life itself. To write it was to keep the faith. To read it was to receive the faith.

2 Thomas Hardy:
The Faithful Imagination

Thomas Hardy's sense of the novel may be resumed in the statement that he didn't keep the faith. If James wanted to be nothing but a novelist, Hardy wanted to be anything but. A largely self-educated man with the self-educated man's snobbish reverence for classical literature and literary values, he celebrated poetry as queen of all the arts and denigrated the novel as something of a shabby court attendant. He regretted that Sir Walter Scott, "the author of 'the most Homeric poem in the English language— Marmion'—should later have declined on prose fiction" and was stunned by the news that the poet laureate himself had stooped in his failing years to reading novels: "Even the best novels I find it hard to read. I have never understood how Tennyson took that downward step." The marriage James conceived as a marriage of true love Hardy accordingly conceived as a marriage of convenience. Infatuated from the first with the muse of poetry, he engaged himself to her plain and prosy sister only reluctantly and after deciding he couldn't otherwise make his way in the world. If his experiment in novel-writing didn't pay off, he assured his first publisher, he would abandon

Thomas Hardy, 1840–1928. (*The Bettmann Archive*)

the nasty business altogether. He might one day become
"a great stickler for the proper artistic balance of the
completed work," he told Leslie Stephen at the outset, but
he was content for the present "merely to be considered a
good hand at a serial." Time itself didn't mitigate his
somewhat churlish contempt for the form that had made
his fame and fortune. "I never wanted to write prose
novels at all," he said toward the end of his life.
". . . Circumstances compelled me to turn them out. All
the time I composed verse . . . Lyrical activity was
essential for my existence."

For all its intransigency, however, Hardy's aversion for
the novel wasn't finally disabling. It didn't prevent him
from arriving at and acting upon a perfectly coherent and
often impressive theory of fiction. On the contrary, it was
responsible precisely for the originality or the eccentricity
of his theory. If it did inspire him to reject the novel, it
also inspired him to revise or refashion it, to make it a
better or braver thing than it was, as he thought, under its
purely realistic dispensation. Not the representationalism
of the artist as scientist and historian but the abstractionism of the artist as poet and philosopher was ultimately
Hardy's aim and ideal.

                                I

The novel wasn't for him, to begin with, the entirely
new thing in the world that it was for James. Bitterly
regretting the unfulfilled poet, steeped in the literature of
classical and medieval antiquity, he couldn't see it as a
wholly new departure in the history of letters. "One fact is
certain," he said discouragingly: "in fiction there can be no
intrinsically new thing at this stage of the world's history."
Convinced there was no essential discontinuity between
the ancient and modern forms of fiction, he was sure the

novel couldn't do better than approximate "the epic,
dramatic, or narrative masterpieces of the past." Convinced in fact that it was "as yet in its youth, if not in its
infancy," he was sure that only by adapting itself to the
enduring forms of the past could it hope to acquire the
status and dignity it couldn't claim, he thought, on its own
poor terms. When he came to judge the fiction of his age,
therefore, it was by the primitive standards of biblical and
classical epic. "How few stories of any length does one
recognize as well told from beginning to end!" he lamented. "The first half of this story, the last half of that,
the middle of another. . . . But in these Bible lives and
adventures there is the spherical completeness of perfect
art."

It was in the light of traditional drama, in the light of
classical comedy and tragedy, however, that he saw the
novel most often. For the novelist as scientist, the world
was neither tragic nor comic but a queer mixture of the
two and hence to make it either one thing or another was
to imitate a mere literary convention, was to imitate not
life but literature. For the true novelist, indeed, the novel
could only be the novel, could only be the unique thing it
pretended to be, to the extent that it liberated itself from
the tyranny of theatrical form. For old-fashioned Hardy,
however, the schematizations of theatrical form, of classical comedy and classical tragedy, continued to be valid.
"Some natures become vocal at tragedy, some are made
vocal by comedy," he said. It was accordingly with no
sense of disapproval that he described Meredith as a comic
artist "in the direct succession of Congreve and the
artificial comedians of the Restoration." He rejoiced,
certainly, in the finding of "one experienced critic" that
The Hand of Ethelberta "was the finest ideal comedy
since the days of Shakespeare" and he would surely have
rejoiced in the finding of another that there breathed once

again, in *The Trumpet-Major*, in the pages of a novel of
all places, the classical strains of Ben Jonson's comedy. It
was the form of tragedy, however, that made his own
nature most often vocal. He gratefully recalled that *The
Return of the Native* had been faithful in its fashion to
the classical unities of time and place, claimed to. see in
the setting of *The Woodlanders* the opportunity for
dramas of Sophoclean dimensions, and was reconciled to
the geographical limits of Wessex by the comfortable
reflection "that our magnificent heritage from the Greeks
in dramatic literature found sufficient room for . . . its
action in an extent of their country not much larger." In
the case of *Jude*, he defended his interest in the marriage
laws on the grounds that they were necessary, and
accessory, to the purposes of tragedy. The difficulty of
getting a divorce served, he said, as the "tragic machinery
of the tale," as "a good foundation for the fable of a
tragedy . . . a presentation of particulars containing a
good deal that was universal, and not without a hope that
certain cathartic, Aristotelian qualities might be found
therein."

A tragic schematization of reality was always more
fundamental to his intention, in fact, than the naturalistic
schematization his work has often accidentally suggested.
If he did sympathize with the French naturalists, it was
only because he thought they were preparing the way for a
revival of high tragedy in his day, for "a revival of the
artistic instincts towards great dramatic motives . . .
formerly worked out with such force by the Periclean and
Elizabethan dramatists." When he attacked the tyrannical
censorship of the time, therefore, it was because it
prevented the consummation not of naturalism but of
tragedy. "The crash of broken commandments is as
necessary an accompaniment to the catastrophe of a
tragedy as the noise of drum and cymbals to a triumphal

march." "But," Hardy bitterly observed, "the crash of broken commandments shall not be heard." He couldn't understand, he said, "why the honest and uncompromising delineation which makes the old stories and dramas lessons in life must make of the modern novel, *following humbly on the same lines*, a lesson in iniquity."

For all his worship of the classics, Hardy was of course more familiar with the literature of the novel than he usually cared to admit. But his preference was for romancers rather than for novelists as such and he was more affected by the liberated imaginations of Poe and Melville than by the soberer imaginations of Howells and James. Indeed, his friendliest feelings were for those practitioners —for Scott and Fielding in particular—who had tried to bring the novel into line with "the epic, dramatic, or narrative masterpieces of the past." Without underestimating Richardson, it was for epic Fielding, the most traditional of the fathers of the form, that Hardy reserved his warmest praise. The critics should have "sneered" at the "coarse" scenes in *Jude* "for their Fieldingism rather than for their Zolaism," he once bitterly remarked. ". . . I am read in Zola very little, but have felt akin locally to Fielding." It wasn't, then, to *the* great tradition of the novel dear to Dr. Leavis that Hardy belonged. It was to the *other* great tradition, to the tradition that questioned the novel's preeminence among all the forms of fiction, that questioned the absolute superiority of its representational approach to things.

If Hardy regretted the novel, it was first of all because it couldn't satisfy his passion for the form of the ideal. As the ordinary novelist saw it, the universal wasn't distinguishable from the particular realities that changed from time to time, from place to place, from individual to individual. But as Thomas Hardy saw it, a universal did exist independently of these ephemeral and fluctuating realities.

He exalted the great monuments of tragic literature, "the triumphs of the Hellenic and Elizabethan theatre," precisely because they scorned the appearance and cherished the essential, because they exhibited "scenes laid 'far in the Unapparent' " and were willing "to look through the insistent, and often grotesque, substance at the thing signified."

Hardy did share, it's true, the novelist's suspicion of the professional philosopher's *a priori* ideas. "After reading various philosophic systems, and being struck with their contradictions and futilities, I have come to this," he announced: "*Let every man make a philosophy for himself out of his own experience.*" Since the world's reality was a very enigmatic one, was immanent in nature rather than transcendent, it was more available to the observation of the scientist than to the cogitation of the philosopher. "The road to a true philosophy of life," as Hardy put it, "seems to lie in humbly recording diverse readings of its phenomena as they are forced upon us by chance and change." At the same time, however, Hardy didn't deny a moral philosophy in order to magnify a scientific one. His novels were products neither of the one nor of the other, he argued, but wholly of his own artistic sense or sensibility. "A novel is an impression, not an argument," he wrote in defense of *Tess. Jude* was "simply an endeavour to give shape and coherence to a series of seemings, or personal impressions," he wrote in defense of that novel. Denying that his works advanced "a scientific system of philosophy," he insisted that "the views in them [were] *seemings* . . . used for artistic purposes because they represent approximately the impressions of the age."

For Hardy, accordingly, the form of the novel was ideally dramatic. The world being more a mystery than a meaning, the good and faithful work of art made no attempt to codify the mystery: it sought not to mean but to be. "Their doctrines are but tentative," he wrote of *The Dynasts*, "and are advanced with little eye to a clear metaphysic . . . warranted to lift 'the burthen of the mystery' of this unintelligible world. The chief thing hoped for them is that they . . . may have dramatic plausibility." This wasn't to say of course that the novelist couldn't teach or preach, couldn't propagate a wisdom of sorts. It was rather to say that the artist could best teach or preach, could most forcibly propagate his wisdom, when his form was dramatic, when the "truth" of his representation was inherent or hidden in the representation itself. "The novels which most conduce to moral profit," as he put it, "are likely to be among those written without a moral purpose. . . . the didactic novel is so generally devoid of *vraisemblance* as to teach nothing but the impossibility of tampering with natural truth to advance dogmatic opinions." Hardy accordingly rejected the opinion that literature "should not be for edification." "It should be so," he said, "but the edified should not perceive the edification."

Dramatic form didn't mean for Hardy, however, what it meant for Flaubert and for the great tradition of the novel that was to issue from Flaubert. When he spoke of the dramatic it was only in the elementary sense in which just about all art and literature were dramatic. It was only in the sense in which even the legend of Joseph in *Genesis* was dramatic. What's more, for all his skepticism of *a priori* dogmas and doctrines, Hardy was always more interested in the philosopher's metaphysic than in the natural scientist's facts and figures. If he was quite sure that what was good enough for Sophocles and Shakespeare was good enough for the novelist, it was because he did believe after all in a rudimentary reality that suffered no change from time to time and from place to place. "New methods and plans may arise," he said, ". . . but the

general theme can neither be changed, nor . . . can the
relative importance of its various particulars be greatly
interfered with. The higher passions must ever rank above
the inferior—intellectual tendencies above animal, and
moral above intellectual . . . Any system of inversion
which should attach more importance to the delineation
of man's appetites than to the delineation of his aspirations, affections, or humors, would condemn the old
masters of imaginative creation from Aeschylus to Shakespeare."

For Hardy, accordingly, the artistic affirmation of truths
permanent and universal was no less the province of the
prose novelist than of the old masters. He was obliged, like
them, "to distinguish truths which are temporary from
truths which are eternal, the accidental from the essential,
accuracies as to custom and ceremony from accuracies as
to the perennial procedure of humanity." He was obliged,
that is, to be less representational and more abstractionist,
to be less concerned with the novelist's outside of things
and more concerned with the tragedian's inside of them.
"I want to see the deeper reality underlying the scenic,"
Hardy said, "the expression of what are sometimes called
abstract imaginings. . . . The exact truth as to material
fact . . . [is] the style of a period when the mind is serene
and unawakened to the tragical mysteries of life." Indeed,
for all that he deplored the novel, he considered it
superior to the modern realistic play because it got nearer,
he thought, "to the heart and meaning of things."

Hardy therefore denounced those novelists who would
serve the outer reality, who would pay "a great regard to
adventitious externals to the neglect of vital qualities."
Certain novels gave, he said, "convincing proof of much
exceptional fidelity, and yet they do not rank as great
productions; for what they are faithful in is life garniture
and not life. . . . the personages are clothed precisely as

you see them clothed in the street, in the drawing-room, at
the assembly. . . . But what of it . . . ? In aiming at the
trivial and the ephemeral they have almost surely missed
better things." For the same reason he denounced the
novelists' infatuation with the social reality, their assumption that life could only be represented and objectified in
a fully particularized social context. As Hardy saw it, the
social was exactly the realm not of "vital qualities" but of
"adventitious externals," not of "life" but of "life garniture," not of the universal but of the particular. He was
accordingly skeptical of the novel and of his adjustability
to it. He was only too certain that being a novelist meant
being a social historian, meant giving up his passion for
"abstract imaginings." What he'd written so far, he noted
ruefully in 1874, hadn't "been novels at all, as usually
understood—that is pictures of modern customs and
observances." And if he wondered whether he had any
reason to go on writing them, it was because, he said, "he
took no interest in manners, but in the substance of life
only." Hence his retreat to the rural fastnesses of Wessex.
As sure as Wordsworth was that the rural life and
character were more quintessential, more universal, than
the urban-social life and character, he hoped, by keeping
his novels "close to natural life," to make them "as near to
poetry in their subject as the conditions would allow," and
by consecrating them to Wessex scenes and subjects, to fill
them with characters "in whose hearts and minds that
which is apparently local should be really universal." Not
that Hardy was entirely indifferent to the novel's value as
social and cultural history. *Under the Greenwood Tree*
and its story of the Mellstock choir were intended, he said,
"to be a fairly true picture, at first hand, of the personages,
ways, and customs . . . in the villages of fifty or sixty years
ago." He had resisted "temptations to exaggerate," he said
of his work as a whole, "in order to preserve . . . a fairly

true record of a vanishing life." But Hardy also suggested that if he had had to do *Under the Greenwood Tree* all over again, he might have aimed "at a deeper, more essential, more transcendent handling" of his historical materials. And he made it perfectly clear, in connection with his works in general, that their value as scientific and historical documents was "quite unintentional and unforeseen" and indeed wholly subsidiary and supplementary. They were primarily "dreams, and not records," he said; "delineations of humanity" and not mere delineations of manners. Hence his indignation when *Jude* was judged as a social novel, when readers couldn't or wouldn't see the lineaments of the universal behind the complication of the particulars. It merely confirmed in 1895 what Hardy had suspected in 1870: that he wasn't "a writer of novels proper . . . that is, stories of modern artificial life and manners," and that his true vocation was, as he'd known from the beginning, the vocation of the poet, the registrar of perennial and quintessential realities.

II

Hardy's quarrel with the novel wasn't only that it excluded the shapes of the ideal and the universal. It was also that it excluded the shapes of the weird and the wonderful. An affection for the average and the commonplace was a vital condition of the novel's realism; but it was just the difficulty of feeling such an affection that made Hardy the most reluctant and eventually the most eccentric of novelists. "We tale-tellers are all Ancient Mariners," he insisted, "and none of us is warranted in stopping Wedding Guests . . . unless he has something more unusual to relate than the ordinary experience of every average man and woman." "The real, if unavowed, purpose of fiction," he declared in what must represent the central statement of his aesthetic, is to give pleasure by gratifying the love of the uncommon in human experience, mental or corporeal.

This is done all the more perfectly in proportion as the reader is illuded to believe the personages true and real like himself.

Solely to this latter end a work of fiction should be a precise transcript of ordinary life: but,

The uncommon would be absent and the interest lost. Hence,

The writer's problem is, how to strike the balance between the uncommon and the ordinary so as on the one hand to give interest, on the other to give reality.

To some extent, Hardy was here endorsing the dictum that the novelist's job was to justify the ways of the world to man by making the ordinary extraordinary. "Art consists," he once observed, "in so depicting the common events of life as to . . . [make] old incidents and things seem as new." In his eagerness "to extract a magic out of the familiar," however, Hardy was ready to take an even stronger line. He may have felt a Wordsworthian attachment to the ordinary; but he felt, even more urgently, a Coleridgean attachment to the extraordinary. He accordingly repudiated the studied sobriety and restraint of the realistic novelists. "They forget in their insistence on life, and nothing but life . . ." he complained, "that a story *must be worth the telling*, that a good deal of life is not worth any such thing."

If he rejected, then, the novel's commitment to a rich social experience, it was because it made no allowance for the marvelous and the wonderful. To go to rustic Wessex for his scene and subject wasn't only to discover "beings in whose hearts and minds that which is apparently local should be really universal." It was also to discover beings in whose hearts and minds the strange and the grotesque could still find expression. "Social refinement operates

upon character," Hardy said, "in a way which is . . .
prejudicial to vigorous portraiture . . . Contrasts are
disguised by the crust of conventionality, picturesqueness
obliterated." But in those provincial hinterlands whose
ancient way of life hadn't yet been corrupted by the
leveling standards of London and Liverpool, the eccentric
and the extraordinary in human character and conduct
were still available. When Hardy elected, then, to leave
London and live in Dorset, it was in part for the reason, he
said, that "residence in or near a city tended to force
mechanical and *ordinary* productions from his pen, concerning *ordinary* society-life and habits." Unlike "the
strained, calculating, unromantic middle classes" who
filled the cities, country folk were naturally, Hardy
thought, "full of character." He didn't, it's true, swallow
whole the Wordsworthian premise that rustic man was
necessarily wiser and more colorful than his urban cousin.
The new metropolitan culture might be powerful enough
to domesticate man's deeds and words, he said, but it had
"as yet but little broken or modified the waves of human
impulse on which deeds and words depend," had "only
affected the surface of those lives with which it has come
in contact, binding down the passions of those predisposed
to turmoil as by a silken thread only." Under these
circumstances, he concluded, "in the portraiture of scenes
in any way emotional or dramatic—the highest province of
fiction—the peer and the peasant [stood] on much the
same level." By painting peasants rather than peers,
countrymen rather than citizens, Hardy proposed, however, to penetrate those merely social appearances which
professional novelists confused with life itself. He proposed to get more easily and more directly at those "waves
of human impulse on which deeds and words depend" and
thus more easily and more directly at all that was

"emotional or dramatic," at all that was spectacular, in life and character.

For the same reason that Hardy rejected an exclusively social reality, he also rejected an exclusively human reality. For the novelist reality was by definition human as surely as it was by definition social. Indeed, it could be the measureable and commonplace reality he assumed it to be only to the extent that it was exclusively human. For the Hardy who heard the voice of Darwin loud and clear, however, a reality did exist that wasn't comprehended by the merely human, a mysterious natural cosmos interesting and glamorous precisely by virtue of its disconnection from the merely human. "Nature [was] played out as a Beauty," as he put it, "but not as a Mystery." He would of course have been the queer novelist indeed if he hadn't felt something of the novelist's feeling for the human. For all the vastness of his cosmic backgrounds, it was the human fate and figure that caught his eye. "An object or mark raised or made by man on a scene is worth ten times any such formed by unconscious Nature," he once wrote. In the last analysis, however, Hardy made a provision for the nonhuman or the extrahuman that more virtuous novelists would have boggled at. Long before and after his discovery of Darwin, he was as eager as any Yeats to believe in the supernatural and at times did half-believe in it. "I seriously assure you," he told William Archer, "that I would give ten years of my life . . . to see a ghost—an authentic, indubitable spectre." "You must not think me a hard-headed rationalist . . ." he wrote another correspondent. "Half my time . . . I 'believe' . . . in spectres, mysterious voices, intuitions, omens, dreams, haunted places, etc., etc." Unlike the novelist, then, Hardy didn't find sufficient a world wholly natural and human, wholly measureable and verifiable. He preferred a world more mysterious and marvelous than the sober, somber realist

could dream of in his philosophy. "The material world is
so uninteresting, human life is so miserably bounded,
circumscribed, cabin'd, cribb'd, confined," he declared. "I
want another domain for the imagination to expatiate in."

In his passion for this domain, Hardy never claimed, it's
true, the romancer's right to forsake the palpable, intimate
present. He might go back thirty or forty years as in *The
Mayor of Casterbridge* or some sixty years as in *Under the
Greenwood Tree*; but with the notable exception of *The
Trumpet-Major* he didn't take his fiction back beyond the
range of his memory or experience. If he didn't choose to
liberate his imagination from the pressure of the present,
however, it was because he didn't really have to. He didn't
have, like a Scott or a Stevenson, to range far and wide
through time and space in search of the exotic. He had it
all at home. The Wessex of his own life and time was after
all an anachronism: its present was the past and its past the
present. "I have seen with my own eyes," he reported,
"things that many people believe to have been extinct for
centuries." His rustics were "full of character" exactly
because, he fondly believed, they were "representatives of
antiquity," descendants of Roman and Norman colonists,
and hence capable of modes of belief and behavior which
antedated the banalities of Victorian England. Indeed, if
Hardy found it necessary to invent a semi-imaginary
kingdom of Wessex, it was to take his fiction out of the
frame of time and space and into a frame where the poetry
of existence was free to assert itself. It was to make more
emphatic the disconnection between the world of his
novel and the world of the present and so, like the
Faulkner of Yoknapatawpha, make still further provision
for a world in which anything, if not everything, was still
possible. Hence, doubtless, his dismay when nature threatened to imitate art, when the Wessex of his imagination
seemed likely to be confused with the advancing Wessex

of time and history. "The appellation which I had thought
to reserve to the horizons and landscapes of a partly real,
partly dream-country, has become more and more popular
as a practical provincial definition . . . But I ask all good
and idealistic readers . . . to refuse steadfastly to believe
that there are any inhabitants of a Victorian Wessex
outside these volumes."

Hardy's aesthetic was accordingly more hospitable to
the Aristotelian first principle of plot than to the novelistic
first principle of character. To recognize beauty of shape
in a novel, he wrote, "the construction of the plot . . . is
to be more particularly observed than . . . the fates of the
chief characters." Fictions might be "remarkable, and even
great, in their character-drawing," he argued, but "quite
second-rate in their structural quality as narratives." Hardy
couldn't of course deny the commitment to character. A
novel's reality could be as fantastical as it liked, but it still
had to have some connection with a known and familiar
reality and hence some concession to the claims of
character had obviously to be made. The writer's problem
being "to strike the balance between the uncommon and
the ordinary," it was essential that "human nature must
never be made abnormal." "The uncommonness must be
in the events," Hardy said, "not in the characters." He was
indeed to find, regretfully, that in its predilection for the
commonplace character, the novel wouldn't always accommodate the sublime ambitions of the tragedian. In the
case of *The Woodlanders*, the tragic consummation
devoutly wished for was confounded, he confessed, by the
sheer perversity of its middle-class heroine. "If she would
have done a really self-abandoned, impassioned
thing . . ." he complained, "he could have made a fine
tragic ending to the book, but she was too commonplace
and strait-laced and he could not make her." Though the
tragic poet did yield here to the novelist, it's obvious,

however, that he did so with no good grace. The man who
loved his Aristotle and would remake the novel in the
image of traditional epic and comedy and tragedy
wouldn't easily surrender the principle of plot to that of
character. In his fondness for storytelling, Hardy was even
willing to sacrifice those laws of probability, of cause and
effect, which constituted one of the very first conditions of
the novel's realism. Certain of his novels showed, he said,
with no embarrassment whatsoever, "a not infrequent
disregard of the probable in the chain of events." The
characters of *The Hand of Ethelberta* "were meant to be
consistent and human," he confessed, but because the
novel was a comedy in the traditional or artificial sense, "a
high degree of probability was not attempted in the
arrangement of the incidents."

Hardy wasn't eager to enter, therefore, as later novelists
were to do, those precincts of the mind where character
loomed large and plot all but disappeared. He did
consider once, in a very rudimentary way, the prospects of
the psychological novel. "A 'sensation-novel' is possible,"
he reflected,

> in which the sensationalism is . . . not physical but psychical.
> . . . The difference between the latter kind of novel and the
> novel of physical sensationalism—i.e. personal adventure,
> etc.,—is this: that whereas in the physical the adventure itself
> is the subject of interest, the psychical results being passed
> over as commonplace, in the psychical the casualty or
> adventure is held to be of no intrinsic interest, but the effect
> upon the faculties is the important matter to be depicted.

Hardy even considered, for a fleeting moment, the possibilities of the stream-of-consciousness method. "They pray
in the litany as if under enchantment," he noted at a
church service: "Their real life is spinning on beneath this
apparent one of calm, like the District Railway-trains

underground just by—throbbing, rushing, hot, concerned
with next week, last week. . . . Could these true scenes in
which this congregation is living be brought into church
bodily with the personages, there would be a churchful of
jostling phantasmagorias crowded like a heap of soap
bubbles, infinitely intersecting, but each seeing only his
own." But no novelist with Hardy's pleasure in the big
broad strokes of the plotmaker, with his abiding interest in
the schematic forms of the epic and tragic poets, was likely
to consider seriously such Joycean and Woolfian humors
as these. He fled the madding crowds of London for the
bucolic fields and forests of Dorset not only because he
didn't want to have to be a social novelist, but also
because he didn't want to have to be a psychological
novelist. Since in his view the social uniformities of urban
life could supply the novelist with no adequate objective
correlatives for the mystery of personality, he thought that
"a subjective system of description [would be] necessitated
for the differentiation of character" and such a prospect he
clearly considered unattractive.

Hardy was equally unwilling to define the lives of his
people in terms of their physical environment, in terms of
their spatial and temporal conditions. As he was to put it
in his "General Preface," his characters were meant to be
the products of a very specific place, of "a province
bounded on the north by the Thames, on the south by the
English Channel, on the east by a line running from
Hayling Island to Windsor Forest, and on the west by the
Cornish coast." But they were meant even more, he said,
"to be typically and essentially those of any and every
place where

Thought's the slave of life, and life time's fool."

Indeed, he professed to prefer the novel to the drama on
the very dubious grounds that it didn't, like the theater,

sacrifice character and action to the representation of
merely material conditions, that it didn't subordinate the
presentation of human passions "to the presentation of
mountains, cities, clothes, furniture, plate, jewels, and
other real and sham-real appurtenances, to the neglect of
the principle that the material stage should be a conventional or figurative arena, in which accessories are kept
down to the plane of mere suggestions of place and time,
so as not to interfere with the required high-relief of the
action and emotions." In Hardy character is indeed
defined as much by the universal conditions embodied in
the plot as by the local conditions embodied in the
physical setting. His heaths and woodlands and dairylands
may act to explain the reality of character, but they also
act to suggest areas of experience not comprehended by
the reality of character. Like the plot, they act to bear
witness to the reality of the nonhuman, to the reality of a
mystery in the universe oblivious of, and impervious to,
the will of the merely human creature. As the agency of
the local and the particular, the trivial and the commonplace, human character was never for Hardy the very heart
and center of the universe that it was for the purest and
most professional of novelists.

III

It wasn't Hardy's idea of fiction, then, that it should
represent life in the novelist's sense, that it should create a
model of the real all but indistinguishable from the real
itself. When he reflected skeptically on the Zolaesque
dictum "that the novel should keep as close to reality *as it
can*" and concluded that it "would no doubt have been
cheerfully accepted by Dumas *père* or Mrs. Radcliffe," he
was opening the door to the boldest departures from the
representational norm. Indeed, by classifying his fictions as

"Novels of Character and Environment," "Romances and Fantasies" and "Novels of Ingenuity," he suggested in effect that he was himself no strict constructionist of the novel, that he felt himself under no obligation to honor a rigid "fidelity-to-life." For him as for classical aestheticians in general, the purpose of art wasn't to compete with science and history but to transcend the limits of science and history. Insofar as it accentuated the universal rather than the particular, the extraordinary rather than the ordinary, it was to make life at once more logical and more fantastic than it was or seemed to be. It was so "to intensify the expression of things . . . that the heart and inner meaning [was] made vividly visible."

Hardy called accordingly for less life and more personality, less world and more self. If the novelist would transcend the slavish verisimilitude of his form, its interest in the mere appearance, he had to assert his individuality, his personal vision of things. "The seer should watch," he said, "that pattern among general things which his idiosyncrasy moves him to observe." To this extent Hardy called for less life and more poetry, less life and more philosophy. Since there did exist a truth of things that wasn't defined by the surface of things, the novelist had to be more than the scientific observer, the man who exercised his senses and sensations. He had to be the poet or philosopher, too, the man who exercised his mind or imagination. Hardy ridiculed the hypothesis "that to write a novel all one had to do was to go to a farmhouse and just describe what happened there during the day." "A sight for the finer qualities of existence, an ear for the 'still sad music of humanity,' are not to be acquired by the outer senses alone . . ." he declared. "What cannot be discerned by eye and ear, what may be apprehended only by the mental tactility that comes from a sympathetic appreciativeness of life in all of its manifestations, this is the gift which renders its possessor a more accurate delineator of human nature than many another with twice his powers and means of external observation." Hence his resistance early and late to the novelist's calling. To be a novelist was, he feared, to be the mere empiricist of life and letters: it was "to go about to dinners and clubs and crushes as a business" and, in general, "to carry on his life not as an emotion, but as a scientific game." Convinced to the very end that the novel asked for nothing more than a mechanical observation, Hardy could thus abandon it altogether in 1895 without remorse or regret: "he had kept, at casual times, a record of his experiences in social life . . . It was now with a sense of great comfort that he felt he might leave off further chronicles of that sort."

Few novelists would have maintained of course that their fiction should be all observation and no imagination whatsoever. In Hardy's theory, however, the imagination was invited to play a more powerful part than any true novelist would have found acceptable. In his passion for the substance of life, in his abhorrence for its mere outer appearance, Hardy in fact demanded a freedom to imagine and invent more peculiar to the ancient forms of fiction, to "the epic, dramatic, or narrative masterpieces of the past." The trouble with realistic novelists, he said with Taine, was that, painting "clothes and places with endless detail," they "renounce[d] free invention" and so were "far removed from the great imaginations which create and transform." "Creativeness in its full and ancient sense—the making a thing or situation out of nothing that ever was before—is apparently ceasing," he complained elsewhere, "to satisfy a world which no longer believes in the abnormal . . . and creative fancy has accordingly to give more and more place to realism, that is, to an artificiality distilled from the fruits of closest observation." The greatest art wasn't, he believed, the product of a careful and conscientious observation of the external world; it was, rather, "the transformation into ideal and imaginative shapes of a predominant system and philosophy of life." That life didn't assume the form of plots would have seemed to most novelists the best possible reason for doing without them; but that life didn't assume such significantly schematic forms would have seemed to Hardy the best possible reason for inventing or imagining them.

In effect, then, Hardy called for less life and more art, less representation and more foreshortening. Art was, he insisted, "a disproportioning . . . of realities, to show more clearly the features that matter in those realities . . . Hence 'realism' is not Art." He recognized, indeed, that in its compulsion to resemble life, the novel's status as art was all too likely to be overlooked. "Every intelligent reader . . . can perceive truth to nature in some degree," he remarked; "but a great reduction must be made for those who can trace in narrative the quality which makes the Apollo and the Aphrodite a charm in marble. Thoughtful readers . . . have no intuition that such an attribute can be claimed by fiction." As the novelist saw it, too, of course, the novel should submit the world to an artistic reshaping in order to reveal its heart and inner meaning. But the kind of reshaping the novelist had in mind had little in common with the kind of reshaping Hardy had in mind. For the novelist, the figure in the carpet of the novel shouldn't be more apparent than the figure in the carpet of life itself. But for the Hardy who loved the artifice of plot and longed for "creativeness in its full and ancient sense," the artist in the novel need observe no such representational restraint. He should be free to make his disproportioning of things as striking as he pleased. Hardy would indeed have been surprised to learn that the obviousness of *Jude the Obscure*'s structural

scheme was an artistic blemish. At the time of its
publication, he feared in fact that it wasn't really obvious
enough. Defining the novel's "idea" as "the contrast
between the ideal life a man wished to lead, and the
squalid real life he was fated to lead," he concluded that
he "must have lamentably failed . . . if this requires
explanation and is not self-evident. The idea . . . is, in
fact, to be discovered in *everybody's* life, though it lies less
on the surface perhaps than it does in my poor puppet's."
Hardy did distinguish, it's true, between the artistic
distortion that "increases the sense of vraisemblance" and
was the mark of "high art" and the artistic distortion that
"diminishes it" and was the mark of "low art." But
vraisemblance didn't mean here for him what it meant for
the novelist pure and simple. What it meant for Hardy
was likeness-to-life not in its local and particular sense but
in its abstract or universal sense. A schematization of
reality of the most obvious and calculated kind, where it
served the purpose of such a vraisemblance, seemed to him
no artistic failure, but the sign, exactly, of the novelist's
superiority to the scientist and historian.

As Hardy saw it, therefore, the novelist was under no
obligation to induce in the reader a total illusion of life. If
novelists denounced the art that openly declared itself, it
was because they conceived the novel as committed, by its
very realism, to the fullest possible illusion of life, to a
nearly total suspension of disbelief. Where the art of the
novel was arbitrary, it falsified life; where it was obvious, it
destroyed the illusion. Hardy himself wasn't wholly unsympathetic to this aspect of the novel. In gratifying the love
of the uncommon, the novelist might legitimately indulge
an extravagance native and natural in a maker of plots; but
he had first to win the consent of the reader's imagination
by carefully consulting likeness-to-life in the making of
characters. The reader must, he said, be "illuded to believe

the personages true and real like himself." No novelist
with Hardy's pleasure in plots and all the other marvelous
fruits of an ardent imagination, however, was likely to
sympathize with the realistic novel's attempt to put the
reader under a deep narcotic spell. If Hardy made little
attempt to disguise the art that ordered his fictions, it was
because he was more ready to grant, with Fielding and
Thackeray and Trollope, that a fiction was only a species
of make-believe, and wasn't to be confounded with life or
history. He accordingly dissociated his work from the
illusionism of the French realists: what he aimed for, he
intimated, was "the mental state when dreaming, interme-
diate between complete *delusion* (which the French
mistakenly aim at) and a clear perception of falsity."
"Scenic perfection such as this," he noted of one of Sir
Henry Irving's elaborate stage productions, "only banishes
one plane further back the jarring point between illusion
and disillusion. You must have it *somewhere*, and begin
calling in 'make believe' forthwith, and it may as well be
soon as late." Hardy didn't expect a novel like *The Hand
of Ethelberta* to be "believed," therefore, in the same way
that a realistic novel was to be "believed." Since he hadn't
attempted "a high degree of probability . . . in the
arrangement of the incidents," he "expected of the reader
. . . a good-natured willingness to accept the production
in the spirit in which it was offered." Indeed, for all their
realism, it's doubtful that he would have expected even
Tess and *Jude* to be believed in the way that most
novelists expected their novels to be believed. He never
contracted to create an illusion of reality so overwhelming
as to reduce the poor reader to a passive state of mind.
Like the Bertolt Brecht who preferred the naïve, nonrepresentational art of the epic to the sophisticated representational art of the dramatic, Hardy invited the active
participation of the "perspicacious reader," asked him to

"see what his author is aiming at, and by affording full scope to his own insight, catch the vision which the writer . . . is endeavouring to project . . . even while it half eludes him."

To say that Hardy celebrated the novelist's personality, his art and imagination, isn't to say, however, that they had for him a special charter to remake the world. Life wasn't for him the struggling, floundering cause. It had an intractable logic of its own, a stubbornly objective and irreducible logic at least indifferent to the merely human will and hence beyond the artist's power to alter and control. There were accordingly limits set in the novelist's freedom to do with the world what he would. He might change "the actual proportions and order of things, so as to bring out more forcibly . . . the idiosyncrasy of the artist," but this, Hardy said, was "a going to Nature" and not a violation of it. A means to an end rather than an end in itself, the artist's personality brought to the world something, he said, "that coalesces with and translates the qualities that are already there,—half-hidden, it may be—and the two united are depicted as the All." The novelist had to have an imagination, then, but it had to be a "faithful imagination," an imagination faithful to the "substance of things." Hardy indeed distinguished between the imagination and the imaginative reason, between the irresponsible imagination that missed "the heart and inner meaning" of things and the responsible imagination that grasped them. Accepting the Wordsworthian dictum that "the more perfectly the natural object is reproduced, the more truly poetic the picture," he went on to say that "this reproduction is achieved by seeing into the *heart of a thing* . . . and is realism, in fact, though through being pursued by means of the imagination it is confounded with invention . . . It is, in short, reached by what M. Arnold calls 'the imaginative reason.' "

For Hardy, therefore, the novelist wasn't free to do what he would with his subject. As he saw it, the novelist's material had a virtue or value that antedated his artistic treatment of it. A subject was either interesting or uninteresting, important or unimportant, and limits were set on the artist's power to make it either more or less so. "The great novels of the future," he prophesied accordingly, with pardonable inaccuracy, after reading James's *The Reverberator*, "will certainly not concern themselves with the minutiae of manners. . . . James's subjects are those one could be interested in at moments when there is nothing larger to think of." "My weakness has always been," he confessed, "to prefer the large intention of an unskilful artist to the trivial intention of an accomplished one." Indeed, in Hardy's view, the whole cult of artistic form was less likely to reveal reality than to refine it out of all existence. If he honored the poet Barnes, it was because he hadn't "become a slave to the passion for form, and . . . wasted all his substance in whittling at its shape." And if he thought Richardson lacked "the robuster touches of nature," it was because his "artistic sense of form was developed at the expense of his accuracy of observation as regards substance." For this reason, Hardy wasn't tempted to transubstantiate the substantial, to enhance his power and freedom as an artist, by dissociating his fictions from their social or historic or geographic sources. Reluctant to refine the things of this world in the crucible of his art and imagination, he willingly exposed himself to the stubborn actualities in which his fictions originated. "I have decided," he wrote from the fastnesses of Upper Bockhampton, "to finish [*Far from the Madding Crowd*] . . . within a walk of the district in which the incidents are supposed to occur. I find it a great advantage to be actually among the people described at the time of describing them." He felt, certainly, no fastidious aversion for the vulgar circumstances, for the "life," out of which his fictions came. The real or historic events upon which *The Mayor of Casterbridge* was based—e.g., the sale of a wife, the failure of the harvest and the visit to Dorchester of a member of the royal family—"Chanced to range themselves," Hardy freely acknowledged, "in the order and at or about the intervals of time here given, in the real history of the town called Casterbridge." The novel should aspire to the heaven of poetry and philosophy, but to a poetry and philosophy that had their roots in the earth of life and history.

Hardy believed as little in the transfigurations of style as he did in the transfigurations of form. Since the novelist's material, whether real or imagined, had an expressive value all its own, the function of his language was less to change his subject than reveal it. Where the substance itself was interesting or important, stylistic transformation was less in demand than stylistic clarity and exactness. The merit of the poet Barnes was thus, Hardy said, that his epithets were "singularly precise, and often beautiful, definitions of the thing signified." The novelist had of course to throw a new and glamorous light over the commonplace; but since this was a feature of the material itself, "a finish of phraseology or incisive sentences of subtle definition" wasn't called for. "The treatment may be baldly incidental . . ." Hardy said. Hardy's conception of the use of style in the novel was, indeed, in the classical tradition of the novel from its very beginnings. For him as for the very first novelists in the eighteenth century, the proper language of the novelist wasn't the highly charged and relatively artificial language of the poet but the natural and supple, the objective and referential, language of the scientific reporter. "The whole secret of a living style," said Hardy, "and the difference between it and a dead style, lies in not having too much style—being, in fact, a little careless, or rather seeming to be, here and there."

For all his passion for poetry and philosophy, then, Hardy didn't relax his hold on reality. He may have demanded, on the novelist's behalf, the freedom to imagine and invent, the power to create in the "full and ancient sense"; but he also demanded, on the world's behalf, a restriction on that power and freedom. He may have submitted the unredeemed facts of life and history to the "religious" transformations of tragedy; but he did so without dishonoring the humble materials in which all transformations begin and without which no transformations are possible. It was indeed an imperative of his aesthetic that no beauty was legitimate that wasn't fully earned, that didn't acknowledge and come to terms with all that was grotesque in life and nature. "If Nature's defects must be looked in the face and transcribed," he had asked himself, "whence arises the *art* in poetry and novel-writing?" It lies, he had answered, "in making these defects the basis of a hitherto unperceived beauty." "To find beauty in ugliness," he said, "is the province of the poet." For that matter the form of tragedy didn't seem to Hardy a merely literary transformation of reality at all. The schematizations of the tragic poet and philosopher constituted for him revelations of the real, not distortions of it. Because a work of fiction wasn't realistic, it wasn't therefore unreal. Because it wasn't representational, it wasn't therefore untrue. On the contrary, it was likely to be more real, more true, than a wholly representational rendering of it in the same way that for the classical aesthetician, poetry and philosophy were more real, more true, than science and history.

Just the same, this wasn't keeping the faith as the novelist understood it. For the novelist, life was neither

tragic nor comic but an undifferentiated mixture of the
two and hence to insist upon a tragic version of life was to
falsify it. It was to make life more beautiful, more heroic
and sublime, than it was; it was to demand that it be more
beautiful, more heroic and sublime, than it could be. To
this extent it was to take a dim view of it. The tragic poet
falsified life because he didn't find it satisfactory on its
own unvarnished terms. Even more incriminating, he
falsified it in this particular way because he wrote from the
darks of a profoundly pessimistic sense of life. It's true that
Hardy repudiated with some energy the charge that he was
unregenerately the pessimist. But the very energy of his
repudiation does arouse some suspicion. With their predominantly and even narrowly tragic vision, his novels do
express a radical and ineradicable disbelief in life, a rather
fundamental failure of faith in its ultimate possibilities.
Indeed, his despair of the novel may figuratively express
his despair of life itself. The very difficulty he had adapting
its subtle rhythms to the more triumphant rhythms of
tragedy may even suggest that there is after all a basic
disparity between the effort of the novel and the effort of
tragedy.

If Hardy didn't keep the faith of the novelist, however,
there is, surely, more faith than one. Who is to say that
the imperatives of realism are any less conventional or
artificial than the imperatives of tragedy, that the novelist's representational rendering of things is more real or
more true than the tragic poet's nonrepresentational
rendering of them? Who is even to say that the faith of
the novelist who finds the mortal world enough, who finds
that it suffices the mind and the imagination without the
transformations of tragedy, is any more honorable than
the faith of the tragedian who would make life more
beautiful than it is and would give it a grandeur and
sublimity it doesn't inherently possess? Beauty is truth and

truth beauty; but there is more than one way of establishing, Hardy would seem to prove, the interdependence of this truth and this beauty.

Joseph Conrad, 1857–1924. (*The Bettmann Archive*)

3 Joseph Conrad:
To Make You See

Conrad's commitment to the novel was every bit as certain and conscientious as James's. Untroubled by a private passion for poetry, he felt none of Hardy's radical reservations about the virtue of his form. He was, he confessed with some complacency, "insensible to verse." He was equally insensible to drama. "I swear by all the gods and all the muses that I have no dramatic gift." He was a novelist, he said, or nothing at all. A novelist, specifically, and not a maker of romances or epics, not a devotee of those traditional forms of fiction dear to Hardy's heart. "I am much more interested in your drama," he assured Edward Garnett, his editor and friend, "than in all the sagas that were ever written." Epics and sagas and such stuff were strictly for children, he said. Nurtured on novels, a matured mankind had outgrown, he liked to think, its frivolous affection for "fairy tales, realistic, romantic or even epic."

If this was so, if novels seemed to Conrad superior in sobriety and seriousness to epics and sagas, it was because they reflected the truth as an age of science defined it. Founded on the existence of physical forms and human sensations, reality for the novelist was a wholly empirical and secular reality, a reality governed by and reducible to no *a priori* metaphysical or religious laws. For the novelist as for Conrad himself, "the aim of creation [could not] be ethical at all. . . . its object [was] purely spectacular." This wasn't to say that it had no meaning at all, no moral significance. The universe was, Conrad believed, "a universe whose amazing spectacle [was] a moral end in itself." The truth that informed it was, that is to say, immanental, not transcendental. The universal was inherent in the particular, the reality in the appearance. To this extent, however, the world was a more mysterious place, its "moral end" a more problematical one, than men had ever dreamed. It was, said Conrad, "a world that . . . [hadn't] been supplied with an obvious meaning." Under the circumstances, man's only wisdom was "to will what the gods will without, perhaps, being certain what their will is." The wisdom of the novel was precisely that it willed what the gods willed without being certain what that will was. Registering not some noumenal reality that transcended time and space but a phenomenal reality wholly conditioned by time and space, it gave artistic form to a meaning that was also a mystery, to a reality of things coexistent and coextensive with the appearance of things. It proposed to find, Conrad said, "in the aspects of matter, and in the facts of life . . . the very truth of their existence." Approaching the world in the spirit of science, in the spirit of a philosophical realism, the novel would *represent* reality, would reveal it on its own scale and its own terms.

I

What this meant was that the novelist couldn't play the part of the systematic philosopher. In his passion for the abstract and the universal, the philosopher scorned the truth that inhered in the physical appearances of things. But, said Conrad disdainfully, this purely phenomenal truth—"the philosopher's 'vain appearances' which yet have endured, poignant or amusing, for so many ages"— was the only truth that mattered to the novelist. He accordingly professed himself entirely innocent of philosophy. "I don't know what my philosophy is," he said only half-facetiously. "I wasn't even aware I had it." *The Secret Agent* was *"purely a work of imagination,"* he assured his publisher. "It has no social or philosophical intention." For the same reason he professed himself entirely innocent of religious or spiritual views of life. In a spectacular universe that was its own moral end, the doctrines of the priests and prophets were just as arbitrary, just as ephemeral, as the doctrines of the politicians and philosophers. "Questions of right and wrong . . . are," he insisted, "things of the air with no connection whatever with the fundamental realities of life." He accordingly detested the great Russian novelists with their willingness to disfigure, in the name of a quasi-moral or -religious sentiment, the fair face of life and nature. Dostoevski was, he confessed, "too Russian for me." He sounded, Conrad said, "like some fierce mouthings from prehistoric ages." He denounced elsewhere, out of the same secular passion, "the gratuitous atrocity" of Tolstoi's *The Death of Ivan Ilyich* and "the monstrous stupidity" of his *Kreutzer Sonata.* Hence his outrage when H. L. Mencken referred to his "Slavonism." "Does he mean by it primitive natures fashioned by a Byzantine theological conception of life, with an inclination to perverted mysticism? Then it cannot possibly apply to me." As the scientist of life and literature, Conrad was, he was sure, no Russian, hadn't hugged his "conceptions of right and wrong too closely," hadn't "flapped any 'message' in the face of the world."

As Conrad saw it, the novelist wasn't even permitted to be the man of letters in any special sense. To the extent that he served a specific literary cause, to the extent that he was bound to "the fettering dogmas of some romantic, realistic, or naturalistic creed," he was, no less than the moral and religious philosopher, disabled from *representing* things. "It is in the impartial practice of life . . ." Conrad said, "that the promise of perfection for his art can be found, rather than in the absurd formulas trying to prescribe this or that particular method of technique or conception." Daudet's distinction was accordingly that he wasn't "in bondage to some vanishing creed" as it was Turgenev's that he worked "independent[ly] of the transitory formulas and theories of art." His own work, Conrad felt sure, defied precise classification, was quintessentially life itself rather than some literary reduction or redaction of it. "I have been called a writer of the sea . . . a romantic writer—and also a realist," he wrote. "But . . . all my concern has been with the 'ideal' value of things, events and people."

To represent life, however, the novelist hadn't only to suppress the philosopher in himself. He had also to suppress the poet. The philosopher sacrificed the world as objective reality to the tyranny of the will as intellect; but the poet sacrificed it to the tyranny of the will as imagination. Like the philosopher, he worked to justify not existence itself, but only his own existence. "The dreams, the passion, the impulses the poet puts into arrangements of verses" were designed, Conrad suspected, to "make his own self appear sublime." The same weakness affected the work of the tragic or comic artist. Like the poet, he did the world less than justice or, what amounted to the same thing, he did it more than justice. Life itself, Conrad argued, was neither comic nor tragic. "In human affairs," he said, "the comic and the tragic

jostle each other at every step." To render life according
to the literary conventions of tragedy or comedy was, then,
to render it in terms that were either more or less than the
terms of life itself. It was to be guilty, like the Russian
novelist, like the moral and religious philosopher, of
exaggeration. "There is . . ." Conrad said of tragedy, "a˚
considerable want of candour in the august view of life.
. . . the blind agitation caused mostly by hunger and
complicated by love and ferocity does not deserve . . . the
artistic fuss made over it." The sign of the novel, on the
other hand, was that it sought not laughter or tears but
"the very fount of laughter and tears," not a comic or
tragic version of life but life itself. For the novelist,
accordingly, the philosopher's intellect and the poet's
imagination were only very doubtful blessings. His proper
work in the world wasn't to conceive *a* reality; it was to
record *the* reality. It wasn't to imagine *a* truth that was the
reflex of his own desire; it was to register *the* truth that was
the reflex of the world's own will and witness.

If the novelist was able to resist the pressures of poet
and philosopher, it was because his program was, like the
scientist's, rigorously objective and inductive. Stimulated
less by formulas than by facts, less by feelings than by
things, he consulted, as poet and philosopher did not, the
physical world before him. The glory of the French novel
was just that it wasn't interested, like the traditional
English novel, in promoting moral ideas and ideals. Like
Maupassant, it paid "a more scrupulous, prolonged and
devoted attention to the aspects of the visible world" and
so derived its realities "from a genuine source, from this
universe of vain appearances." Hudson's *Green Mansions*
had proved, Conrad hoped, that the English novel could
absorb the virtue of the French, that "the pure love of
rendering the external aspects of things [could] exist side
by side with the national novel."

By definition, then, the novelist was less the man who thought or imagined than the man who observed. Like Galsworthy, he was "no theorist but an observer." Like him, he had "an extremely keen and faithful eye for all the phenomena on the surface of the life he observes." The weakness of English novelists like Dickens and Thackeray was that they neglected "to use their powers of selection and observation," but the strength of French novelists like Flaubert and Maupassant was that they permitted themselves no eloquence but the eloquence of observed facts. For Conrad, indeed, the novelist necessarily *saw* the world even more vividly than he *touched* or *heard* it. Reality was what was palpable and provable to the human senses, but since it was primarily a surface of *appearances*, it was palpable and provable most of all to the sense of sight. The task of the novelist was "by the power of the written word to make you hear, to make you feel," Conrad said in his most celebrated statement, but it was also and, "before all, to make you *see*." By rendering the world in its sensual or sensational form, the novelist acted to circumvent the imagination of the poet and the intellect of the philosopher. He acted, in effect, to *represent* the world.

What distinguished the novel, accordingly, was its particularity, its specificity, its saturation in data and detail. The trouble with the theater, Conrad decided, was that it didn't permit the fullest possible notation of life's surface phenomena: ". . . at the end one wishes there were more of it . . . It is as if the subject had been treated too summarily." The beauty of the novel, on the other hand, was just that it did: ". . . you must never be afraid of remote connections: you must let your mind range widely about your subject. . . . You must try to say things fully." Conrad may have gone for his scenes and subjects to the strange shores of the Far East, but it wasn't, he swore, to escape the pressure of particular realities. "The

picture of life, there as here," he wrote in defense of
Almayer's Folly, "is drawn with the same elaboration of
detail." Such elaboration of detail could of course make
the novel as boring and tedious as life itself, but, Conrad
insisted, the novel's need to represent the real justified no
less a risk. "I am long in my development. What of that?"
he wrote on behalf of his form. ". . . Sir Walter, himself,
was not the writer of concise anecdotes I fancy. And G.
Elliot [sic]—is she as swift as the present public . . .
requires us to be at the cost of all honesty, of all truth, and
even the most elementary conception of art?"

The novelist's picture could, however, be roundly and
richly particular only if it registered life as it fulfilled itself
at some specific point in time and space. For the moral
and religious philosopher reality might behave independently of time and space, but for the novelist as scientist,
reality could have no existence independently of them.
The novelist's wisdom wasn't the philosopher's abstract
wisdom which was, Conrad said, "no more immortal than
any other delusion." It was, rather, "the changing wisdom
of successive generations [that] discards ideas . . . [and]
demolishes theories." At the same time, not any point in
time and space would do. The novelist could be the
historian of such a moment in time and space only where
that moment made itself available in an abundance of
observable detail. For Conrad, therefore, the novelist's
proper province was his own time and place, the only time
and place whose particular terms he knew or could know.
The novelist was indeed superior to the historian, Conrad
said, because he was more under the impression of the
immediate present and its teeming realities, because his
work was "based on the reality of forms and the observation of social phenomena, whereas history is based on
documents . . . on second-hand impression."

In his passion for particulars, the novelist was especially

concerned to explore the data of his personal experience. In the private history of his own life even more than in the public history of his own time, he had at his disposal an inexhaustible fund of particular and verifiable realities. "Youth" and "Heart of Darkness" and "The End of the Tether" represented life instead of merely imagining or inventing it because, Conrad said, "they [were] the product of twenty years of life—my own life." Indeed, it troubled him at times to think that he hadn't lived enough, experienced enough, to satisfy the novel's appetite for facts and figures. "I have spent half my life knocking about in ships . . ." he complained to Edward Garnett. "I know nothing, nothing! except from the outside." Accordingly, many of his fictions had, he ruefully confessed, only the most tenuous connection with the actualities of his life and observation. "As with many of my longer stories," he wrote, "the first hint for *Nostromo* came to me in the shape of a vagrant anecdote completely destitute of valuable details." As the conscientious novelist, however, Conrad hardly rejoiced in this freedom from the terms of his own experience. "I am dying over that cursed *Nostromo* thing," he wrote in despair. "All my memories of Central America seem to slip away. I just had a glimpse 25 years ago . . . That is not enough *pour bâtir un roman dessus.*"

What Conrad lamented, however, was less the quantity than the quality of his experience. For him, that is to say, experience was by definition social experience. The novelist had to be the objective observer of things; but he could only be the objective observer where reality had already objectified itself in a rich and various social reality. When Conrad wrote Edward Garnett, then, it wasn't to regret that he hadn't lived but to regret that he hadn't lived ashore; it wasn't to regret that he'd had no experience but to regret that he'd had no social experience. He may have recorded life as it materialized on distant seas and islands, may have taken his subjects "out of the beaten path of organized social life," but he hadn't done so in order to free his people from "the pressure of worldly circumstances" and so give "a larger scope to [his] imagination." He had done so for the simple reason that the limits of his personal experience had left him no alternative. He was too sensible of the novel's link with the social reality to regard his accidental freedom as anything but a serious liability.

To deliver a realistic notation of life, however, it wasn't enough that the novelist register a particular time and particular place. He had to register, too, his own individual sense of that time and place. The reality that changed from time to time and from place to place also changed, it seemed, from individual to individual. For the novelist as for the scientist, there was therefore no real truth that didn't emanate from the individual's sense or sensation of it. Indeed, when a novel wasn't some particular person's understanding of life, it was only too likely to be a traditional or *a priori* understanding of it. "Everyone," said Conrad, "must walk in the light of his own heart's gospel. No man's light is good to any of his fellows. . . . That's my view of life,—a view that rejects all formulas, dogmas and principles of other people's making." The defect of the theater was, he argued accordingly, that its "inferior poetics" played havoc "with that imponderable quality of creative literary expression which depends on one's individuality." The merit of the novel, on the other hand, was that it did minister to the individual sense of things, to "the truth which every death takes out of the world." "A writer of imaginative prose (even more than any other sort of artist) stands confessed in his works," Conrad declared.

The novel valued originality, therefore, in a way that no

other literary form did. If it would offer life itself and not
just a stale or conventional version of it, the novel had
necessarily to be novel. It had to imitate life not as it was
yesterday, not as it was always, but as it was now, today,
for some specific individual who felt or experienced it as it
had never been felt or experienced before. When it
presented itself as realistic or romantic or naturalistic,
when, that is, it repeated already established literary
models, it was no longer that direct and individual
impression of things which was the source of its representational value and vitality. The law of the novelist was thus,
Conrad said, that he imitated no one, that he "expect[ed]
nothing from gods or men." "I don't resemble anybody . . ." Conrad said of himself. "There is nothing in
me but a turn of mind which, whether valuable or
worthless, cannot be imitated." Indeed, in his rage for
representation, for a reality undisfigured by a dogma or a
doctrine, Conrad pushed the cult of originality even
further. The truth that changed from individual to individual also changed *for* the individual from time to time,
from moment to moment. Ideally, therefore, not only
should the novelist not imitate other novelists. He
shouldn't even imitate himself. "Some critics have found
fault with me for not being constantly myself," Conrad
complained. "But they are wrong. I am always myself . . .
but I am no slave to prejudices and formulas, and I shall
never be. My attitude . . . will, within limits, be always
changing—not because I am unstable or unprincipled but
because I am free." For Conrad, consequently, an essential
condition of the novel's enduring life was its freedom from
all external and internal constraints. Since of all literary
forms it was most dependent for its vitality on the
individual impression and expression of things, its right to
the fullest possible freedom from the tyranny of custom or
habit or precedent had to be uncontestable. "Where a

novelist has an advantage . . ." Conrad wrote, "is in his privilege of freedom—the freedom of expression and the freedom of confessing his innermost beliefs."

It followed from all this that the novel's proper subject was the ordinary and the commonplace. Committed to what was known or could be known, it couldn't legitimately have commerce with the supernatural and the superhuman, with what denied or defied a rational explanation. Its business was to keep, as Conrad put it, "within the limits of the visible world and within the boundaries of human emotions." He was accordingly offended by the accusation that he had tried in *The Shadow-Line* to smuggle in the supernatural. The hallucinations of the character Burns hadn't come, he argued, "from beyond the confines of this world"; they had been wholly produced and were wholly explained by the conditions of this one: "Whatever falls under the dominion of our senses must be in nature and, however exceptional, cannot differ in its essence from all the other effects of the visible and tangible world." Not surprisingly, therefore, Conrad found Wells's *The Invisible Man* a little hard to take and was only reconciled to it by the reflection that Wells had somehow managed "to give over humanity into the clutches of the Impossible and yet . . . keep it down (or up) to its humanity."

The same respect for the ordinary processes of nature made him repudiate the whole cult of the heroic. "The incapacity to achieve anything distinctly good or evil is inherent in our earthly condition," he said with Marlow. "Mediocrity is our mark." This was even more true under the bourgeois dispensation of today, he suggested, than under the aristocratic dispensation of yesterday. If he honored James's refusal to give his characters "Titanic proportions," it was because he too recognized that "the earth itself [had] grown smaller in the course of ages." The

measure of Marryat's fidelity to things was thus that he
gave us "a glimpse of the everyday life" of his time as it
was Daudet's that he took pleasure in "the joys of
commonplace people in a commonplace way." It was,
Conrad believed, the measure of his own fidelity to things.
When a critic complained of the "lack of heroism" in *The
Nigger of the "Narcissus,"* he replied that as a novelist he
wasn't obliged to produce what life itself couldn't produce. He may have written of faraway seas and strands, he
wrote elsewhere, but he hadn't done so in order to enjoy a
"special imaginative freedom," in order to flee the average
and the trivial in human experience. On the contrary, he
had conscientiously resisted the temptation to exploit the
exotic aspects of his subject matter. "I am content," he
said, "to sympathize with common mortals, no matter
where they live; in houses or in tents, in the streets . . . or
in the forests."

Hence his contempt for plot and his interest in character. To make characters instead of manufacturing plots, to
put the stress not on what happened but on those it
happened to, was to be in touch with the ordinary and the
commonplace. The critic who complained of the lack of
heroism in *The Nigger of the "Narcissus"* also complained
of its lack of story. But, said Conrad, life wasn't normally
heroic and hence didn't normally assume the form of
stories: ". . . the incomplete joy, the incomplete sorrow,
the incomplete rascality or heroism . . . Events crowd and
push and nothing happens." The mark of the novelist was
thus that he produced characters, was that he depicted the
fate of humanity "as illustrated in individuals." Even more
specifically, it was that he depicted character as the
product of certain social and natural conditions. For the
novelist as for the scientist, human creatures weren't "the
outcome of malevolence," couldn't be explained by the *a
priori* notions of good and evil cherished in the melodra-

matic imaginations of moral and religious philosophers. More modestly, less spectacularly, they were produced and explained by empirically measurable and identifiable conditions, i.e., by "their education, their social status, even their professions." "The kingdom of this earth itself" was, Conrad said of the novelist, "the ground upon which his individualities stand, stumble, or die" and had, therefore, to "enter into his scheme of faithful record." Like the scientist's, the novelist's reality had nothing to do with the heroic and the miraculous. His world was the purely sublunary world where the exceptional had no dominion whatsoever.

II

To say that the novelist celebrated the particular wasn't of course to say that he denied the universal. To say that he addressed himself to the surface of life wasn't to say that he denied its heart and inner meaning. It was rather to say that, for him as for the scientist, what life meant was inherent in what life was, that there was no "reality" that didn't actualize itself in an "appearance." The world being a spectacular world that was its own moral end, the novelist had only to record with studious fidelity the spectacle itself—"its vibration, its colour, its form"—and the moral end it concealed—"the *substance* of its truth" —must inevitably emerge. He had only to make the reader "see" the spectacular universe in the sense of physically apprehending it and he must also make him "see" it in the sense of spiritually comprehending it. Like every other artist, the novelist must "get through the veil of details at the essence of life," but for him as for no other artist, the essential wasn't distinguishable from the existential, the universal from the particular.

To this extent the aesthetic peculiar to the novel was

necessarily an aesthetic of ambiguity and even obscurity. In its purely phenomenal character, the world remained enigmatic and inscrutable. To represent it, the novel had to be no less so. What it meant had to be more suspected than seen, more implicit than explicit. Conrad felt "an ineradicable mistrust of the theater" just because it seemed to him the "destroyer of all suggestiveness." The appeal of the novel, on the other hand, was that it managed, by virtue of its richer and more wide-ranging form, to suggest much more than it stated. Like Proust's, its power derived from "its inexplicable character." Conrad accordingly denounced whatever acted to destroy its veil of ambiguity. A novel's title shouldn't be "too literal—too explicit—too much of a definition." Its dialogue shouldn't translate too plainly and too openly the feelings of its characters: ". . . instead of disclosing themselves, which would be art, [they] are made to give themselves away, which is neither art nor life." It shouldn't analyze its characters too closely and too carefully, shouldn't "drag out for public inspection the very entrails of [its] characters." Above all else, the novel shouldn't permit itself the simple delights of plot-making or storytelling. Since life hadn't been supplied with an obvious meaning, to manufacture plots, to insist on their factitious consummations and climaxes, was to make life more systematic and symmetrical than it was in fact. In both Marryat and Cooper, Conrad complained, "the stress of adventure and endeavour must end fatally in inheritance and marriage." In the work of his friend Edward Noble, it must end, still more fatally, in death. "All the truth of it," he wrote him, "[is] thrown away . . . by the mechanism . . . of the story which makes it appear false." More exemplary, more conscientiously novelistic, was the procedure of Henry James, who made his characters renounce their opportunities, who refused them the easy victories of death and marriage. "A solution by rejection must always present," Conrad granted sardonically, "a certain lack of finality, especially startling when contrasted with the usual methods of solution by rewards and punishments, by crowned love, by fortune, by a broken leg or. a sudden death." But such a solution was the only one that honestly consisted with the mixed and mysterious law of life itself: "One is never set at rest by Mr. Henry James's novels. His books end as an episode in life ends. You remain with a sense of the life still going on." To ask for more, to ask for a finality that life itself couldn't offer, was to ask for a picture less suggestive, less ambiguous, than life itself.

In effect, then, representational form was for Conrad nothing other than dramatic form. A universe whose meaning was inherent in its appearance was by definition a dramatic universe and hence, to be representational, the form of the novel must be no less so. It must not mean but be. It had to have a figure in its carpet, but that figure had to be as elusive as the figure in the carpet of life itself. The novelist wasn't therefore permitted to assume the mantle of the omniscient author, to present himself as the intelligent god of an intelligible creation. His office wasn't to explain the world away but to let the world explain itself. That novelist was best who governed least, who took to his trade, as Conrad had taken to his, "without any moral intention but that which pervades the whole scheme of this world of senses." For the same reason, that novel was best which governed least, whose figure or whose fable was more expressed than explained, more suspected than seen. His own novels, Conrad confessed, weren't designed to mean this thing or that, to be less suggestive and inexplicable than the world they mirrored. He would have found it difficult, he said of *The Nigger of the "Narcissus"* "to give my complex intentions the form of a concise and definite statement." "A piece of literary work may be

defined in twenty ways," he wrote in defense of *The Secret
Agent*. He considered himself in fact no more responsible
for the way his readers read his works than for the way they
read the world his works imitated. "I have given there all
the truth that is in me . . ." he said. "But as to 'final
effect' my conscience has nothing to do with that." When
fiction was as dramatic in form as the form of life itself, its
effect must be as problematical as the effect of life itself.

It was for the sake of a dramatic rendering of life that
Conrad embraced the aesthetic of the symbolist. Insofar as
the universal actualized itself in the particular, life itself
was symbolic in the same sense and for the same reason
that it was dramatic, and hence to be the novelist, to
represent, was necessarily to be the symbolist. Conrad
didn't have in mind of course "the Symbolist School of
poets or prose writers" whose subjective and artificial
system of symbols he dismissed as "only a literary proceeding." What he had in mind, he said, was "something
much larger," was that natural and mysterious symbolism
which, deriving from the world itself rather than from the
author's mind or imagination, dramatized rather than
defined. If "a work of art [was] very seldom limited to one
exclusive meaning . . ." Conrad wrote, it was "for the
reason that the nearer it approaches art, the more it
acquires a symbolic character."

Conrad was "haunted by the *necessity* of style" for the
same reason that he was haunted by the necessity of form.
To record a world whose truth was easier embodied than
known, the novelist's style had to be as presentational, as
dramatic or symbolic, as his form. It had to be rather than
mean, to suggest rather than state. In their rational or
discursive character, words were "the great foes of reality,"
but words were also, Conrad said, "symbols of life,"
dramatic or objective correlatives of life, and, as such, had
"the power in their sound or their aspect to present the

very thing you wish to hold up before the mental vision of
your readers." If he would represent life, then, the novelist
as stylist had to be something of the poet or musician: he
had, by "an unremitting never-discouraged care for the
shape and ring of sentences," to bring to play "the light of
magic suggestiveness . . . over the commonplace surface
of words" and so dramatize the truth that couldn't be
defined. This was far from saying of course that the
novelist should cultivate style for the sake of style. Conrad
was just as skeptical of a studied and elaborate prose that
drew attention to itself as he was of a studied and
elaborate symbolism that drew attention to itself. He
deprecated "the elegant verbiage" of Bulwer-Lytton's
pages and put Stevenson down as "a conscious virtuoso of
style." Like Galsworthy's, the novelist's prose should be
"clear, direct, sane" with "not a single phrase in it written
for the sake of its cleverness." In its obligation to suggest
the truth that couldn't be stated, the best style, like the
best art, was the style that concealed itself.

III

Though the novelist was primarily concerned with the
world's external reality, he wasn't therefore indifferent to
man's internal reality. The world was a world of physical
forms and colors; but it was also a world of human feelings
and sensations. Indeed, if the universe of physical forms
and colors was accessible at all, it was only insofar as it was
accessible to the human feelings and sensations. Life
wasn't after all the one or the other. It wasn't even the
sum of the one and the other. It was the product of their
vital reciprocity. They belonged in one single continuum,
comprehended one single unified experience. Just as the
universal was contained in the particular, so the world or
object was contained in the self or subject. To express the

individual sense and sensibility of things wasn't therefore
to deny or dishonor the objective reality of things. It was
the only way there was to affirm and honor their objective
reality. "Our appointed task on this earth," as Conrad put
it, was to pay "unwearied self-forgetful attention to every
phase of the living universe reflected in our consciousness."

He insisted for this reason on the priority of character
and psychology over plot and action. When life was
represented, what materialized wasn't events, incidents,
episodes, which were, said Conrad, only *accidental* signs of
life, but experience, feelings, sensations, which were *essential* signs of life. Hence, again, his impatience with the
traditional climaxes of marriage and death. "Death is not
the most pathetic,—the most poignant thing," he reminded Edward Noble, ". . . treat events only as illustrative of human sensation,—as the outward sign of inward
feelings . . . which alone are truly pathetic and interesting." Not what character did but what character thought
and felt was accordingly all Conrad's own concern. "As in
most of my writings," he wrote of "Falk," "I insist not on
the events but on their effect upon the persons in the
tale."

The novelist's primary obligation to the external universe of physical shapes and colors didn't necessarily
involve, therefore, the total effacement of his personality.
Life wasn't only a function of this external universe. It was
also a function of the human mind and imagination, of
the human consciousness in which alone the reality of the
external universe was entered and registered. Conrad
could accordingly concede that the novelist should have
some imagination. The mysterious truth that inhabited
the appearances of things couldn't be deciphered alone by
the scientist's observation. It demanded the active collabo-
ration of the poet's vision. "The road to legitimate realism

[was]," Conrad said, "through poetical feeling." Stephen
Crane had reached "within life's appearances and forms,
the very spirit of life's truth" because he had applied "a
wonderful power of vision . . . to the things of this earth."
Indeed, Conrad was at times troubled by the thought that
he hadn't himself applied to things the same wonderful
power of vision. *Lord Jim* lacked "illuminating imagination," he feared; he hadn't, he decided, "been strong
enough to breathe the right sort of life into my clay—the
revealing life." The novelist's imagination might legitimately serve, Conrad could even suggest, not only as an
aid to his observation and experience but as a *substitute*
for them. Crane's "ignorance of the world at large—he
had seen very little of it—did not stand in the way," he
noted, "of his imaginative grasp of facts, events, and
picturesque men." An ignorance of the world hadn't even
stood, Conrad claimed, in his own way. "Anarchy and
anarchists are outside my experience," he wrote of *The
Secret Agent*; "I know almost nothing of the philosophy,
and nothing at all of the men."

Conrad was even willing to concede that the novelist
could have *some* intellect, could apply to things the force
of his ideas or conceptions. To disclose the reality that
lurked in the appearance, a novel had to be more than the
product of the novelist's observation. It had also to be the
product of his philosophical intelligence. The defect of
Dostoevski's *Brothers Karamazov* was that it was all thing
and no thought: it was only, Conrad said, "an impossible
lump of valuable matter. . . . I don't know what D stands
for or reveals." It was thus for the idea, for the figure in the
carpet, that Conrad declared himself. What should stand
out in 'The End of the Tether,' he said, wasn't the fiction
but the fable, wasn't "the miserable threadbare warp and
woof of the thing," but "the Figure in the Carpet of the E
of this T."

For Conrad, however, the novelist's personality, his intellect or imagination, existed to justify not his own reality but the world's. Since man's "appointed task on earth" was to pay "unwearied self-forgetful attention to every phase of the living universe," the novelist's task should be no less. His attention should be no less "unwearied" and, above all, no less "self-forgetful." Accordingly, the imagination Conrad had in mind wasn't the irresponsible imagination that disdained the world but the responsible imagination that maintained it. If novelists were comparatively rare, it was, he said, because "the seduction of irresponsible freedom [was] very great; and to be tied to the earth . . . in the exercise of one's imagination . . . [was] a lot hard enough not to be lightly embraced." That he was himself a novelist in this rare, this rigorous, sense, Conrad didn't seriously doubt. He may have written of people "who go to sea or live on lonely islands untrammelled by the pressure of worldly circumstances," but it wasn't, he argued, "because such characters allowed freer play to my imagination." It was an accident, rather, of his life and experience: "I have not sought for special imaginative freedom." He liked indeed to boast that he didn't have a very strong imagination, that for "the sustained invention of a really telling lie" he had no talent at all. He could therefore admit to "an intense and unreasoning affection" for Dickens' *Bleak House* and to a perennial delight in the charm of Fenimore Cooper and still remain skeptical of the romance, of the fiction that licensed the imagination to make or remake the world. "There is more than one aspect," he wrote of Don Quixote, "to the charm of that exalted and dangerous figure. . . . After reading so many romances he desired naïvely to escape . . . from the intolerable reality of things. . . . Who would not succumb to such a consoling temptation? Nevertheless it was a form of self-indulgence

. . . The priest and the barber were not unreasonable in their strictures."

Conrad was just as skeptical of the irresponsible intellect as of the irresponsible imagination. When he talked about the idea as the animating principle of his fiction, he was more likely to have in mind a percept than a concept, a feeling or sensation than a specific theory or theorem. As he saw it, the greatest works of literature were unified by something much more pervasive and enigmatical than an idea. Like Galsworthy's *The Man of Property*, they were harmonized by something that couldn't be put into words, by "something altogether more subtle, more remote, whose excellent and faithful unity is reflected rather than expressed in the book, yet is as absolutely . . . present in it as the image in the mirror." Where an idea as such did inhabit his work, Conrad hoped it was too diffuse or diffused to be identifiable. Like the idea of *The Rescue*, it should have "the bluish tenuity of dry wood smoke," should get "lost in the words, as the smoke is lost in the air." The novelist's proper procedure, in short, wasn't the philosopher's deductive procedure but the scientist's inductive one. As the mature artist, the novelist should work, Conrad said, "through inevitable moments to the final situation" instead of "creating the moments for the illustration of the idea."

The novelist was best advised to write, then, *not* from his imagination or his intellect but from his senses or sensations, from what Conrad called his temperament. The world as object, "the surrounding vision of form and color," had its first and most immediate reality in the human senses and sensations and hence to register it in their terms was to register it in its most elemental form. Individuals lived and died; personalities came and went; intellects perished and imaginations withered. But the senses, the sensations, the temperament, lived forever, and to see and record the world according to their simple imperatives was to see and record it without any of those perversions for which a personality or a philosophy or an imagination were responsible. "One's own personality [was]," Conrad said, "only a ridiculous and aimless masquerade of something hopelessly unknown." There remained, he concluded, "nothing but the surrender to one's impulses . . . which is perhaps a nearer approach to truth than any other philosophy of life." He accordingly reviled the enterprises of Shaw and Wells, their eagerness to make the earth a reasonable and therefore possible place. "The grave of individual temperaments is being dug by G. B. S. and H. G. W. with hopeful industry . . ." he sourly observed. ". . . but for the saving of the universe I put my faith in the power of folly." More admirable was the Maupassant whose mode was "more temperamental than rational," whose method was to trust "his senses for information and his instinct for deductions." His own mode and method were, Conrad was sure, no different. If his novels did represent life, it was because they were written, he said, "with a conscientious regard for the truth of my own sensations."

Such a principle of life and art had of course its terrible liabilities. To be the individual and only the individual in the vast universe of form and color, to bear true witness to its spectacle and to do so armed only with the evidence of one's mere senses and sensations, was no ordinary obligation. It was under just such a fearful obligation that Conrad's Decoud, the type of the novelist, the creature "with no faith in anything except the truth of his own sensations," was destined eventually to sink. It was indeed an obligation under which Conrad himself could believe himself sinking. "I am frightened when I remember that I have to drag it all out of myself," he wrote Edward Garnett. "Other writers have some starting point. . . .

They lean on dialect—or on tradition—or on history . . .
they trade upon some tie or some conviction of their time
. . . they know something to begin with—while I don't. I
have had some impressions, some sensations—in my time
. . . And it's all faded." Dire and cruel as it was, however,
the novelist's necessity was also his opportunity. To
represent life, to render it on a scale that didn't diminish
or disfigure it, the novelist must, like Decoud, like human
creatures always and everywhere, abide in the elemental
seas of life without the consolation of traditional or
theoretical readings of it.

To this extent, Conrad's novelist described himself, like
Wordsworth's poet, as an ordinary man addressing other
ordinary men. Faithful to those sensations "felt in the
blood, and felt along the heart," writing from the part of
himself that united him with the great undifferentiated
mass of humankind, the novelist was in touch with that
irreducible reality which all men received and which,
indeed, all men continuously created. To be art, as
Conrad said it, fiction must constitute "the appeal of one
temperament to all the other innumerable temperaments
whose subtle and resistless power endows passing events
with their true meaning, and creates the moral . . .
atmosphere of the place and time." Though Conrad liked
to think, then, that he was too individual to be imitated,
he also liked to think that he wasn't *too* individual, that he
wasn't "specialized enough to call up imitators." He
fancied himself in fact as a perfectly ordinary agent, as
something of a man-in-the-street. "I stand much nearer the
public mind than Stevenson . . ." he boasted. "My point
of view, which is purely human, my subjects, which are not
too specialized . . . cannot possibly stand in the way of a
large public."

If the novelist was empowered to represent reality,
however, it wasn't only because he wrote as a normal man

addressing other normal men. It was also because he wrote
from a sensibility in its perfectly normal state. In his effort
"to move others deeply," to move them to laughter or
tears, the artist as tragic or comic poet was himself "carried
away beyond the bounds of our normal sensibility" and so
became "the victim of his own exaggeration." But the
novelist, the artist as scientist, kept within "the bounds of
our normal sensibility," "[looked] on with undimmed eyes
and [kept] laughter out of his voice," and so maintained
his hold on that elemental and elementary reality for
which the poet had no use. "I, too," Conrad said, "would
like . . . that command over laughter and tears which is
declared to be the highest achievement of imaginative
literature. Only, to be a great magician one must surrender
oneself to occult and irresponsible powers, either outside
or within one's breast. . . . I have a positive horror of
losing even for one moving moment that full possession of
myself which is the first condition of good service." He
took up his first novel, he boasted accordingly, in no
inspired, no Dionysiac, mood: "I charged my pipe in the
usual way and I looked for the matchbox with glances
distraught indeed but exhibiting, I am ready to swear, no
signs of a fine frenzy." Forbidden to write in a state of
abnormal excitement, it followed that the novelist was
also forbidden to awaken in others a state of abnormal
excitement. Fallen creatures that they were, ordinary
readers artlessly demanded to be moved or touched or
otherwise entertained. But the true novelist, Conrad
insisted, stubbornly refused their vulgar desire "to be
edified, consoled, amused . . . frightened, or shocked, or
charmed." Hence his bitter chagrin when some artless
readers found "The End of the Tether" *affecting*.
"Touching, tender, noble, moving. . . . Let us spit!"
Conrad wrote in a rage of artistic virtue.

It was with the studied sobriety of the French, then, and

not with the humor and pathos of the English, that
Conrad chose to be associated. "I mustn't exaggerate," he
instructed himself. "It is not my speciality. I am not a
humoristic writer." Like Maupassant, the novelist must
resist, Conrad said, "the seductions of sentiment, of
eloquence, of humour, of pathos; of all that splendid
pageant of faults that pass between the writer and his
probity." Like the scientist himself, he must write. in a
spirit of critical detachment and impartiality. If he would
represent life, if he would "bear true testimony to . . . the
abiding mystery of the sublime spectacle," he had to
assume in its presence that attitude of skepticism which
Conrad extolled as "the tonic of minds, the tonic of life,
the agent of truth."

In the long run, then, the novel's realism was a
condition less of the subject itself than of the author's
treatment of it. "Subjects in themselves," Conrad maintained, "never appear revelatory to me . . . It depends
really on him who picks it up." That many of his fictions
were exotic or tropical, were African or Malaysian or
Indonesian, didn't really matter, didn't make them romances. What really mattered, what made them novels
and nothing else, was that they had been treated tempera-
mentally or sensationally, was that they had been exam-
ined and recorded in the rigorously skeptical spirit of the
scientist. "The mere fact of dealing with matters outside
the general run of everyday experience," as Conrad put it,
"laid me under the obligation of a more scrupulous fidelity
to the truth of my own sensations." Conrad was accordingly distressed by his reputation as a specialist in sea
stories. His life at sea had, he protested, "about as much
bearing on . . . my quality as a writer as the enumeration
of drawing-rooms which Thackeray frequented could have
had on his gift as a great novelist."

IV

So far as the novel, according to Conrad's strict interpretation of it, issued from the author's senses or sensations, the artistic process, the process that brought the novel into being, was less conscious than unconscious. "Switch off the critical current of your mind and work in darkness," he once exhorted Edward Garnett. "For me," he confided to Wells, "writing . . . is just simply the conversion of nervous force into phrases . . . when the nervous force is exhausted the phrases don't come—and no tension of will can help." There were times, it's true, when he conceived the creative act as an anxiously meditated or premeditated one. The trouble with the novelist in the good old English tradition, Conrad said, was that he regarded his books "simply as an instinctive . . . outpouring of his own emotions" instead of "building [them] up with a precise intention and a steady mind." Indeed, when he was justifying his work to the son of the publisher Blackwood—"I know exactly what I am doing" —he described himself as a writer in the conscientious tradition of the French and specifically repudiated the cause of temperamental writing for which he had elsewhere declared himself so passionately. "I am not writing 'in the air,' " he wrote angrily. "It is not the haphazard business of a mere temperament. There is in it as much intelligent action guided by a deliberate view of the effect to be attained as in any business enterprise." As the devotee of the *mot juste*, certainly, he couldn't help feeling that novels were made, not born. Not one of his own successful stories, Conrad declared, "was achieved without much conscious thought bearing . . . on the problems of their style."

By and large, however, the artistic performance was for

him more Dionysiac than Apollonian. "How mysteriously independent of myself is my power of expression . . ." he wrote his publisher. "I am not as the work men who can take up and lay down their tools. I am . . . only the agent of an unreliable master." He liked to believe, therefore, that what he'd produced had been produced by no process of conscious art, that it was the work of a mysterious tact not entirely his own. "The Secret Sharer . . . is *it*. Eh?" he wrote Garnett in a moment of elation. ". . . Every word fits and there's not a single uncertain note. Luck my boy. Pure luck." "Things get themselves written," he told Garnett earlier. ". . . when I do consciously try to write or try to construct then . . . the quality of my miserable and benighted intelligence is disclosed." Conrad didn't see himself, then, as the rigorous reviser in the Flaubertian sense. What had been committed to paper by the power of unconscious art it was beyond the power of a conscious art to alter or improve. "Nothing now can unmake my mistake . . ." he wrote of *The Outcast*, "because all my work is produced unconsciously . . . It isn't in me to improve what has got itself written."

To this extent, to the extent that it was the product of unconscious writing, a novel was less something made than something experienced, was less something built than something lived. It was, as Conrad described it, "a creative effort in which mind and will and conscience are engaged to the full, hour after hour, day after day, away from the world." It wasn't to make-believe in the playful spirit of the English novelist nor was it to negotiate in the deliberate manner of the French novelist. It was almost literally to believe and even live one's novel; it was to become the victim of one's own illusion. "There had been moments . . . when I was an extreme revolutionist . . ." Conrad wrote *a propos The Secret Agent*. "I don't say this to boast. I was simply attending to my business . . . It

would have bored me too much to make believe." He
would appear, indeed, to have believed *Under Western
Eyes* all too intensely. After its completion he lived for
days, his wife disclosed, under the spell of his own illusion:
". . . he lives mixed up in the scenes and holds converse
with the characters." To write a novel wasn't to pretend; it
was to believe. It wasn't to invent something; it was to live
it.

In spite of his reputation, then, as a novelist in the
rigorously professional tradition of the French, Conrad
declared himself surprisingly indifferent to matters of craft
and technique. Neither in his essays and prefaces nor in his
letters and memoirs did he show much interest in the
specific strategies of the novelist's art. Since the novelist
proceeded less consciously than unconsciously, it was less
important to have the right technique which was conscious
than to have the right character which was unconscious. It
was less important to have an artistic apparatus than to
have an artistic temperament. The success of Galsworthy's
The Man of Property had much to do, Conrad considered, with the author's character, his artistic or temperamental response to the world, and very little to do with
"considerations of subject and method fascinating to the
limited nature of human literary minds." Conrad professed the same indifference to questions of literary style.
"To have the gift of words is no such great matter," he
said. It was more important to express the right attitude in
the presence of the surrounding vision of form and color.
Its "amazing felicity of conception" was, Conrad said of
Galsworthy's *Strife*, "a thing infinitely greater than mere
felicity of expression." The defect of Bennett's *Man from
the North*, on the other hand, was that its felicity was all
of the expression and not of the conception. "I am
profoundly impressed with the achievement of style. . . .
The thing as written is undeniable. . . . [but] the book (as

a novel, not as a piece of writing) *is* disputable." When Conrad came to the defense of his own fiction, then, it wasn't at all on the grounds of the sophistication of his art and style, but on the grounds of the stability of his moral character. "I've rejected the idea of [my own] worthlessness . . ." he said. ". . . given my talent, the fundamental and permanent failure could only be the outcome of an inherent worthlessness of character. Now my character is formed . . . I have looked upon the worst life can do—and I am sure of myself."

Conrad declined, therefore, to take an exalted or esctatic view of the artist and his art. If it was true that the novelist worked unconsciously, that he was an instrument of a power greater than himself, that the reality he created was not from his own intellect or imagination but from the senses or sensations of the human millions living and dead, then he could rightfully claim for his office, Conrad believed, no especial glory or grandeur. "Literary creation . . . has no value," he maintained, "but on the condition of not excluding the fullest recognition of all the more distinct forms of action. This condition is sometimes forgotten by the man of letters, who often . . . is inclined to lay a claim of exclusive superiority for his own amongst all the other tasks of the human mind." Alphonse Daudet was accordingly approved because he went about his work "with the disinterestedness of the toiler," because he never sought to claim for his art a special significance, religious, philosophical or otherwise. As for himself, Conrad declared himself indifferent to literature regarded as anything but a form of humble, self-forgetful toil. "I had no conception of what a literary ambition may be," he recalled in his later years, "and I don't know that I understand it even now." In his role as the historian of the great life, not the pride of the artist but the humility of the worker was the novelist's only proper posture.

V

To some extent the "morality" of the novel, its status as an appraisal as well as a description of life, was coextensive with the nature of the universe itself. Since this universe was an amazing spectacle that was its own moral end, the novelist had only to be faithful to the spectacle and its meaning must inevitably disclose itself. For Conrad, accordingly, the novel's realism wasn't in itself morally inactive. To represent the world wasn't simply to record its surface of "vain appearances." It was, by that very token, to reveal its inner meaning. It's true of course that the novel also expressed the novelist's individual sense of things. Since, however, self and world, subject and object, composed one single circuit; since, moreover, the novel expressed that part of the individual that united him with other men and things; since in fact the novelist existed only to bear true witness to the supreme and abiding reality of the world around him: the novel affirmed not a "morality" eccentric to the novelist as individual but a "morality" essential to the universe itself.

If the novel wasn't morally indifferent, however, it was also because it reflected, as a form of realism, a specific moral attitude before the world. To represent this world wasn't only to describe it fully and accurately. It was also to express a sympathy and solidarity with it. The philosopher or theologian who fixed the real in the frame of an *a priori* theory declared in effect his impatience and dissatisfaction with it. But the novelist who placed the real in its own sufficient frame declared a "God-sent form of trust in the magic force and inspiration belonging to the life of this earth." Like the Maupassant who trusted "his senses for information and his instinct for deductions," he offered himself as "a true and dutiful lover of our earth."

Hence one of the more recurrent and more resonant motifs in Conrad's apologetics of the novel: it is, he said, "the spirit of piety towards all things human which sanctions the conceptions of a writer of tales."

Accordingly, the failure of the lyric and tragic poet wasn't only a representational failure, a failure of truth: it was also a moral failure, a failure of piety. It wasn't only that the poet falsified, out of a lyrical emotion, the great world of man and nature. It was also that he asked of man and nature more than man and nature had to give and so offended against that piety for all things human and natural that sustained the novelist. "That's your poet," Conrad said with Marlow. "He demands too much from others." That was your tragic poet, too, Conrad said in effect. Instead of interpreting life, in the sober terms of the scientist, as a "blind agitation caused mostly by hunger and complicated by love and ferocity," he interpreted it, in the exaggerated terms of the poet, as a sublime event and so dishonored the truth of human life. "It may be consoling . . . but it is scarcely honest," Conrad protested, "to shout at those who struggle drowning in an insignificant pool: You are indeed admirable and great to be the victims . . . of such a terrible ocean!" It was indeed to sacrifice life to art, to sacrifice a helpless humankind to the vanity of the artist. Man's misfortunes were "tragic enough in their droll way," Conrad conceded, but they weren't "so momentous and profound as some writers—probably for the sake of Art—would like to make us believe."

While the tragic poet demonstrated his failure of sympathy by making his picture of life more beautiful than life, the comic poet demonstrated it by making his picture less beautiful than life. If it wasn't our business to "praise [mankind] for what it is not," said Conrad, neither was it our business to "reprove mankind for what it is." Satirical comedy he therefore rejected as "a vain use of intelligence," as the sign of a cold and callous contempt for the human condition. The proper office of the artist was to pity and accept, not ridicule and reject. It was to take survey of all· the world "with a large forgiveness." The inadequacy of English novelists like Dickens and Thackeray, Conrad said, was that they hated what did exist and so "emotionally excelled in rendering the disagreeable." But the true novelist came to terms with what did exist, with the disagreeable: his, Conrad said, was the "graver task" of finding "beauty, grace, charm in the bitterness of truth." Conrad was accordingly anxious to dissociate his novels from a satiric intention. He had no desire, he said, to ridicule the Evangelical cook in *The Nigger of the "Narcissus"*: "Nothing was further from my thoughts than irreverence. It would have been untrue to my convictions. The worst that can be charged against me is artistic failure,—failure to express the mixed sentiments the men . . . awakened in me."

If the novelist was required to particularize, then, it wasn't only because the particular was the condition of the real. It was also because it was the condition of a sympathetic appreciation of the real. James wasn't, Conrad argued, the heartless witness of the world Galsworthy accused him of being. "His really wide sympathy" was visible, Conrad said, in his loving attention to detail: "his heart shows itself in the delicacy of his handling." It was indeed this loving attention to detail that defined for Conrad the moral superiority of novelist to tragedian. "The history of men on this earth . . ." he wrote, "may be resumed in one phrase of infinite poignancy: They were born, they suffered, they died . . . But in the infinitely minute stories about men and women it is my lot on earth to narrate I am not capable of such detachment." The same moral logic explained the novelist's preoccupation with human character and with the ordinary in human character. The priority of character over plot, of the ordinary over the extraordinary, revealed in the novelist an acceptance of all that was natural and human. Conrad could despise the supernatural in life and literature, could passionately deny that it had ever entered *The Shadow-Line*, not only because it falsified life, but also because, as a falsification, it insulted "the world of the living, suffering humanity," was "insensitive to the intimate delicacies of our relation to the dead and to the living." "The world of the living," he said, "contains enough marvels and mysteries as it is." Conrad scorned the spiritual in literature for the same reason that it affronted the world of the living. The sign of Turgenev's "essential humanity," of his moral superiority to "the convulsed terror-haunted Dostoevski," was, he said, that "all his creations . . . [were] human beings, not . . . damned souls knocking themselves to pieces in the stuffy darkness of mystical contradictions." Conrad attacked heroic literature—the aristocratic literature of love and war—from the same ethical position that it offended against the human and the natural. Like Defoe and Richardson before him, he questioned it not only on the representational grounds that it was out of all relation to life, but also on the moral grounds, on the humane and humanitarian grounds, that its values were uncivilized. "A world of inflammable lovers of the Romeo and Juliet type," he believed with Marlow, "would very soon end in barbarism and misery." He accordingly took pleasure in reporting that his own life at sea hadn't been at all heroic. "My life . . . was far from being adventurous," he disclosed. ". . . its colouring wears the sober hue of hard work and exacting calls of duty, things . . . not much charged with a feeling of romance."

The novelist best expressed his feeling for life not by making it *more* marvelous than it was but by making it *as* marvelous as it was. Like Wordsworth's, his mission was to

prove the ordinary extraordinary, was to prove that the
ordinary was extraordinary enough. It was to prove that
the modern or moral form of heroism was just as
remarkable in its way as the ancient or physical form of it.
"The struggles Mr. Henry James chronicles . . . [were]
none the less heroic . . . for the absence of shouted
watchwords, clash of arms and sound of trumpets . . . The
fiercest excitements of a romance *'de cape et d'épée,'* the
romance of yard-arm and boarding pike so dear to youth,
whose knowledge of action . . . is imperfect and limited,
are matched, for the quickening of our maturer years, by
the tasks set . . . to the sense of truth, of necessity—before all, of conduct—of Mr. Henry James's men and
women." Conrad indeed suggested that the real hero of a
novel wasn't any of the characters but the novelist himself.
The novelist himself was the model of that moral or
psychological heroism of which every human soul, however
commonplace, was capable. By representing life, by es-
chewing the easy solutions of tragedy and comedy, philosophy and religion, the novelist as novelist affirmed his
heroic confidence in the appeal of life itself, in its power
to sustain the human mind and imagination. By proving
the novel was fit to read, he proved that life itself was fit to
live. "Is it such a very mad presumption," Conrad said, "to
believe in the sovereign power of one's art, to try for other
means [than the literary distortions of tragedy and com-
edy] . . . of affirming this belief in the deeper appeal of
one's work?"

Insofar as he saw the world with the clinical detachment
of the scientist, the novelist did expose himself, it's true, to
the charge of heartless indifference. "There are those who
reproach me with the pose of brutality," Conrad said. "I
am suspected," he complained, "of a certain unemotional,
grim acceptance of facts—of what the French would call
sécheresse du coeur." But to practise the disinterestedness

of the scientist, to decline the laughter and the tears of comedy and tragedy, wasn't to be guilty of indifference, he said. On the contrary, it was to betray a feeling for the world unknown alike to the comic and the tragic poet. "I have approached the object of my task, things human, in a spirit of piety," he declared. ". . . I've neither grinned nor gnashed my teeth . . . I've tried to write with dignity, not out of regard for myself, but for the sake of the spectacle." He accordingly defended with some feeling the Maupassant who had neglected "to qualify his truth with the drop of facile sweetness." "The disregard of these common decencies lays him open to the charges of cruelty, cynicism, hardness," Conrad said. "And yet . . . this man wrote from the fullness of a compassionate heart." The detachment of the novelist was more after all than a method, than a way of representing the nature of things. It was also an ethic, was a way of expressing a tender regard for this nature more impressive in the end than the "attachment" of poet, priest or philosopher.

The same moral value was connected in Conrad's mind with temperamental writing. To write from the senses and sensations wasn't only to represent, wasn't only to establish the most sensitive contact with an unconditioned and unconditional reality. It was also to sympathize, to establish the most compassionate contact, with that reality. It was to render, as Conrad put it, "his own deeper and more sympathetic emotions in the face of his belief in men and things." For Conrad, indeed, the novelist was as much the democrat as the scientist of life and literature. If he was faithful to those Wordsworthian sensations "felt in the blood, and felt along the heart," it wasn't only because he would represent, would feel the same rudimentary reality that all men felt. It was also because he would affirm his affiliation with all men. "I am sufficient of a democrat," Conrad claimed, "to detest the idea of being a writer of

any 'coterie' of some small self-appointed aristocracy . . .
As a matter of feeling—not as a matter of business—I
want to be read by many eyes." The aristocratic cast of his
mind and character did sometimes make, it's true, for a
species of antipopulism. He professed a disdain for "the
inconceivable stupidity of the common reader." "One
writes for a chosen little group . . ." he told Arnold
Bennett. "The public comes in or stays away—and really it
does not matter." This wasn't his usual line, however. He
could hardly claim to write from that temperamental part
of himself where he was one with all men without wanting
to have a "distinct sense of my work being tangible to
others than myself." His pleasure was accordingly pure and
unfeigned when he became for the first time, with the
publication of *Chance*, a popular author. What he'd most
feared, he confessed, was becoming "a writer for a limited
coterie; a position which would have been odious to me as
throwing a doubt on the soundness of my belief in the
solidarity of all mankind."

The moral value of temperamental writing wasn't only,
however, that it demonstrated the novelist's own essential
community with men and things. It was also that it
demonstrated the reader's own essential community with
them. Writing from those deeps or darks where thought
and theory had no place, from those levels of experience
where he was sympathetically one with man and nature,
the novelist aroused in the reader "that feeling of unavoidable solidarity . . . which binds men to each other and all
mankind to the visible world." Called "decivilized" because they dealt with the exotic in peoples and places,
Almayer's Folly and *Within the Tides* were defended
exactly on the grounds that, written with a "scrupulous
fidelity to the truth of my own sensations," they had made
"unfamiliar things credible" and so "created a bond
between us and that humanity so far away." "What is a

novel," Conrad asked, "if not a conviction of our fellow-men's existence strong enough to take upon itself a form of imagined life clearer than reality?"

For Conrad, in short, the novel was urgently moral in the sense that it was urgently social. If it presented itself as a form of science or history, it was because it was moved by a missionary impulse to quicken man's knowledge of and communion with the sensible world about him. It sought to enlarge, as Conrad said of Proust, "the general experience of mankind by bringing to it something that has not been recorded before." He accordingly insisted that the novel's form be dramatic not only on the representational grounds that the form of life itself was dramatic, but also on the moral grounds that only dramatic form had the power to arouse a vivid and sympathetic knowledge of life. The thing dramatized not only made the reader *see* it in the sense of visualizing it; it also made him *see* it in the sense of connecting with it. The omniscient author who stood outside or above his handiwork assumed, Conrad charged, "the hieratic and imbecile pose of some cheap god whose greatness consists in being too stupid to care." But the dramatic author who disappeared into or behind his handiwork assumed the more humane position of a man whose greatness consisted exactly in his having the intelligence or imagination to care.

The novelist, the artist as realist, was involved in something more, then, than a purely scientific enterprise. He was involved in a religious enterprise, too. To represent, to render the real without deforming or transforming it, was to express not disbelief but belief, not irreverence but reverence. It was to approach life with an emotion almost indistinguishable from a religious emotion. If the novelist took himself and his art seriously, if he declined to regard them as forms of fun or play or make-believe, it was just because he took life seriously. "I was never one of those wonderful fellows," as Conrad put it, "that would go afloat in a wash-tub for the sake of the fun, and . . . it was ever just the same with my writing." For Conrad, indeed, the novelist was by definition the optimist. Insofar as he represented life, insofar as he rendered it not as it might be or as it might have been but as it really was, he affirmed in effect his tender faith in its possibilities. "The pursuit of happiness . . ." Conrad said, "is the only theme that can be legitimately developed by the novelist." Fidelity-to-life was more after all than a representational imperative. It was a moral imperative, too. To be true to it in the artistic sense was to be true to it in the moral sense. It was to cast a vote of faith, of belief, of confidence, in the entire sufficiency of this life, this time, this world.

James Joyce, 1882–1941. Portrait by Jacques Emile Blanche, 1935. (*The Bettmann Archive*)

4 James Joyce:
It's All Won

James Joyce wasn't, like James and Conrad, to the manner born. His first loyalties were to poetry and the drama. They weren't, however, the lasting loyalties of Thomas Hardy. The young poet defected to prose with none of the older man's bitter reluctance and regret. "He always spoke disparagingly of himself as a 'pote' . . ." his brother Stanislaus recalls; "he considered prose the higher literary form." He didn't share, moreover, Hardy's veneration for the narrative and dramatic masterpieces of the past. Describing it as "a syllabus of greenroom proprieties . . . which in after ages were foolishly set up as the canons of dramatic art," he decided that "Greek drama [was] played out." Shakespeare himself didn't survive the Joycean purge. Though he had delivered the *coup de grâce* to the prestige of Greek drama, his tyranny over the present was no less oppressive. "Both of these dramas," Joyce flatly announced, ". . . may be relegated to the department of literary curios."

Joyce didn't reject the literary forms of the past, however, in order to affirm the special claims of the novel. He never talked about the novel as a special form of fiction in the reverential way that James and Conrad did. If he did repudiate the authority of traditional drama, it was in Ibsen's name and in the name of Ibsen's prose drama. Nevertheless, by declaring the independence of drama in prose, Joyce also declared the independence of fiction in prose. Indeed, he extolled Defoe precisely on the grounds that he was the first to liberate English literature from the baneful influence of Italy, from the baneful influence of classical and medieval literary models. For him as for James and Conrad, the modern art of fiction, like the modern art of drama, owed nothing whatsoever to the narrative and dramatic masterpieces of the past.

I

If this was so, it was because the scientific epistemology upon which the novel was founded had displaced, he recognized, the religious epistemology upon which tragedy and epic had been founded. For Stephen Dedalus, for the artist as a very young man, the world was a theorem of universality, was "one vast symmetrical expression of God's power and love." But after his fall from grace, after his exposure to Ibsen and the vulgarity of experience, he would come to doubt that everything rehearsed the same single design, that "everything [was] the same as everything else." "Though humanity may not change beyond recognition during the short eras known as the ages of man," he argued, "yet these ages are the preys of different ideas in accordance with which every activity . . . which they engender is conceived and directed." Reality didn't flourish independently, that is, of time and space; it flourished in and through time and space. It didn't remain unchanged from time to time and from place to place; it changed its character from time to time and from place to place. This wasn't of course to say there was no universal

at all, no law or logic in the world. Joyce didn't reject
traditional system and belief in order to reject all system
and belief. The world of physical appearances might shift
and alter in the flux of time and history but, he maintained, "the deathless passions, the human verities . . . are
indeed deathless, in the heroic cycle, or in the scientific
age." The verities he had in mind, the verities of a
scientific age, were, however, immanental, not transcendental. The world was still a theorem of universality, but
that universality was natural and terrestrial, not divine and
supernatural. In Nature, as in a perfect poem, Joyce
believed with Saint Augustine, nothing was accidental or
unintended. He was accordingly confident that without
the aid of gods or priests or fathers, man could seize the
logic that lurked inside and linked together the things of
this world, that the artist could, as secular seer, "arrive at a
sane understanding of so-called mysteries if [he] only had
patience enough." What devoted him to Ibsen was just his
"wilful resolution to wrest the secret from life." And what
devoted him to the philosopher Bruno was just this same
wilful resolution: "Inwards from the material universe . . .
he passes, and from heroic enthusiasm to enthusiasm to
unite himself with God."

The new epistemology called of course for a new
methodology, for an empirical and inductive methodology. "The ancient spirit accepted phenomena with a bad
grace," Joyce complained with Stephen Dedalus. "The
ancient method investigated law with the lantern of
justice, morality with the lantern of revelation, art with
the lantern of tradition. But all these lanterns have
magical properties: they transform and disfigure. The
modern method examines its territory by the light of day."
If Joyce embraced prose fiction, then, it was because its
method was modern. It was because of all the literary
forms it seemed most willing to accept phenomena with a

good grace. Dispensing with those magical lanterns that would transform and disfigure, it proposed to look at life in the light of day, to see and record it in its own strong light. It proposed, in a word, to *represent* reality.

Joyce was therefore hostile to all those *a priori* valuations that would compromise the novel's representational rôle. Since nature had a logic of its own, the logic brought to bear upon it by the philosopher and the propagandist could only be impertinent in both senses of the term. "Balzac's reputation rests on a lot of neat generalizations about life," Joyce scornfully observed. "Why had I written about ideas, why had I condescended to make generalizations?" Yeats recalled being asked at their famous meeting. Joyce was accordingly pleased to report that he had no political convictions of any kind. "I have no wish," he told his brother, "to codify myself as anarchist or socialist or reactionary." He had even less wish to codify himself as the patriot and the priest in literature. Expected, as a good Irishman, to put his art to the service of church and state, he appealed to the authority of old Aquinas in whose theory of beauty he could find no trace "of this Puritanic conception of the esthetic purpose." "I hear no mention of instruction or elevation," Stephen Dedalus said. Hence the logic of Joyce's repudiations. Ibsen's early play, *Catilina*, savored, he said, "of dogma—a most proper thing in a priest but a most improper in a poet." Kipling hadn't lived up to his great natural talents, Joyce said, because he had had, like Tolstoi and D'Annunzio, "semifanatic ideas about religion or about patriotism." He wasn't himself likely, Joyce considered, to make this mistake. If he deemed himself "an artist by temperament," it was because, "neither *savant* nor saint," he didn't, like Renan, have "the temperament of a philologist" or, like Newman, "the temperament of a theologian."

Nor would he have, for this reason, the temperament of a poet. The savant and the saint would visit on the world a mind too powerful and impatient; but the poet would visit on it an *imagination* too powerful and impatient. "In works of fancy," the young Joyce had written, "a too prolific imagination literally flys [sic] away with the author, and lands him in regions of loveliness unutterable" and hence must be "subdued by vigilance and care." For Joyce, accordingly, the romantic artist was no match for the classical. As the romantic artist saw it, nature didn't exist in any stubbornly objective sense and so could offer no serious resistance to the urgencies of his imagination. But as the classical artist saw it, nature did have its own irrefutable existence and so set very definite limits on the activity of his imagination. Like Henrik Ibsen, he must labor to unite "his strong, ample, imaginative faculty . . . with the things present to him." Joyce was therefore happy to admit that he had as little imagination as he had philosophy. "Unfortunately I have very little imagination," he wrote Ezra Pound; but without suggesting thereby that he was really missing anything. Not beauty but truth, not poetry but science, was after all the artist's only true vocation. "Beauty is the swerga of the aesthete," Joyce declared; "but truth has a more ascertainable and more real dominion. Art is true to itself when it deals with truth." Under the circumstances, the artist's only proper attitude before the world wasn't the passionate imagination of the poet but the sober sense of the scientist. There was, Joyce implied, a special connection between Ibsen's "perfect vision" and his "angelic dispassionateness." There was or ought to be a special connection, he elsewhere implied, between the "artistic inclination" itself and the "state of indifference." It was, accordingly, with the rigorously objective tradition of the French novel and not with the moralizing and idealizing tradition of the English

that Joyce aligned himself. "Without boasting," he said,
"I think I have little or nothing to learn from English
novelists." "Je confesse que je dois beaucoup," he wrote
later, "aux écrivains français."

To represent life, to avoid the perils and penalties of the
poet and the philosopher, the artist had, like the scientist,
to consult the concrete and the particular. He couldn't
choose, like the romantic artist, to behold his ideals
"under insensible figures" or "adventures lacking the
gravity of solid bodies." He had instead, like the classical
artist, "to bend upon these present things." Joyce indeed
insisted on a nearly fanatical fidelity to literal fact. When
he was writing *Dubliners*, he asked his brother to authenticate the host of trivial details he couldn't himself authenticate from his exile. "Can a priest be buried in a habit?";
"Can a municipal election take place in October?"; "Are
the police supplied with provisions by government or by
private contracts?" And when he was writing *Ulysses*, he
asked his aunt Josephine to perform the same painful
service. "I want . . . all the information you can give,
tittletattle, facts etc about Hollis Street maternity hospi-
tal," he wrote her in the throes of the "Oxen of the Sun"
episode. "Get an ordinary sheet of foolscap and a pencil,"
he instructed her in a rage of creation, "and scribble any
God damn drivel you may remember about these people."
For Joyce it wasn't enough that a novel be *like* history; it
was necessary, it seemed, that it *be* history. Indeed, as
Joyce understood it, the novelist's facts should come as
abundantly as the facts of history. Since life was by its very
nature inexhaustible and encyclopaedic, the work of art
should seem no less so. When Wyndham Lewis denounced Gothic architecture as "a fussy multiplication of
accents, demonstrating a belief in the virtue of *quantity*,"
Joyce came accordingly to its defense: ". . . as a matter of
fact," he said, "I do something of that sort in words." "I

want," he confessed, "to give a picture of Dublin so complete that if the city one day suddenly disappeared from the earth it could be reconstructed out of my book." The novelist was by definition the artist whose model of the world was nearly as exquisite and immense as the world it imitated.

It was especially crucial for Joyce, therefore, that art be directly the product of his personal experience and observation. When a writer relied on the verifiable materials of his own life, he was less likely to imagine in the fashion of the poet, to generalize in the fashion of the philosopher. He was more likely to particularize in the conscientious fashion of the scientist. Joyce was sure, his brother Stanislaus reported, that even the greatest artists "offered the world a make-believe" because they "belied the life they knew." He accordingly rated D'Annunzio's *Il Fuoco* the highest achievement of the novel to date because it asserted, he said, in his brother's paraphrase, "the inalienable right of the artist to use his own life and the lives of those around him as material for his art without consideration for people." Indeed, Joyce's normally unshakable confidence could at times be shaken by the sense that his own immediate experience wasn't sufficient, that he hadn't lived and seen enough to do Dublin a novelist's justice. "If I knew Ireland as well as R. K. [Rudyard Kipling] seems to know India I fancy I could write something good," he wrote ruefully from exile. "But it is becoming a mist in my brain rapidly. I have the idea of three or four little immortal stories in my head but I am *too cold* to write them." Joyce solved his problem, however, by ruthlessly exploiting the lives of others, by claiming and exercising the artist's inalienable right to use "the lives of those around him." He mightn't know the Irish well enough; but others did. He may not have lived enough himself; but others had. In composing the stories in *Dubliners*, he accordingly helped himself, with or without permission, to his brother's diaries and letters. For Joyce as for perhaps no other novelist, past or present, the novel depended for its representational authority not on the fabrications of the author's imagination but on the established facts of real life and history.

To be the scientist of life, to prevent the poet and the philosopher, the novelist hadn't only to be faithful to his own particular *experience* of the world. He had also to be faithful to his own particular *sense* of it. If he wasn't to be betrayed by the siren songs of dogma and beauty, he had to depend exclusively on the evidence of his own unaided sensibility. Stephen Dedalus must contravene the traditions and conventions of his time in order to express himself; but it's even more true that he must express himself in order to contravene the traditions and conventions of his time. He must rigorously repudiate the rabblement because the rabblement was the repository of precisely those *a priori* moral and political convictions that stood between the artist and his probity. If the Irish poet Mangan had "no urgent need to become a shouter, or a preacher, or a perfumer," it was, said Joyce, because he was "one of those strange abnormal spirits . . . who believe that their inner life is so valuable that they have no need of popular support . . . who believe, in sum, that the poet is sufficient in himself, the heir and preserver of a secular patrimony." Hence Joyce's own insistence on the purely personal derivation of his own work. "His own little book," he assured the patriotic folklorist Yeats, *a propos Chamber Music*, "owed nothing to anything but his own mind which was much nearer to God than folklore." "I have certain ideas I would like to give form to," he told his brother: "not as a doctrine but as the continuation of the expression of myself which I now see I began in *Chamber Music*." To be a private person, to have a private personality to express, was to write from a level of being where politics and philosophy and all that came between the writer and the naked form of the truth could have no influence.

To express himself fully and freely, however, wasn't only to liberate the novelist from all moral and political conventions. It was also to liberate him from all literary and artistic conventions. Like investigating "law with the lantern of justice" and "morality with the lantern of revelation," investigating "art with the lantern of tradition" made for misrepresentation. What Joyce called "literature" was inferior to what he called "drama" exactly because it produced not life itself, but a merely literary or conventional version of it: "literature is a comparatively low form of art. . . . it flourishes through conventions in all human relations, in all actuality. Drama will be for the future at war with convention, if it is to realize itself truly." Joyce accordingly refused to associate himself with any specific literary party or program. To repeat the achievements of others, to conform to the literary modes or models of the past, was to create not life itself but only a reprise of it. For Joyce as for James and Conrad, every novelist had necessarily to be different, original. For him as for them every novel had necessarily to be novel. The proverbial pride of the Joycean artist wasn't after all a mere empty pose, a mere affectation, a mere symptom of personal vanity and conceit. His freedom to be himself and express himself without shame or restraint was the absolutely necessary condition of his power to represent the world.

Because reality was for Joyce coextensive with the particular, with all that touched the human senses and sensations, it was also by definition coextensive with the ordinary and the commonplace. What made the world go round wasn't the extraordinary grace of God, the miraculous and unpredictable interventions of the supernatural and the superhuman, but the perfectly ordinary necessities of cause and effect, the unmiraculous and predictable operations of the natural and the human. "Drama," as Joyce defined it, was superior to all other artistic forms just for the reason that it explained all things in terms of wholly human passions and perceptions, in terms of wholly natural causes and conditions. Because it forsook the natural for the supernatural, the human for the superhuman, the later art of William Blake didn't qualify as drama: "the continual strain of these voyages into the unknown and the abrupt return to natural life slowly but inexorably corrode his artistic power." The art of the religious painter, Munkacsy, on the other hand, limited itself to the record of the natural and the human and so did qualify as "drama": "It would have been easy to have made Mary a Madonna and John an evangelist but the artist has chosen to make Mary a mother and John a man . . . If there is to be anything superhuman in the picture . . . it will appear in Christ. But no matter how you view Christ . . . there is nothing superhuman. . . . Consequently his work is drama." The appeal of Homer's Ulysses for Joyce was thus that he was "profoundly human," was that his story didn't invoke the supernatural and so was "more human than that of *Hamlet, Don Quixote,* Dante, *Faust.*"

If an age of science required the artist to renounce the supernatural, an age of democracy required him to renounce the superhuman. The same age that denied the existence of gods and defined reality as human also denied the existence of heroes and defined reality as ordinary. Joyce recognized indeed that the very character of life had changed, that in a civilization governed by burghers and merchants, the heroics of epic and tragedy could have no place. "Epic savagery is rendered impossible by vigilant

policing," the young Joyce said, "chivalry has been killed
by the fashion oracles of the boulevards. There is no clank
of mail, no halo about gallantry, no hat-sweeping, no
roystering!" Even as a young man, however, Joyce was
hardly disturbed by the disappearance of the ancient
heroism. Romantic art was anathema to him precisely
because it was still in love, he said, with "the monstrous or
heroic." Greek drama was anathema to him because it was
romantic, he said, not classical and, as such, "heroic,
monstruous" [sic]. "Eschylus [sic] is not a classical writer,"
he declared with magnificent perversity. Ibsen was, however. It would have been easy, Joyce said, for him "to have
written *An Enemy of the People* on a speciously loftier
level—to have replaced the *bourgeois* by the legitimate
hero," but here as in all his later plays he had chosen
instead "the average lives in their uncompromising truth."
He accordingly denounced an aristocratic literature that,
dressing itself in the gaudy feathers of epic and romance,
scorned the drab domestic realities of a bourgeois civilization. "The people who regulate the demand for fiction,"
he wrote scornfully, "are being day by day so restricted by
the civilization they have helped to build up that they are
not unlike the men of Mandeville's time, for whom
enchantments, and monsters, and deeds of prowess were
so liberally purveyed." For Joyce, indeed, the particular
wasn't just interchangeable with the ordinary and the
commonplace. It was interchangeable with the trivial and
the vulgar. "He deliberately chose," his brother said, "the
base things of the world, the things that are despised . . .
and made himself the paladin of pariah thoughts and
emotions."

For Joyce, therefore, not the plot with its intimations of
the universal and the marvelous but the character with its
intimations of the particular and the trivial was the
novelist's true Penelope. Like "wideawake language" and

"cutandry grammar," "goahead plot," as Joyce called it, made life more rational and schematic than it was and so, his brother said, "he came to consider a well-ordered plot in a novel or story as a meretricious literary interest." In an age that had discountenanced the absolute, Joyce declared, "the writer of dramas must remember now more than ever a principle of all patient and perfect art which bids him express his fable in terms of his characters." Indeed, he considered the play inferior just for the reason that its form didn't permit, as the ampler form of the novel did, a full and detailed notation of character. Not even Shakespeare had created a really complete character, he said, because the conditions of the theater demanded not "complete all-round beings, but only three hours of passionate conflict."

II

To say that the Joycean artist addressed himself to the local and the particular, to character and the conditions of character, wasn't however to say that he had nothing to do with the universal. Since the nature he would represent had its own internal law or logic, the artist as novelist had still, under a secular as under a religious dispensation, to disengage the essential meaning of things. What defined for Joyce the inferiority of "literature," of "the wide domain which lies between ephemeral writing and poetry," was that it was content to register the mere surface appearance: ". . . its merit lay in its portrayal of externals; the realm of its princes was the realm of the manners and customs of societies." The superiority of "poetry" or "drama," on the other hand, was that it "had to do with the underlying laws first, in all their nakedness and divine severity, and only secondarily with the motley agents who bear them out." The novelist had, in short, like any other artist, to "disentangle the subtle soul of the image from its mesh of defining circumstances."

As Joyce saw it, however, the universal wasn't separable from the particular; the soul of the image wasn't separable from the image itself. What Aquinas called "claritas" wasn't, he was sure, "the artistic discovery and representation of the divine purpose in anything or a force of generalization which would make the esthetic image a universal one." By "claritas," said Joyce, Aquinas meant "the scholastic *quidditas,* the *whatness* of a thing," what happened when an object was seen as "that thing which it is and no other thing." Before the soul or whatness of the image could declare itself, before it could achieve its "epiphany," as Stephen christened Aquinas' "quidditas," it had to be recognized first as *one* thing and then as one *thing,* which is to say that its particularity antedated and was a precondition of its universality. The image was the necessary vehicle of the soul of the image; the particular was the necessary vehicle of the universal. If Turgenev was, then, for Joyce, "a great international writer," it was because he was first of all a great local writer. And if it was true that Tolstoi was strong for the soul, it's also true that he was strong, in spite of himself, for the image: "Unlike Saul, the son of Kish," Joyce mordantly observed, "Tolstoy seems to have come out to find a kingdom and to have found his father's asses." As for himself, Joyce was certain he knew what was what. Asses first, kingdoms later. "If I can get to the heart of Dublin," he said, "I can get to the heart of all the cities of the world. In the particular is contained the universal." Hence his admiration for what he called classical art. Choosing as it did "to bend upon these present things and so to work upon them . . . that the quick intelligence may go beyond them to their meaning," it represented, he said, "the only legitimate process from one world to another," from the particular to the universal, from the world of appearance to the world of reality.

Just as a preoccupation with the particular didn't exclude the universal, so a preoccupation with the real didn't exclude the ideal. For all that he admired the fiction of the French, Joyce had his reservations about a realism that made no concession at all to what was fair in life and nature. He preferred the Flaubert of *La Tentation de Saint Antoine* to the Flaubert of *Madame Bovary* and believed that the novel had passed beyond the realistic sobriety of *Madame Bovary* to the lyric exaltation of D'Annunzio. In the throes of *Dubliners*, he felt indeed a rare spasm of self-mistrust, a sneaking suspicion that he may have given too much to truth and not enough to beauty. "The preface to *The Vicar of Wakefield* . . . gave me a moment of doubt," he confessed, "as to the excellence of my literary manners." The doubt, however, was only momentary. Truth and beauty had for Joyce the same essential unity as universal and particular. If Aquinas and Aristotle were right, if "those things [were] beautiful the apprehension of which pleases" and if the activity of perception and recognition was, "like every other activity, itself pleasant," then, said Joyce, "even the most hideous object can be said . . . to be beautiful in so far as it has been apprehended" or, more accurately, could be made so by the artist, by the sheer exactitude and rectitude of his labor. It wasn't for the artist to register a truth divorced from beauty. His sacred office, as the secular priest of the imagination, was to solemnize their marriage, was to stand "in the position of mediator between the world of his experience and the world of his dreams." By the same token, it wasn't for him to register a beauty divorced from truth. As Joyce described him, the artist wasn't, like the common priest, "a fellow who dangles a mechanical heaven before the public." Like William Blake, he con-

nected "the visionary faculty . . . with the artistic faculty"
and so proposed no heaven that wasn't rooted in this
earth. The romantic artist could accept, in a mood of the
darkest despair, the necessary irreconcilability of truth and
beauty, could therefore seek fulfilment in the easy world
of his imagination. But the classical artist refused to accept
as final the separation of truth and beauty and would forge
in the smithy of his art their reconciliation, their remarriage.

To embrace the ordinary in life and nature wasn't
therefore to refuse the extraordinary. For Joyce the
ordinary and the extraordinary were no less inseparable
than the real and the ideal. If Blake was right and eternity
was in love with the products of time, then the very
lowliest of creatures and objects, the very commonest
manifestations of a scientific and democratic age, could be
the vehicles of the vastest meanings and mysteries. "Out of
the dreary sameness of existence," Joyce early maintained,
"a measure of dramatic life may be drawn. Even the most
commonplace, the deadest among the living, may play a
part in a great drama. . . . *Ghosts*, the action of which
passes in a common parlour, is of universal import." What
was suggested in the practice of Ibsen was confirmed in the
theory of Aquinas. For if the sense for beauty was
appeased by "the most satisfying relations of the sensible,"
then it couldn't matter whether "the sensible" belonged
to the category of the ordinary or the extraordinary, to the
category of cabbages or kings. Hence Stephen's denial that
by the beautiful Aquinas meant the sublime. His theory of
beauty, Stephen said, "would apply to a Dutch painter's
representation of a plate of onions." The literary epiphany, the moment when the "claritas" or whatness of a
thing announced itself, he could define therefore as "a
sudden spiritual manifestation, whether in the vulgarity of
speech or of gesture or in a memorable phase of the mind

itself." At such a moment, he said, "the soul of the commonest object . . . seems to us radiant." What accounted for the ineffectuality of romantic art was just its refusal to accommodate the commonest objects. "Imperfect and impatient as it is," Joyce wrote of it, "[it] cannot express itself adequately unless it employs the monstrous or heroic." It was the virtue of classical art, on the other hand, that it scorned the easy way out of the monstrous and heroic and sought in the substance of the ordinary the form of the extraordinary. It proposed to give pleasure, Joyce said, by "transmuting the daily bread of experience into the radiant body of everliving life." Hence the significance of good old Leopold Bloom. To discover in his prosy odyssey the heroic odyssey of Homer's man wasn't only to assert the interdependence of the particular and the universal, the real and the ideal. It was also to assert the interdependence of the ordinary and the extraordinary.

Though the novelist couldn't legitimately lust after the wonders of plot, then, he wasn't therefore condemned to a perfectly plain and prosy reality. Joyce couldn't believe in the end that the world was a world devoid of all marvel and mystery. He couldn't believe that the human creature was everything, that it played no part in a dream or drama greater than itself. The interest of Ibsen's plays didn't depend on the action but neither did it depend, Joyce noted, on the characters themselves. It depended, he said, on "the naked drama—either the perception of a great truth, or the opening up of a great question, or a great conflict which is almost independent of the conflicting actors." Joyce accordingly rejected the notion that reality was by definition social, that character could be explained in the wholly fixed and stable terms of a social reality. The inferior form of "literature" might be satisfied to derive human life from "the customs and manners of societies,"

but the superior form of "poetry" or "drama" was concerned with a larger reality that wasn't comprehended by
the social. As his friend Budgen recalled it, Joyce "attached greater weight to race, nation, and to some real yet
indefinite thing one might call type" as determinants of
human character than to such categories as "trade or
caste."

If life and character weren't for Joyce defined by the
conventional social norms, neither were they defined by
the conventional human norms. He would indeed submit
them to the terms of a new abstractionism, would do for
the human figure what Cézanne and Picasso had done or
were doing for it. Even before he wrote *Stephen Hero,* he
contemplated not the stable character of traditional
realism, but what he called an "individuating rhythm," not
"an identificative paper but rather the curve of an
emotion." In the final episode of *Ulysses,* he hadn't tried
to present Molly Bloom "as a human apparition," he said.
"In conception and technique I tried to depict the earth
which is prehuman and presumably posthuman." What
had been the emphasis of this last section of *Ulysses* was
evidently to be the emphasis of *Finnegans Wake* as a
whole. "There is no connection," Joyce said, "between the
people in *Ulysses* and the people in [*Finnegans Wake*].
There are in a way no characters. . . . If one had to name
a character, it would be just an old man. But his own
connection with reality is doubtful." This nonrepresentational emphasis didn't call, however, for the total extinction of the human image. The human character still
constituted "the only legitimate process from one world to
another," the only legitimate process from the particular
to the universal, from the human to the nonhuman. "The
last word (human, all-too-human) is left to Penelope,"
Joyce wrote Budgen *a propos Ulysses.* "This is the
indispensable countersign to Bloom's passport to eter-

nity." Hence, though there were "in a way no characters" in the pages of *Finnegans Wake*, yet, as Joyce pointed out, "the elements are exactly what every novelist might use: man and woman, birth, childhood, night, sleep, marriage, prayer, death." Whatever his feeling for the wondrous and the wonderful, it obviously involved no rejection of the human and the natural, no failure of confidence in the radical community of particular and universal, character and "drama," human and nonhuman.

The novelist had to be a great deal more, then, than the scientist. To separate the universal from the particular, the subtle soul of the image from its mesh of defining circumstances, he had to be the philosopher as well. The traditional explanations of the universe may have lost their force and their function, but explanations were as necessary today as yesterday, and hence Joyce repudiated a "poetry" that wasn't also a "philosophy." "It must be asked," he said, "concerning every artist how he is in relation to the highest knowledge and to those laws which do not take holiday because men and times forget them." Blake may in his later years have been too much the philosopher and not enough the artist, but this was not, Joyce insisted, to discredit the philosopher in life and literature: "if we must accuse of madness every great genius who does not believe in the hurried materialism now in vogue . . ." he declared indignantly, "little remains for art and universal philosophy." Hence Ibsen's special claim to Joyce's admiration and affection. As great a thinker as he was an artist, he had united the world of his intelligence with the world of his experience and so established an art that joined the universal and the particular.

For something like these reasons, the artist had also to be no less the poet than the scientist. To perceive the ideal and the universal that lay hidden in the real and the particular, the artist had to feel and imagine as much as he observed. If there was "no poetry in French literature," it was, Joyce decided, "because the Kingdom of God cometh not with observation." Though he loved, then, "to fetter his imagination with chains," as his friend Italo Svevo put it, he sometimes feared he didn't have enough imagination. He envied the "pure imagination" he ascribed to Kipling and Emily Brontë and even conceded that Yeats might be a greater writer than himself because the poet had so much imagination and he himself so little. In the long run, however, the human imagination, like the human intellect, seemed to Joyce a means to an end rather than an end in itself. It existed not to create a universal independent of the particular or a beauty independent of the truth, but to define the universal immanent in the particular, the beauty immanent in the truth. "When . . . the gift . . . of a poetic sense . . . has been subdued by vigilance and care . . ." Joyce wrote as a very young man, "the true and superior spirit . . . interprets, without mysticism, for men the great things that are hidden from their eyes." The Joycean artist would unite the poet and the scientist in the same way and for the same reason that he united the philosopher and the scientist. If, as scientist-philosopher, he mediated between the world of his experience and the world of his intelligence, as scientist-poet he mediated "between the world of his experience and the world of his dreams."

To say, then, that the artist expressed the world wasn't to say that he suppressed the self. It was rather to say that the artist's personality, like his intellect or imagination, was a means to an end, not an end in itself. It existed to bear true and faithful witness to the objective reality of the surrounding universe, to act as a species of conductor or transmitter by means of which the world of things passed, and made itself real, to the world of men. "In every other art," Joyce wrote, *a propos* the superiority of "drama," "personality, mannerism of touch, local sense, are held as adornments, as additional charms. But here the artist forgoes his very self and stands a mediator in awful truth before the veiled face of God." What the artist expressed, in short, wasn't his will or ego, but, more elusively, his deeper self or sensibility. The artist was thinker as well as artist, but, Joyce proceeded to say, this wasn't "to look for a message." It was, he said, "to approach the temper which has made the work." The artist expressed himself by uniting himself with the world, with the things present to him, in the same way that the intellect and imagination expressed themselves by uniting themselves with the world, with the things present to them. For all his determined assertion of his own personality, Joyce's aesthetic wasn't quite the "egomaniac" aesthetic his brother called it. "I shall express myself as I am," Stephen says, but he says so only after he has said, "this race and this country and this life produced me." Which is to say that the revelation of self he had in mind was also inevitably a revelation of race and country and life itself. For Joyce subject and object, self and world, particular and universal, weren't mutually exclusive. In the subject was contained the object; in the self was contained the world; in the particular was contained the universal.

Hence the emphasis in Joyce's aesthetic on the principle of dramatic form. To insist that subject and object, particular and universal, were organically continuous with each other was in effect to insist that the form of life itself was identical with the form of drama. Nature wasn't, Joyce said on Aristotle's authority, "a collection of unconnected episodes, like a bad dream (or *drama?*)." It was actuated by the same internal connections that actuated a good drama. "Drama arises spontaneously out of life and is coeval with it," Joyce declared. To be representational, therefore, the form of fiction had necessarily to be dramatic. Like life itself, it had to have its own coherence, a logic not superimposed upon it from without but inhering in and issuing from its own material. Like the world which hadn't been created but which had created itself, it should assume or should seem to assume, like a good play, a life of its own. Put differently, the work of fiction had to have an author but an author inherent in his materials and not arbitrarily imposed upon them. Since the real world was the work not of a Divine Author but of its very own materials, the fictitious world designed to resemble it couldn't legitimately assert itself as the act of an omnipotent author. Like a good play, it should assume or should seem to assume a life of its own. If for Joyce as for Stephen, then, art had progressed as it moved from lyric through epic to dramatic form, it was just for the reason that with each stage in its evolution the artist himself had become increasingly invisible: "The personality of the artist, at first a cry or a cadence or a mood and then a fluid and lambent narrative, finally refines itself out of existence, impersonalizes itself . . . The artist, like the God of the creation, remains within or behind or beyond or above his handiwork, invisible, refined out of existence, indifferent, paring his fingernails." The form of fiction achieved the dramatic form of life itself when its law or its logic and the author who stood behind it were immanent rather than transcendent, consubstantial with things rather than transubstantial.

Indeed, life's law or logic didn't articulate itself as a specific moral or message at all. What unified life wasn't an idea but a form, the form of drama. The dramatic form life took was, that is to say, its only unity, its only universal. Like drama, life was, as Joyce put it, "strife, evolution, movement in whatever way unfolded; it exists before it takes form, independently; it is conditioned but not controlled by its scene." To be really representational, then, fiction had to imitate not an idea but a form, not a theory of life but an instinct for it. It wasn't the office of the artist to preach or instruct openly and explicitly. He had to work through the particular to the universal, but to a universal that remained less a statement than a form. He had to "bend upon these present things . . . [so] that the quick intelligence may go beyond them to their meaning," but to a meaning, Joyce added, which was "still unuttered." Indeed, when art achieved the condition of drama, when it manifested itself "through suggestion rather than direct statement," it acquired, Joyce believed, such a parity with life itself as to be all but irrefutable. "It is hardly possible to criticize The Wild Duck . . ." he declared; "one can only brood upon it as upon a personal woe."

But if the dramatic work of art resembled life, it wasn't only in the sense that its form was the form of life itself. It was also in the sense that its process was the process of life itself, that it came into being in exactly the same way that life itself came into being. When Aristotle said "Art imitates Nature," he didn't mean, Joyce proposed, that "Art is an imitation of Nature." What he meant was that "the artistic process [was] like the natural process" or that "the artistic process was a natural process," which is to say that the work of art formed itself in the same pragmatic and instinctual way that life itself did. "Literature" was an inferior form of art because it rehearsed a merely artistic, a merely conventional, process. But "drama" was superior because it rehearsed the natural process, willed itself into being instead of getting itself willed into being. "Whatever form it takes," Joyce said of it, "must not be superimposed or conventional." He liked accordingly to think that his own work not only *seemed* to create itself but *did* in fact create itself, that like Ibsen's, it was the product of "an artistic manner which was itself almost a natural phenomenon." "Joyce never tried to force his preliminary sketches into a rigid pattern," we're told of the author of *Finnegans Wake*, "but patiently waited for relationships to develop," referring to them as "active elements" which would "fuse of themselves" in time. In the literal as well as in the figurative sense, Joyce in fact refused to behave as the omnipotent god of his creation. According to his friend Eugene Jolas, *Finnegans Wake* seemed "a collective composition in the end, for he let his friends participate in his inventive zeal, as they searched through numberless notebooks with mysterious reference points to be inserted in the text." Indeed, when Joyce's blindness threatened to prevent the completion of *Finnegans Wake*, he conceived the bizarre plan of turning the whole project over to the Irish poet, James Stephens, on the grotesque assumption that anybody could do it and that it didn't really matter who did: "If he consented to maintain three or four points which I consider essential and I showed him the threads he could finish the design." This wasn't, moreover, the aberration of an ailing and troubled man. "Six medical students under my direction will write *Paradise Lost* except 100 lines," he once boasted. Since, like the world, the play had a life of its own, the play, not the playwright, was the thing.

For all his reputation as the arch-egomaniac of modern letters, then, Joyce declined to take a mystical or miraculous view of the artist, declined to see him as the inspired genius of life and literature. Like Stephen Dedalus, "he persuaded himself that it is necessary for an artist to labour incessantly at his art . . . and . . . that every moment of inspiration must be paid for in advance." For Joyce, indeed, that artist was best who wrote as an ordinary man in a perfectly ordinary mental or emotional condition. "Jim says that he writes well because when he writes his mind is nearly as normal as possible." What disabled the romantic artist was that he couldn't behold his ideals in the things of this world and so wrote out of "an insecure, unsatisfied, impatient temper." But what enabled the classical artist was just that he could behold his ideals in the things of this world and so wrote from "a temper of security and satisfaction and peace."

If the Joycean artist wasn't expected to write in an inspired condition, neither was he expected to arouse in the reader an inspired condition. "The feelings excited by improper art," Stephen Dedalus said, "are kinetic, desire or loathing." But in a work of art that was properly a work of art, "the mind [was] arrested and raised above desire or loathing." Tragic art was honored because it "arrest[ed] the mind in the presence of whatsoever is grave and constant in human sufferings" and so exempted it from desire or loathing. Comic art was honored because it aroused not "the feeling of desire" which "urges us from rest that we may possess something," but "the feeling of joy" which "holds us in rest so long as we possess something." Hence Joyce's certainty that the only legitimate form was the form of drama, the form not of statement but of total presentation. Because what it meant was fully and finally expressed in what it was, because it was complete and sufficient in itself, it didn't urge the mind to seek something outside or beyond itself. Putting the reader in full possession of something and therefore holding him in rest, it was static, not kinetic, inspired security and satisfaction, not desire and loathing. Insofar as it was true, insofar as it had to do with intelligible and sensible matter and even with vulgar and squalid matter, it should theoretically arouse an anguish of disgust or longing. But because it was beautiful as well as true, because it converted "the bread of everyday life into something that has a permanent artistic life of its own," because it was "the human disposition of sensible or intelligible matter for an esthetic end" and so created "the most satisfying relations" of sensible or intelligible matter: it raised the mind above the anguish of disgust and longing and arrested it in an act of pure contemplation. Dramatic form was nothing less, in short, than the artist's sanity and satisfaction given artistic form and, in this form, transmitted to the reader. Insofar as it reconciled the particular and the universal, the real and the ideal, the ordinary and the extraordinary, it made the reader see and understand the world, produced in him a sense of peace and satisfaction with it.

III

To say, then, that the work of art should advance no specific moral cause wasn't to say that it could claim no specific moral effect. In the same way that it should be personal without seeming to be personal, philosophical without seeming to be philosophical, the work of art should be moral without seeming to be moral. Stephen Dedalus may have insisted that art be "free from missionary intention," but he never insisted that it also be free from missionary result. In spite of his sinister reputation as the great immoralist or amoralist of modern letters, Joyce's theory of art was in fact an urgently moral one.

The morality of the work of art derived, first of all, from the artist's personality, from his personal vision or version of things. It wasn't the art of Henrik Ibsen that seduced the young poet of *Stephen Hero* but the man and morality behind the art: "the very spirit of Ibsen himself . . . moving behind the impersonal manner of the artist . . . a mind of sincere and boylike bravery, of disillusioned pride, of minute and wilful energy." Conversely, it wasn't the art of Maupassant that Joyce found inadequate but the man and morality behind the art: "Maupassant writes very well, of course, but I am afraid that his moral sense is rather obtuse." It wasn't enough to be a good artist: one had to be a good man as well. It wasn't enough to write well: one had to write to some good moral purpose. What the artist was invited to express wasn't, however, his ego or moral theory of life, but his character or moral feeling for it, wasn't the part of him that separated him from the universe but the part of him that united him with it. Since the world did have a moral end of its own, the novel's morality was coextensive with the artist's personality only insofar as that personality diffused itself in and became one with the form of life itself. This isn't to say that it could be formulated as a specific meaning or message. What unified the novelist's personality wasn't a specific moral idea but a character whose moral idea remained unuttered and unutterable; what unified the world itself wasn't a specific moral idea but a form whose moral idea remained unuttered and unutterable. The novel's morality was a function neither of a moral idea inherent in the author nor of a moral idea inherent in the world. More elusively, it was a function of the artist's moral relation to the world, of his organic and sympathetic relationship to that world.

Hence for Joyce the special significance of the novel's representational form. For him as for James and Conrad, it wasn't morally indeterminate. For him as for them, it revealed in the writer a moral connection with the world, an organic and sympathetic connection with it. To misrepresent it, to make its truth either more or less beautiful than it was, was to declare in effect one's disaffection with it. But to represent it, to see it and show it in its own strong light, was to publish a profound affection for it. The "Arcadian grace" of Goldsmith's treatment of the rural life Joyce identified with "lack of

true insight and sympathy," but the rugged realism of
Crabbe's treatment of it he identified with "appreciation
and fidelity." For Joyce, the essentials of realistic form
were ethical as well as epistemological and aesthetic. To
represent the world was to celebrate the world. Truth-to-
life in the artistic sense meant truth-to-life in the moral
sense.

When Joyce repudiated all traditional approaches to
life, then, it wasn't just because they falsified nature. It was
also because, in so doing, they dishonored it. To be a
Christian was to see the world as "a place of probation";
to be a Neo-Platonist was to see it as "the kingdom of the
soul's malady." But to be a Giordano Bruno, to cast away
religious tradition and approach things as "an independent observer," was at once to see nature as it is and to feel
an "ardent sympathy for nature as it is." What was true for
the philosopher as realist was also true for the artist as
realist. "So long as this place in nature is given us,"
Stephen Dedalus reflected, "it is right that art should do
no violence to the gift." Hence the logic of Joyce's stress
on the novel's particularity. The particular wasn't only a
condition of a vivid sense of the real. It was also a
condition of a keen sympathy for the real. Seeing "no fit
abode here for its ideals and [choosing] to behold them
under insensible figures," a romantic art was unfaithful to
life, artistically in the sense that it didn't register life as it
was, morally in the sense that, by corollary, it showed no
confidence in life as it was. But a classical art did bend
itself on present things, did express its ideals under
sensible figures, and so achieved a fidelity to life at once
artistic and moral, treating all things, as Joyce said of
Ibsen, "with large insight . . . and sympathy." Indeed,
because a romantic art could see "no fit abode here for its
ideals," it approached the world in a mood of despair and
despondency; but because a classical art did see such an

abode here for its ideals, it approached the world in a
"sane and joyful spirit." To generalize reality in the
fashion of the religious philosopher or to imagine it in the
fashion of the romantic artist was to reject reality; but to
particularize reality in the fashion of the classical or
realistic artist was to rejoice in it.

Hence also the logic of Joyce's contention that art
should be a form of vigorous self-assertion. It wasn't just
that to assert the self was to represent, was to render
reality undisfigured by convention and tradition. It was
also that to assert the self fully and fearlessly was to deny
the claims of gods and priests, was to proclaim the
sufficiency of one's own humanity. "To walk nobly on the
surface of the earth, to express oneself without pretence,
to acknowledge one's own humanity": these belonged, for
Stephen and for Joyce himself, in the same logical series.
This indeed was the source of their feeling for Ibsen. To
be an Ibsen, to give expression to "a mind of sincere and
boylike bravery" and to do so in a spirit of "wonderful
calm," was to set a moral example, was to prove that even
in a world without God, human dignity was still possible:
"Let the world solve itself in whatsoever fashion it pleased,
let its putative Maker justify Himself by whatsoever
processes seemed good to Him, one could scarcely advance the dignity of the human attitude a step beyond this
answer." Such an assertion of the personality had nothing
to do of course with the arrogant stance of some omniscient author. To assume such a stance wasn't only to
predicate the existence of a power that stood outside this
world. It was also to militate against a truly sympathetic
relation to this world. For to approach things human from
a standpoint of omniscience was to play god, was to deny
one's humanity and, by inference, the humanity of others.
It was to take a lofty *a priori* view, which is to say an
unsympathetic view, of things human. For Joyce therefore,

the attitude of detachment and dispassion assumed by the
dramatic author, by the author who imitated the indifferent god of the creation, was by no means inconsistent
with sympathy. The Ibsen he admired he admired because
he conjoined "artistic restraint and sympathy." A work of
art shouldn't be solved "according to an ethical idea,"
Joyce said; it should be solved "according to that indifferent sympathy . . . which is so often anathematized by
theologians of the street."

If Joyce espoused the cause of dramatic form, then, it
wasn't only because dramatic form was realistic form, the
form of life itself. It was also because, as such, it created
the basis for a real knowledge of and sympathy with the
form of that life. Insofar as it was complete and sufficient
in itself, insofar as it didn't urge us "to seek something
beyond itself," dramatic art was, Joyce said, an art of
satisfaction. But the satisfaction wasn't just a satisfaction
in the novel as a work of art. Because the dramatic form
was a model of the universe itself, the satisfaction it
produced was also a satisfaction in the form of that
universe. As dramatic form, it placed not only itself but
the world it imitated beyond the pale of criticism. "When
the art of a dramatist is perfect," Joyce said, "the critic is
superfluous. Life is not to be criticized, but to be faced
and lived." In effect if not in intention, the dramatic work
of art performed a species of moral therapy. It inspired in
men and women not an impatience with the form of
things but a perfect patience.

It was as the poet laureate of the ordinary in men and
affairs, however, that Joyce acknowledged most often the
humane and humanitarian values implicit in the aesthetics
of realism. For if he scorned the "legitimate" hero of
traditional drama and fiction, it wasn't just from a rage of
realism, from a rage to define the world as it ordinarily
was. It was also to declare his solidarity with the world as it

ordinarily was. Unlike the Hardys and the Yeatses, Joyce felt no nostalgia for the lusty manners of the ancient kings and heroes, felt perfectly at home in the good safe life of the modern metropolis. He was "more a Dubliner than an Irishman," Frank Budgen observed; "he would rather," Joyce told him, "be burgomaster of a city like Amsterdam than emperor of any empire." If he disparaged Greek epics and Norse sagas, it was thus because the heroic values they cherished were incompatible with the sober values he shared with the modern middle class community. "In the sagas of Norway, in ancient epics in the tales of 'knights and barons bold' . . ." he wrote disdainfully as a young man, "we have abundant examples of the havoc that men's passions make, when they are allowed to spend their force in Bersirk freedom." "At school," his brother Stanislaus tells us, "he always made fun of the heroes of the *Iliad* and the *Odyssey*, who seemed to have made their bodies as strong as a bull only at the expense of their heads." For Joyce, for the artist as burgomaster, the only authentic heroism was indeed moral, not physical. "Physical courage, which man shares with animals, never aroused his admiration," his brother recalled. ". . . for Joyce, only moral courage was truly virile." He accordingly dismissed, in a scornful review, "that immature brutality which is always so anxious to be mistaken for virility." If Homer's *Odyssey* alone escaped his general censure of epic fiction, it wasn't because the hero was physically heroic, but precisely because he wasn't. "Don't forget," he told his friend Budgen with considerable satisfaction, "that he was a war dodger who tried to evade military service by simulating madness." "Odysseus didn't want to go off to Troy," he told another. ". . . [he is] the only man in Hellas who is against the war."

The moral impulse behind Joyce's elucidation of the common wasn't just humane and humanitarian, however.

It was also democratic and fraternal. He may have envied the "beauty" of Goldsmith's *The Vicar of Wakefield* but he eventually rejected it as a "beauty" only possible to a culture aristocratic and therefore careless of the great democracy of human creatures: "I saw the extreme putridity of the social system out of which Goldsmith had reared his flower." He felt the same way about the "beauty" of Meredith. In spite of his early respect for him, he eventually dismissed him as a royalist and shocked his brother "by deriving him from Lytton and Disraeli." "He was altogether out of sympathy," Stanislaus reported, "with the class of people Meredith wrote about." Indeed, his disaffection with the English literary tradition had probably a great deal to do with what he considered its fixation with class or caste. "Even the best Englishmen," he said mockingly, "seem to love a lord in literature." Joyce resisted, for the same reason apparently, the current enthusiasm for Russian fiction which he put down as an "essentially feudal art." "The chief thing I find in nearly all Russians," he said disparagingly, "is a scrupulous instinct for caste. . . . I suspect that [Tolstoi] speaks the very best Russian with a Saint Petersburg accent and remembers the Christian name of his great-great-grandfather."

If Joyce insisted on the trivial and even the squalid in men and things, however, it wasn't just because they defined the terms of life itself. It was also because the novelist had to prove, in his moral effort to justify the form of life, that even the trivial and the squalid were convertible to the terms of the ideal and the beautiful. As the scientist and historian, the novelist had to register the truth in even its meanest and most wretched states. But if he did so, it was to free the human spirit, not enslave it, was to exorcise its loathing or disgust, not arouse it. For all his skepticism of the English novel, Joyce had in him a strain of its moral idealism, a feeling for its moral subtlety and sensitivity. He didn't admire the "moral sense" of Maupassant whom he found "frequently brutal in judging the characters of his stories." And he didn't admire, it seemed, "a certain scrupulous brute force" his brother found in Russian fiction. "Rousseau, confessing to stealing silver spoons he had really stolen, is much more interesting," he told Frank Budgen, "than one of Dostoevsky's people confessing to an unreal murder." He had, in short, some fairly English reservations about a realism that made no concession to the romance of the real. Leopold Bloom may suggest his commitment to the real, but he also suggests his concession to the ideal. "I see him from all sides, and therefore he is all-round . . ." Joyce said. "But he is a complete man as well—*a good man.* At any rate, that is what I intend that he shall be." There's no question that the maker of *Dubliners* and *The Portrait* wrote primarily in the hard tradition of the French novel, the novel of Flaubert and Maupassant; but there's more than a grain of truth in the observation that the maker of *Ulysses* and *Finnegans Wake* also wrote in the more genial tradition of the English novel, the novel of Sterne and Dickens.

In the end of course the novelist should belong, Joyce said, neither to the one nor to the other, should be neither all for truth nor all for beauty. He best testified to his belief in the sufficiency of life itself by showing the perfect community of its truth and its beauty. His mission wasn't to lull the conscience after the fashion of English Goldsmith, but neither was it to encumber the conscience after the fashion of French Flaubert. Stanislaus had feared that the people in *Dubliners* were not only "below literary interest but even below human interest," but his brother had proven to his satisfaction that through the agency of a scrupulously faithful art, "one could liberate one's soul from the contagion of that experience and contemplate it from above with tolerance, even with compassion." And though this seems like art for the artist's sake, it was also art for everybody's sake. "It is my idea of the significance of trivial things," Joyce told his brother, "that I want to give the two or three unfortunate wretches who may eventually read me." To represent life wasn't to betray it; it was to justify it. It wasn't to weaken the will to live, it was to strengthen it. "If *Ulysses* isn't fit to read," as Joyce put it, "life isn't fit to live."

For Joyce, then, art was urgently moral in the sense that it was urgently social. By creating in the smithy of his art a faithful image of his time and place, the artist not only liberated himself from the contagion of that time and place but liberated others, too. Hence the logic of his egomaniac aesthetic, his celebration of the novel as an expression of the self. "He wished to express his nature freely and fully," he could say with Stephen Dedalus, "for the benefit of a society which he would enrich." For the benefit, more specifically, of the Irish nation. By creating in the smithy of his art a faithful image of his nation, the artist liberated his countrymen from the contagion of their experience. In the same way that art should be moral without being moralistic, it should be national without being nationalistic. Accordingly, when Stephen pledged "to forge in the smithy of [his] soul the uncreated conscience of [his] race," there is no good reason to believe he wasn't speaking for the author himself. His intention in *Dubliners*, Joyce wrote his reluctant publisher, was to write a "chapter of the moral history of my country" and so take "the first step towards [its] spiritual liberation." "You will retard the course of civilisation in Ireland," he warned that unhappy man, "by preventing the Irish people from having one good look at themselves in my nicely polished looking-glass." In his letters to his wife, Joyce recorded his ambitions in strains even more exalted. "O take me into your soul of souls," he wrote her, "and then I will become indeed the poet of my race." "I am one of the writers of this generation," he boasted, "who are perhaps creating at last a conscience in the soul of this wretched race." Joyce may indeed have mocked the epic form as the celebration of a merely physical heroism; but he took it perfectly seriously as the celebration of racial or national character. He may have intended *Ulysses* to be epic in the mock sense, but he also intended it to be epic in the serious sense, in the sense that it did embody the "virtues" of the Irish nation, did mark yet another step in the creation of the hitherto uncreated conscience of his race. In his own queer and perverse way, Joyce even worked in the idealizing tradition of the Spenserian and Miltonic epic. As the "good man" Joyce intended him to be, what is Leopold Bloom if he isn't the image of a moral virtue after which all men are instructed to strive? Joyce would do for men and Irishmen what Spenser and Milton would do for men and Englishmen. He would "cast his shadow over the imaginations of their daughters . . . that they might breed a race less ignoble than their own."

Joyce's conception of the artist's moral and social mission in the world was almost traditional, then. There would seem to be no continuity at all between a reverend Victorian like Matthew Arnold and an irreverend modern like James Joyce. But the fact of the matter is that Joyce's theory of art was every bit as moral and social, as humane and humanistic, as Arnold's. For him as for Arnold, art was a criticism or appraisal of life. Its business was to create a picture of the age so much more real than the age itself that it gave men and women the knowledge and the power to live it. It was in fact to reconcile man's instinct for knowledge with his instinct for beauty and his instinct for conduct. It shouldn't, certainly, express and inspire a disgust of life. It should express and inspire a faith in it. For Joyce as for Arnold, it should make men strong for life. Even Joyce's language suggests Arnold's. When he returned from London it was to announce "that the music-hall, not poetry, was a criticism of life." It is the virtue of Ibsen that "he sees it steadily and whole." "Every age," says Stephen Dedalus, "must look for its sanction to its poets and philosophers . . . The age, though it bury itself fathoms deep in formulas and machinery, has need of these realities which alone give and sustain life and it must await from those chosen centres of vivification the force to live." Indeed, recognizing with Arnold the disintegration of those traditional religious systems that had hitherto mediated between man and his world, Joyce, like Arnold, conceived poetry as the religion of the future and poets as its priests and prophets. "He believed," Stanislaus reported, "that poets . . . were the repositories of the genuine spiritual life of their race, and that priests were usurpers." Hence when the hero of *The Portrait* conceived himself as "a priest of the eternal imagination, transmuting the daily bread of experience into the radiant body of everliving life," Joyce wasn't being entirely facetious at his expense. The day of the priest and of the religion he served was departed; but the day of the secular priest and of the art he served was only begun. Joyce was accordingly contemptuous of an art that could stoop to amuse and entertain, that could approach the world and its work in the world with less than total seriousness. "People who want to be amused by what they read . . ." he wrote grimly of *Dubliners*, "will not find many of them to their taste." "For him," said Stanislaus, "literature was not a comforting pastime that half lulls, half encumbers the conscience. It offered . . . grim realizations that dethrone tyrannical secrets in the heart and awaken in it a sense of liberation. And of sympathy, too."

Hence the justification for Joyce of the representational in art and literature. In effect, an art or literature that didn't represent life didn't take itself seriously and didn't take life seriously. Seduced by the magic of *The Vicar of Wakefield*, by a beauty that had no connection with the truth of things, Joyce's faith in art as a form of moral knowledge could be temporarily troubled. "Is it possible that, after all, men of letters are no more than entertainers?" But in the end he kept the faith that had sustained the Jameses and the Conrads. For him as for them, realism was more than a morally neutral way of describing the world. It constituted a sharply defined moral attitude in the presence of that world. To represent it was to take it seriously and sympathetically, was to insist that it was worth taking seriously and sympathetically. For all its showy secular and skeptical emphasis, Joyce's private passion for life and art was no less religious in its way than the great public passion of D. H. Lawrence himself.

D. H. Lawrence, 1885–1930. (*The Bettmann Archive*)

5   D. H. Lawrence:
The One Bright Book of Life

Lawrence's theory of fiction urged the faith of the novel in its most naked and most uncompromising form. Even more aggressively than for James and Joyce and Conrad, the novel's enterprise was for him a missionary enterprise, a religious enterprise. Acutely aware of a crisis in western civilization, passionate to find or create the values that would sustain a new one, he conceived the novel as nothing less than an instrument for the refreshment of the human spirit and the regeneration of human institutions. By writing books, he assured his wife, he hoped to "make a new heaven and earth" for her children. "I shall change the world for the next thousand years," he told her. Lawrence worked, indeed, not in the disinterested tradition of continental novelists like Flaubert and Maupassant but in the activist tradition of native English novelists like Dickens and Wells. He was less passionate to define life than to redefine it, was less passionate to achieve its form than to achieve its re-form. Where for Dickens and Wells, however, reality was primarily social and political and economic, for Lawrence it was primarily psychological. There could be no reorganization of human institutions without a more fundamental reorganization of the human psyche. In a world between two worlds, one dead, the other powerless to be born, "the vast importance of the novel" was, Lawrence believed, that it could enter "the *passional* secret places" where "the tide of sensitive awareness needs to ebb and flow, cleansing and freshening." "The great social change interests me and troubles me, but it is not my field," he said. ". . . My field is to know the feelings inside a man, and to make new feelings conscious." It wasn't as the dispassionate scientist of life and literature that Lawrence saw the novelist, then, but as the passionate priest or prophet, the medicine man. A reformer in the great *Prote*stant and pro*test*ant tradition of Bunyan and Blake, he exalted the novelist as the destroyer of a dead or dying world and as the creator of an entirely new world, a New Jerusalem, otherwise powerless to be born.

As the refugee from the Congregationalist chapel, Lawrence could hardly have tolerated the artist and his work on any other terms. Like all millennial dreamers, like all architects of Heavenly Cities, like Platonists and Puritans and Soviet Realists, too, he felt the old anxiety, the ancient paranoia, about sensuous artistic representations, had a highly developed sense of their power for evil. As a young man he "earnestly begged" his friend Jessica Chambers not to read *The Picture of Dorian Gray*, made her promise not to read *Wuthering Heights* ("It might upset you") and regretted having exposed her to Maupassant ("You mustn't allow yourself to be hurt by Maupassant"). Art had, he said, the power to "glorify the most corrupt feelings." It could be, he believed, "an unparallelled perverter of men and women . . . like 'Lead, Kindly Light,' which [has] helped to rot the marrow in the bones of the present generation." Indeed, during the First World War, when he entered a stage of nearly hysterical depression, he was tempted to give art up altogether. "The pure abstract thought interests me now at this juncture more than art," he wrote. "I am tired of emotions and squirmings and sensations. Let us have . . . a little perfect and detached understanding." This mood was only a transitory one, however. The same assumptions that made it possible for him to conceive the artistic representation as a powerful force for evil also made it possible for him to conceive it as a powerful force for good. If it could demoralize the hearts of men and women and strike dead their capacity to live, it could also invigorate the hearts of men and women and reawaken their capacity to live. If it could excite "spurious sympathies and recoils," it could also "lead into new places the flow of our sympathetic consciousness, and . . . lead our sympathy away in recoil from things gone dead." Hence the sense of urgency that was to inform so much of his literary creation and criticism. For him, the artistic image wasn't a static thing, an invitation to contemplation and satisfaction and, as such, beyond good and evil. For him it was a dynamic thing, an incitement to action, and, as such, pregnant with all the possibilities for good and evil.

He accordingly abominated as heartily as any evangelical Christian an art that was content merely to entertain the world. Its business being to build a better and braver life, it had to approach that world in a mood of the most religious consecration. "Damn 'holiday reading!'" he exclaimed in one of his puritanical rages. "They take even Dostoevsky to the sea-side now, and eat a horn of ice-cream while they read him." He didn't, however, condemn an art that didn't take itself seriously enough in order to condone an art that took itself too seriously. The professional art of Flaubert and his kind, the art that took itself too seriously, was just as guilty of a religious disrespect for life and nature as the amateur art of Dickens

and his kind, the art that didn't take itself seriously
enough. To be anxious to produce literary masterpieces
was, Lawrence believed, to venerate art rather than life,
was to feel that one's art was somehow more important
than life itself. It was to justify the Christian superstition
that artistic creations, competing as they did with the
creation itself, were somehow wicked or impious. Lawrence accordingly disaffiliated himself from the cult of the
"masterpiece." "I never starved in a garret . . ." he
insisted belligerently, "nor did I struggle in sweat and
blood to bring forth mighty works, nor did I ever wake up
and find myself famous." As the transmitter of a truth that
had the power to save the world, the novel was more for
Lawrence than a mere profession or vocation. It was,
exactly, a religious calling. "Primarily I am a passionately
religious man," he declared, "and my novels must be
written from the depth of my religious experience."

I

The moral imperatives which had been variously implicit in the poetics of James and Joyce and Conrad were
accordingly explicit in the poetics of Lawrence. For him
the artist's first and fundamental obligation was to establish a reverential feeling for life. It was to create a bond of
sympathy between the author and his fellowmen, between
the reader and his fellowmen. "The essence . . . of true
human art," he wrote in an early essay, "is that it should
convey the emotions of one man to his fellows. It is a form
of sympathy." The virtue of Balzac was, he said, that "he
was vastly sympathetic;" the trouble with H. G. Wells was
that he lacked "the subtle soul of sympathy of a true
artist." The note of satire was accordingly detestable to
Lawrence. It wasn't compatible, he believed, with a
sympathetic relation to things. Satire, he declared, "just

dries up one's bowels—and that I don't like." A writer should write, he said, "in a spirit of respect for the struggling, battered thing which any human soul is, and in a spirit of fine, discriminative sympathy." Indeed, Lawrence rejected the first version of *The Rainbow* just for the reason that it was "flippant and often vulgar and jeering." Satire was what happened, he explained, when his deeply religious response to life didn't materialize, "when the deep feeling [didn't] find its way out, and a sort of jeer [came] instead." Love, not hatred, praise, not blame, was for Lawrence the artist's only proper attitude in a universe of men and things: "the Cherubim who are nearest God and palpitate with his brightness are *absorbed in praise.*"

For Lawrence the best testimony art could offer of its religious affections was a deep-rooted faith in the possibilities of human life and the chances of human happiness. For him as for Gissing's Henry Ryecroft, "the essence of art [was] to express the zest of Life." If he was impatient with much of the fiction of his time, it was accordingly because it didn't have "enough energy, enough sanguinity." "I hate Bennett's resignation," he said. ". . . *Anna of the Five Towns* seems like an acceptance—so does all the modern stuff since Flaubert. I hate it. I want to wash again quickly, wash off England, the oldness and grubbiness and despair." For Lawrence, therefore, the whole cult of tragedy was unacceptable. It affirmed not faith in life, but despair, not the possibility of human success but the certainty of human failure. "The more Dostoevsky gets worked up about the tragic nature of the human soul," he said, "the more I lose interest." From Rozanov, Dostoevski's more sanguine compatriot, we got, he declared, "what we have got from no Russian, neither Tolstoi nor Dostoevsky nor any of them, a real, positive view on life."

Indeed, as Lawrence saw it, artists had no business making as much of death as they did. To end the work of

art on the climactic note of a death might be cathartic all
right, but since the artist's only proper concern was with
phenomena, with life as it materialized in time and space,
such a merely artistic gratification constituted a rank
betrayal of natural experience. "Death is so *easy*, in
novels," he noted scornfully. "It never kills the novelist:
though it is pretty risky for the artist." "If you are making
a great book on Egotism . . ." he accordingly rebuked a
young novelist, "give us the death of Egotism, not the
death of the sinner." "For God's sake follow your novel,"
he went on to say, "to its *biggest* close—further than
death, to the gladness." Lawrence believed, in short, as
ardently as any Philistine, that the work of art should end
happily or, if not happily, then at least positively. If it was
to register and restore a religious faith in things, it had to
record the triumph, not the defeat, of man and life. It
should make hearts, not break them. Under the dispensa-
tions of a rigorous and sterile realism, moderns like
Flaubert and Hardy preferred "to end insisting on the sad
plight." "But the great souls in all time did not end there,"
Lawrence protested. "In the mediaeval period, Christian-
ity did *not* insist on the Cross: but on the Resurrection."
Increasingly, therefore, Lawrence was himself resolved to
end insisting on the happy plight. "I hate miserable
endings, now," he wrote in 1926. *Lady Chatterley's Lover*
was "good and sun-wards, truly sun-wards," he said, "not
widdershins nor anti!"

For Lawrence, however, the novel's value as a moral
affirmation of life was inevitably bound up with its social
or cultural utility. By serving as a species of secular priest
or prophet, the artist made vividly visible the truth of his
day and so liberated men and women from their bondage
to it. In the end, indeed, he asked of the artist even more
than this. To fulfill his religious mission in the world, he
hadn't only to define life and nature as they were. He had

also, like Shelley's poet-legislator, to imagine life and
nature as they should be. He had in effect to predict, to
prophesy. Lawrence accordingly endorsed Oscar Wilde's
dictum that nature always imitates art. "The thing called
'spontaneous human nature' does not exist, and never
did," Lawrence stated. ". . . Men *can* only feel the
feelings they know how to feel." Hence the motive of
novels like *The Rainbow* and *Lady Chatterley's Lover*. By
solving "*the* problem of today, the establishment of a new
relation . . . between men and women," by expressing and
inspiring an "*adjustment in consciousness* to the basic
physical realities," they were expected to do nothing less
than create a whole new human nature, a whole new
epoch in human life and culture. It wasn't enough that the
artist register the disintegrating shape of the Old Jerusalem. If he was to foster an enabling faith and belief in life,
he had also to register the emerging shape of the New
Jerusalem.

Lawrence did of course recognize the value of those
artists who were destroyers of Old Jerusalems rather than
builders of new ones. "Moralists have always wondered
helplessly," he wrote, "why Poe's 'morbid' tales need have
been written." "They need to be written," he said,
"because old things need to die and disintegrate . . .
before anything else can come to pass." He accordingly
felt a grudging admiration for the demolition work of
writers like Flaubert and Hardy, commended in the books
of Aldous Huxley "a sort of desperate courage of repulsion" and recommended Forster's *A Passage to India* for
its "repudiation of our white bunk": "Negative, yes. But
King Charles *must* have his head off. Homage to the
headsman." At the very last, however, Lawrence wasn't
satisfied to destroy the old without creating the new. The
mark of the very greatest art, he said, was that it yielded to
"the stirring half-born impulse to smash up the vast lie of

the world, and make a new world." *Women in Love* might be "end-of-the-world" but it was "the beginning of a new world too." *Lady Chatterley's Lover* might be "a bomb" but it was also "to the living, a flood of urge."

Indeed, Lawrence was always more than half in love with the ideal, with intimations of the beatific and the beautiful. "I am tired of life being so ugly and cruel," he wrote his sister Ada. "How I long for it to turn pleasant. It makes my soul heave with distaste to see it so harsh and brutal." For Lawrence, accordingly, a novel didn't have to be the record of what one *saw*; it could also be the record of what one *dreamed*. It didn't have to be an *imitation* of life; it could also be a *creation* of life. "I long to be a dear little God," he wrote of the heroine of *The White Peacock*, "and evolve her soul, or metempsychose it. I want to have my own way somewhere." He was hardly out of sympathy, then, with the literature of "romance." As a young man he reveled in Scott and Stevenson and the Samuel Butler of *Erewhon* ("It's so fresh, so romantic, such a sense of a new country"). Even after his initiation in the more somber mysteries of the "novel" and, in fact, to the very end of his days, he could still feel an old affection for the lovely habitations of fable and romance. "Both of [these] works," he said of *A Christmas Carol* and *Silas Marner*, "are 'ridiculous,' if you like, without thereby being wiped out of existence." "Perhaps my taste is childish," he wrote, fondly forgiving Fenimore Cooper his evasions of the actual, "but these scenes in *Pioneers* seem to me marvellously beautiful." For Lawrence, Cooper's novels weren't after all versions of the real; like *A Christmas Carol* and *Silas Marner*, they were visions of the ideal, and, as such, "as presentations of a deep subjective desire, real in their way, and almost prophetic." To register the world as it was was to be the scientist of life and literature; but to register the world as it could and should and would be was to be the priest or prophet.

Lawrence wasn't intimidated, certainly, by the French conception of the novel, by its more rigorously empirical sense of what was comprehended by the real. "The French are essentially critics of life," he said, "rather than creators of life." If Balzac alone was found worthy, it was because his realism was "fair" as well as "unrelenting." "Balzac," he said, "can lay bare the living body of the great Life better than anybody in the world. . . . unlike de Maupassant or Zola, he doesn't inevitably light on a wound, or a festering sore." The otherworldliness of the Russians wasn't less distasteful to him, however, than the worldliness of the French. Their Byzantine mysticism seemed to him as vulgar an insult to the body and blood of life as the crass materialism of the French. For if the French offended by asking less of life than life had to offer, the Russians offended by asking more of life than life had to give. Turgenev, Tolstoi and Dostoevski had "meant an enormous amount" to him, Lawrence acknowledged, but "now, with something of a shock, I realize a certain crudity and thick, uncivilized, insensitive stupidity about them, I realize how much finer and purer and more ultimate our own stuff is." It was, in short, to the Anglo-American tradition of the novel with its more civilized religious perception, its more delicate moral aspiration, that Lawrence was loyal. "It amazes me," he said, "that we have bowed down and worshipped these foreigners as we have. Their art is clumsy, really, and clayey, compared with our own. I read *Deerslayer* just before the Turgenev. And I can tell you what a come-down it was, from the pure and exquisite art of Fenimore Cooper—whom we count nobody—to the journalistic bludgeonings of Turgenev. They are all—Turgenev, Tolstoi, Dostoevsky, Maupassant, Flaubert—so very *obvious* and coarse, beside the lovely, mature and sensitive art of Fenimore Cooper or Hardy. It seems to me that our English art, at its best, is by far the subtlest and loveliest and most perfect in the world."

II

The same missionary zeal that made Lawrence strain against the limits of life also made him strain against the limits of the novel. As a purely representational form, it was up to defining reality; but it wasn't quite up to redefining it. It did suffice to document the conditions of the Old Jerusalem; but it scarcely sufficed to create the conditions of the new one.

Lawrence quarreled, first of all, with its commitment to the familiar, with its refusal to entertain the marvelous and the wonderful. For the novelist as usually understood, the virtue of his form was precisely that it did commemorate the commonplace in people and events. But for Lawrence, for the novelist as the priest or prophet, the problem was to transcend a kind of fiction in which the commonplace predominated. For citizenship in the Old Jerusalem, no special qualifications were necessary; but for citizenship in the New Jerusalem, man had to be more than the average creature who crept about in the pages of the average novel. He had to be the hero in the Carlylean or Nietzschean sense, had to be nothing less than the man "who touches and transmits the life of the universe." Lawrence could accordingly believe it was still possible to rehabilitate the "legitimate" hero, the hero in the ancient or traditional sense. For all that he condemned the pessimism of tragedy, he could even believe it possible to rehabilitate the tragic hero. The trouble with the realistic novel, he argued, was just that it wouldn't or couldn't

produce heroes on the aristocratic scale of tragedy, was
that it forced the "truly exceptional man like Flaubert or
like Verga . . . to read his own sense of tragedy into
people much smaller than himself." "You can't put a great
soul into a commonplace person," Lawrence insisted, but
the Bovarys and Malavoglias "were deliberately chosen
because they *were* commonplace, and not heroic." In spite
of his predilection for the aristocratic hero, Hardy himself
had fared no better, Lawrence observed. "The glory of
mankind is not in a host of secure, comfortable, law-abid-
ing citizens, but in the few more fine, clear lives." But
Hardy, making "every exceptional person a villain," must
show "the times of the Average in triumph." In his ardor
for the New Jerusalem and for a people qualified to
populate it, Lawrence wasn't even willing to settle for a
psychological or moral form of heroism. He objected to
the vogue of psychological fiction exactly for the reason
that it offered only the palest substitute for the real thing.
"The realistic-democratic age has dodged the dilemma of
having no heroes," he charged, "by having every man his
own hero. This is reached by what we call subjective
intensity . . . That is almost the whole of Russian
literature: the phenomenal coruscations of the souls of
quite commonplace people."

In effect, then, Lawrence rejected the conscientiously
antiheroic values of that urban middle class culture
traditionally chronicled and commemorated in the pages
of novels. Like Hardy as well as Yeats and Synge, his
sympathy was all for the primitive in people and places, for
those conditions of life that, remaining untouched by the
subtleties of soul and psychology, could still produce the
heroic in human experience. Recalling ancient Greece in
their freedom from soul, Verga's "Sicilians simply don't
have any subjective idea of themselves . . ." Lawrence
said. "The self-tortured Jesus, the self-tortured Hamlet,

simply does not exist. . . . Anything more un-Russian than Verga it would be hard to imagine: save Homer." Hence the special significance of *The Plumed Serpent*, Lawrence's most strenuous attempt to correct the failure of the realistic novel. Heroism in the "legitimate" sense mightn't be possible for the citizens of a sophisticated modern society, but it was possible, Lawrence hoped, for the people of a primitive Mexico. "I thought there *were* no really great men any more," muses the awestruck heroine—who is, however, more convinced of the greatness of the Don Ramons and Ciprianos than the reader has any reason to be. No Sicilian, Lawrence didn't have, after all, the luck of a Giovanni Verga. Nottinghamshire lying, for all its proximity in space, centuries away from Hardy's antique Wessex, he didn't even have Hardy's luck. Willingly or not, he was committed by birth and experience to a democratic, urban-industrial community and to the perfectly ordinary humanity that walked the streets of its Old Jerusalem.

If such a humanity couldn't rise to the heroic and the marvelous, however, humanity, fortunately, wasn't everything. For the realistic novelist, life was by definition human life. For him human experience marked the limits of what was real or realizable. But for Lawrence, for the artist as religious reformer, such a life, such an experience, just wouldn't do. For him, man's salvation, his citizenship in a New Jerusalem, depended upon his being more than man, on his emerging "into something clear and new, beyond humanity." Lawrence bitterly refused, therefore, the novelist's predicate that life was merely human life, that "man [was] the chief environment of man." "Man is related to the universe in some 'religious' way, even prior to his relation to his fellow man," he insisted. At one point, indeed, he seemed ready to give up on the novel altogether. "Philosophy interests me most now—not novels or stories," he told his friend Murry. "I find people ultimately boring: and you can't have fiction without people." In the end, however, Lawrence chose rather to correct the novel than to reject it, chose to believe that it didn't *have* to be about people and their relations and nothing else. Forster's *A Passage to India* might be all about "people, people and nothing but people: *ad nauseam*," but Melville's fiction constantly revealed "the sense of vastness and mystery of life which is non-human" and Hardy's constantly revealed "a great background, vital and vivid, which matters more than the people who move upon it." Which is to say that man might be hopelessly unmarvelous, but life, the natural universe in which he lived and participated, wasn't. The merely human world out of which the heroine of *St. Mawr* comes may be a mean and trivial world; but the world out of which the great horse comes suggests "another darker, more spacious, more dangerous, more splendid world than ours." If there was in Melville something "bigger than life, more terrific than human activity," it was because he was "more spell-bound by the strange slidings and collidings of Matter than by the things men do." And if there was in Hardy "some primal morality greater than ever the human mind [could] grasp," it was because it, too, incorporated the mighty and irreducible forms of the nonhuman world: "Not Egdon is futile, sending forth life on the powerful heave of passion. . . . What is futile is the purpose of man." Hungry for marvels and miracles, Lawrence himself would make the same provisions. In *Aaron's Rod* the great plains of Lombardy become, like the weird geographies of Melville and Hardy, attestations of the wonder of the nonhuman universe. "There was something big and exposed about it all," the hero thinks. "No more the cosy English ambushed life . . . It was all exposed, exposed to the sweep of plain, to the high strong sky, and to human gaze. A kind of boldness, an indifference." Dear to the English novelist just because it was so human, so cozy, English life was abhorrent to Lawrence because it was all-too-human, all-too-cozy.

This isn't to say, however, that Lawrence would or could *depopulate* the world and the novel. The natural universe of bird, beast and flower, of seascape and mountain-scape, wasn't the sole repository of the marvel and the mystery of existence. "Man is nothing . . ." Lawrence declared, "unless he adventures. Either into the unknown of the world, of his environment. Or into the unknown of himself." Which is to say that the nonhuman, the *fantasia* of the unconscious, existed inside man as well as outside him. As a mere human being, man was doomed to the death-in-life of the average and the commonplace; but as something other than human, as something vitally in touch with his own sexual or unconscious nature, he was capable of transcending the death-in-life of his own humanity. Hence Lawrence's determination to revolutionize the whole concept of character in the novel. His fiction would have people all right, since it was in the nature of fiction, it seemed, to have them, but they would be such people as had never entered the pages of fiction before. They would look as little like people as possible. Like the Cézanne whose paintings of the "human" figure he admired, he was intent on "deliberately painting *out* the so-called humanness, the personality, the 'likeness,' the physical cliché." "That which is physic—non-human, in humanity, is more interesting to me than the old-fashioned human element," he wrote Edward Garnett. ". . . I don't so much care about what the woman *feels* . . . I only care about . . . what she IS—inhumanly, physiologically, materially . . . what she *is* as a phenomenon (or as representing some greater, inhuman will), instead of what she feels according to the human conception." In effect, then, Lawrence strove to smuggle back into the wholly secular and godless world of the novel a renewed sense of the divine, of the universal. Under a novelistic dispensation of things, reality was by definition particular: hence the novel's necessary accent on the human, on human characters and their relations. But Lawrence's passion was all for the universal, for a universal that would replace the old universals destroyed by scientific and democratic modes of thought: hence his contempt for the merely human, for particularities of characters and their relations. Man might not be great but the Universe was. Man as man might be trivial and insignificant, but man as the agent of "some greater, inhuman will" could rediscover meaning and nobility again. Lawrence declined, therefore, to be the novelist of character in the usual sense. He maintained, according to his friend Murry, "that the novel was *not* creation of character." "If one is to do fiction now," he declared, "one must cross the threshold of the human people."

For the same reason that Lawrence rejected the purely human emphasis of the novel he also rejected its purely social emphasis. The traditional novelist worked on the assumption that reality was social, that the relations between man and man, between class and class, best guaranteed the objective authority of his record of life. For Lawrence, however, the social values of the western world were valid no longer. "One simply must stand out against the social world," he stated bitterly, "even if one misses 'life.' Much life they have to offer!" If he would rediscover the remarkable in experience, the novelist had to study not man in his social relation to other men but man in his religious relation to the deity, the universe, the living natural world both outside him and inside him. "The proper study of mankind is man in his relation to the deity . . . We have come to the end . . . of the study of

man in his relation to man." The failure of H. G. Wells
was thus that he couldn't see his people in other than
simply social terms. "He is really a writer of books of
manners," Lawrence complained. "He seizes the typical
manners of a class. . . . Not one of his characters has got a
real *being*—*Wesen*—is a real being." Hardy's merit, on
the other hand, was that his characters refused to behave
as merely social creatures: "they are people each with a
real, vital, potential self . . . and this self suddenly bursts
the shell of manner and convention."

If man's salvation didn't have its source in the external
world of social forms, neither did it have its source in the
external world of physical forms. For the novelist as
scientist, the primary obligation was to the universe of
ordinary "appearances," the visible universe of physical
shapes and colors. But for the novelist as religious
reformer, that universe was a dead one, an old Jerusalem.
"It is just the life outside, and the outside of life," as
Lawrence said of America. "Not *really* life." The Kingdom of God was after all inside man, not outside him. "I
am not so much concerned," he said, "with the things
around . . . but with the mystery of the flame forever
flowing . . . and being *itself*, whatever there is around it."
Hence for him the special appeal, the special excitement,
of *Women in Love*. "The world crackles and busts," he
wrote in the throes of that novel, "but that is another
matter, external, in chaos. One has a certain order
inviolable in one's soul." He accordingly mistrusted the
realistic novelist's preoccupation with those laws of cause
and effect that were said to rule the external world. "The
universe isn't a spinning wheel," he said on Einstein's
authority. "It is a cloud of bees flying and veering round."
The novel itself, then, shouldn't be a spinning wheel, but a
cloud of bees flying and veering round. Poe was "rather a
scientist than an artist," he suggested, in the sense that his

tales were "a concatenation of cause and effect." It was
Verga's virtue, on the other hand, that "he had come to
hate the tyranny of a persistently logical sequence, or even
a persistently chronological sequence." It was Hardy's
virtue, too. "Nowhere, except perhaps in *Jude*," Lawrence
observed, "is there the slightest development of personal
action in the characters: it is all explosive."

For Lawrence, then, the novelist had to be less the
scientist than the poet. From the point of view of a
traditional realism, the novelist was primarily the conscientious observer of physical and social objects. But with the
bankruptcy of these objects, Lawrence's novelist had
increasingly to bring to them the dynamic resources of his
vision and imagination. "Why," he complained, with the
realistic strategy of the Impressionists perhaps in mind,
"do all the painters have to sit in front of what they paint?
. . . it should all be brought from inside oneself." Hence,
once again, the special passion that went into the making
of *The Rainbow*, the sense that he was doing something
never done before. "I shan't write in the same manner as
Sons and Lovers again . . ." he wrote Edward Garnett,
"in that hard, violent style full of sensation and presentation." "I don't care much more," he said, "about accumu-
lating objects in the powerful light of emotion, and
making a scene of them." Anxious to break with the
unrelenting objectivity of the French novel, Lawrence was
even willing to expose the world as object to the philosophic mind. *The Rainbow* and *Women in Love* were
meant, he suggested, to be frankly philosophical, to be
more the products of thought than of sensation. "It is all
analytical," he wrote of his work-in-progress, "quite unlike
Sons and Lovers, not a bit visualised." To defeat the
vulgar tyranny of the external world, it wasn't enough, it
seems, to have a touch of the poet. The novelist had to
have a touch of the philosopher, too. Lawrence indeed

derided those current writers who disdained didactic
novels, novels that would teach or preach a message. A
"didactic purpose" was *not*, he insisted in their despite,
"like catarrh, something to be ashamed of."

Lawrence's marriage to the realistic novel was always,
then, a rather uneasy one. Its epistemological assumptions
and formal procedures required restraints that his passionately religious temperament could only chafe under. As
the representational form *par excellence*, it seemed readier to repeat the terms of the old dispensation than to
create the terms of the new one, seemed readier to serve
and satisfy a scientific conscience than a religious one.

III

In the last analysis, however, Lawrence wasn't disabled
as a novelist by his religious passion. His visionary longings
were for worlds unrealized, not for worlds unrealizable.
The New Jerusalem he contemplated was of this world,
not the next. His theory of the novel may have strained
against its representational necessities, but it never repudiated them outright. Like his quarrel with the world, his
quarrel with the novel was a lover's quarrel. He was never
the reluctant novelist, the antinovelist, in the radical and
ineradicable sense that Thomas Hardy was.

If this was so it was first of all because his epistemological assumptions didn't differ markedly from those of other
novelists. He may have clamored more loudly for a new
universal, for a renewed sense of the universal; but the
universal he had in mind was, like theirs, immanental, not
transcendental, was inherent in the particular, not independent of it. There was, he was sure, "*a principle* in the
universe"; but that principle was *in* the universe, not
outside it. "The proper study of mankind is man in his
relation to the deity," he said; but the Laurentian deity

was *in* man and nature, not outside them. It acted in and through time and history, not independently of them. "There is no absolute good, there is nothing absolutely right," he announced. "All things flow and change." For Lawrence, then, the principle at work in the world was more mysterious and problematic than men had dreamed of in their philosophies. Things didn't receive their reality from their fixed relation to some absolute in the universe or to some absolute theory of the universe. More elusively, they achieved their reality from their relations to each other, from their dynamic relations to the rest of things in the flux of time and history. In "knocking that eternal axis out of the universe," Einstein hadn't, Lawrence insisted, abolished the universal itself. He had only established that it was infinitely more complex and more difficult than had ever been imagined. "We should like, vulgarly, to rejoice and say that the new Theory of Relativity releases us from the old obligation of centrality. It does no such thing. It only makes the old centrality much more strange, subtle, complex, and vital. It only robs us of the nice old ideal simplicity."

Lawrence accordingly denounced all attempts to make the world obey some "nice old ideal simplicity." "The Ten Commandments which Moses heard were the very voice of life," says the charismatic leader in *Kangaroo*. "But the tablets of stone he engraved them on are millstones round our necks. Commandments should fade as flowers do." The commandments of the scientists, Darwinian or Freudian, Lawrence denounced equally with the commandments of the religious and philosophical idealists. "There never was," he said, "any universe, any cosmos, of which the first reality was anything but living, incorporate individuals . . . it is time for the idealist and the scientist —they are one and the same, really—to stop his monkey-jargon about the atom and the origin of life and the mechanical clue to the universe." For Lawrence, then, reality was characterized not by its simplicity but by its multiplicity, not by its universality but by its particularity. "Beware of absolutes," he said. "There are many gods." "There is a certain life concord," he suggested elsewhere. "But life-expressions are *so* different, it is idiocy to count them like cash. Give me *differences*."

Not surprisingly, therefore, Lawrence was hostile to all those forms of abstraction that denied the differences, the multiplicity of things. He ridiculed those idealists who feared "the flesh-pots of artistic 'representation,'" who would purify themselves "of all low lust for likenesses." "Most puerile," he said of the abstractionist painters, "is this clabbing geometric figures behind one another, just to prove the artist . . . is not attempting representation of the object." To represent the object, to register its "whatness," the universality implicit in its particularity, was, he considered, the only proper purpose of the artist. "What Cézanne himself wanted," he contended, "*was* representation. He *wanted* true-to-life representation. Only he wanted it *more* true to life." If Lawrence's zest for the novel was eventually greater than his impatience with it, then, it was because he recognized it as the most radically representational of all artistic forms. "The highest form of human expression so far attained," it resisted, he said, as no other form did, the generalizing tendencies of moralists and philosophers. "Men get ideas into their heads, of what they mean by Life, and they proceed to cut life out to pattern," he said. ". . . What then? Turn truly, honourably to the novel." The trouble with the Russian novelist was just that he had sinned against the novel's special genius, had tried, as Hardy had, "to push events into line with his theory of being." "The certain moral scheme is what I object to," Lawrence wrote. "In Turgenev, and in Tolstoi, and in Dostoevsky, the moral scheme into which all the characters fit . . . is, whatever the extraordinariness of the characters themselves, dull, old, dead." If he was himself a novelist in the representational tradition, it was because he was, he said with Conrad, no moral philosopher in the Russian sense and indeed no philosopher in any sense. "For my part," he said, "life is so many things I don't care what it is. It's not my affair to sum it up."

In spite of his exasperation, then, with the restrictions the novel placed upon his restless religious emotion, Lawrence did accept the essentials of its realism. He accepted, for one thing, its commitment to the particular reality of its own time and place. Since the eternal had no real existence, there could be no truth that wasn't conditioned by wholly temporal and spatial circumstances. "Truth lives from day to day," he declared, "and the marvellous Plato of yesterday is chiefly bosh today." Inevitably, therefore, the artist was or should be the historian of a particular time and of his own particular time. "An artist is usually a damned liar," he said, "but his art, if it be art, will tell you the truth of his day." The novel had accordingly to express the author's own sense and experience of the world. If it was to keep up with life's rapid evolutions and mutations, it had to insist on the novelist's personal testimony of things. One man's time and space wasn't after all another's. The truth that changed from time to time and from place to place also changed from individual to individual. For Lawrence, therefore, the novel's power to represent life was contingent upon its novel-ty, its originality. "I don't want to write like Galsworthy nor Ibsen, nor Strindberg, nor any of them," he announced. "Tell Arnold Bennett," he wrote indignantly, "that all rules of construction hold good only for novels which are copies of other novels." Indeed, as Lawrence saw it, the novelist hadn't only to refrain from imitating other novelists. He had even to refrain from imitating himself. Since life changed not only from individual to individual but from moment to moment in the life of the individual, the novelist had to register his immediate, his momentary, his changing, apprehension of the real. "Even change is not absolute . . ." Lawrence declared. "My yea! of today is oddly different from my yea! of yesterday. My tears of tomorrow will have nothing to do with my tears of a year ago." "It is my transition stage," he wrote in defense of *Women in Love*, "but . . . it must produce its flowers, and if they be frail or shadowy, they will be all right if they are true to their hour." For Lawrence, accordingly, the artist's lot was intensely and excruciatingly a lonely one. He was asked to do nothing less than enter the immensity of the universe with no external aids to help him, with nothing but the resources of his own small self to depend upon. "Isn't it hard, hard work to come to real grips with one's imagination,—throw everything overboard. I always feel as if I stood naked for the fire of Almighty God to go through me—and it's rather an awful feeling."

To say that the novelist expressed the self wasn't however to say that he denied the world. To record that world from the lonely solitude of the free individual was the only way to record it without any of those perversions for which literature and tradition were responsible. As the priest or prophet, Lawrence may have rejected the tyrannous external world that threatened the extinction of his inner light, of his religious feeling for men and things. But, as the novelist, he recognized that it was exactly this tyrannous external world that he was primarily accountable to, that he was primarily accountable for. Indeed, he ridiculed the Impressionist painters precisely because they sought to deny, it seemed to him, the world of physical appearances. "Probably the most joyous moment in the whole history of painting," he wrote sardonically, "was the moment when the incipient impressionists discovered light, and with it, colour. Ah, then they made the grand, grand escape into freedom, into infinity, into light and delight. They escaped from the tyranny of solidity." But not for long, Lawrence said. "Back comes the truant, back to the old doom of matter, of corporate existence, of the body sullen and stubborn and obstinately refusing to be transmuted into pure light, pure colour, or pure anything. It is not concerned with purity. Life isn't. Chemistry and mathematics and ideal religion are, but these are only small bits of life, which is itself bodily, and hence neither pure nor impure." Lawrence accordingly honored those artists who refused to bruise the body in order to pleasure the soul. He honored Van Gogh for establishing that "instead of being nice and ethereal and non-sensual," landscape was "overwhelmingly substantial and sensual." And he honored Cézanne for establishing that "there *was* substance still in the world, a thousand times be damned to it!", that "there *was* the body, the great lumpy body." Lawrence may have cherished, then, as an essential part of the novelist's equipment, the creative imagination of the poet, but if he did so it was on the same restrictive terms that he cherished the intellect of the philosopher. Its function was to actualize the world as object, not idealize it; it was to accomplish what the senses and sensations of the empirical observer couldn't of themselves accomplish.

He accordingly repudiated the alchemical art that would turn the stubbornnest stones of life into the finest and purest aesthetic gold. Believing as he did in the integrity of physical matter, he believed also in the integrity of "subject" or "content." The theoreticians of Post-Impressionist painting he anathematized precisely because they "had renounced the mammon of 'subject' in pictures." For them as for Loerke, the perverse artist in

Women in Love, objects in nature existed only in order to serve the demands of form in art: "that horse is a certain *form* . . . it is part of a work of art, it has no relation to anything outside that work of art." For Lawrence, however, life didn't exist for the sake of art; art existed for the sake of life. Hence his impatience with the mystique of form in modern fiction, with "that will of the writer to be greater than and undisputed lord over the stuff he writes, which is figured to the world in Gustave Flaubert." Like the mystique of form in painting, it seemed to him an arrogance in the face of life and nature. For all his visionary's impatience with the external world of physical fact and matter, he wouldn't sacrifice it to the whim of the artist's will and imagination.

If Lawrence didn't reject the novel's commitment to an external physical reality, neither did he reject its commitment to a predominantly human reality. In spite of his dissatisfaction with a world exclusively human, he did recognize that if man wasn't quite the measure of all things, he was at least the point where all things intersected and, as such, the necessary clue to the universe. "Landscape is always waiting for something to occupy it," he said. He could therefore challenge the novel's fixation with human character and still subscribe to the principle that human character was what the novel was all about. The novel needn't, like E. M. Forster, make the human creature *everything*. But it must, if it was to be a novel at all, make *something* of it. Wells's *The World of William Clissold* wasn't "good enough to be called a novel," he decided, because it offered the reader "no created characters at all." "One would welcome," he wrote, "any old scarecrow of a character on this dreary, flinty hillside of abstract words." When he opposed the ancient tyranny of the plot, then, it was because it frustrated the novel's special genius, its genius for producing characters. "You

have written drama so much," he wrote one writer, "you
are more concerned with the mechanism of events and
situations, than with essential human character." Indeed,
for all his irritation with what was merely personal or
individual in character, what was merely personal or
individual in character mattered as much to Lawrence as
to other workers in the novel. To approach life from the
standpoint of a universal idea or ideal was to be interested
"in humanity rather than in men." It was, like Walt
Whitman, to take "that generalised thing, a woman, an
athlete, a youth," instead of this particularised thing,
"Gretchen, or one Henry Wilton." To be the novelist, on
the other hand, was to find the universal in the particular,
Woman in a woman, Man in a man. Hence, when
Lawrence entered the fantasia of the unconscious in his
quest of the nonhuman, it wasn't on the assumption that
he was making character less human, less individual, but
on the assumption that he was making it more so. To
render character in wholly social or external terms was to
deny all that was human and individual in character: "the
fatal change today" was, Lawrence said, "the collapse from
the psychology of the free human individual into the
psychology of the social being." But to render character in
terms of its sexual or unconscious life was to reaffirm in
effect its authentic humanity and individuality. It was to
reach, Lawrence believed, the secret place where character
existed in its irreducibly single and singular form. "By the
unconscious," as he put it, "we wish to indicate the
essential unique nature of every individual creature, which
is, by its very nature, unanalysable, undefinable, inconceivable."

Hence his determined refusal to be identified with the
Freudian school of psychoanalysis. As the great legislator
of the unconscious, Freud had, according to Lawrence,
simply mechanized and idealized it. He had reduced to a

principle of static unity what truly exemplified a principle of dynamic variety and made the repository of the universal what was more accurately the repository of the individual. He had tried, Lawrence charged, "to superimpose an ideal nature upon the unconscious," had talked about it "as if it were a homogeneous force like electricity." As Lawrence saw it, the unconscious was more remarkable for "its unfolding incarnations" and "its unaccountable evolutions." "It is all the time moving forward," he said, "beyond the range of its own fixed laws or habits." For Freud the unconscious was where all men were the same, but for Lawrence it was where all men were different. His quarrel with the naturalists and the futurists was nearly identical with his quarrel with the Freudians. As social or physical scientists, they substituted for the living human being the theoretical or universal one. In his secondary or material reality, man did submit, Lawrence acknowledged, "to all the laws of the material universe." But in his primary or spontaneous reality, he was a law unto himself and had "ascendance, truly, over the material laws of the universe." Accordingly, it was only in his secondary reality that man was subject to the laws of heredity. "The nature of the infant is *not* just a new permutation-and-combination of elements contained in the natures of the parents," Lawrence argued. "There is in the nature of the infant that which is utterly unknown in the natures of the parents." He did of course sympathize with the naturalists insofar as they delivered character from the bondage of Christian and Platonic idealism. But he didn't propose to release man from the prison house of the old idealism to place him in the prison house of the new materialism. He refused to believe that, like Zola, Verga had made his characters "merely physical-functional arrangements." "Verga's people," he insisted, "are always people in the purest sense of the word. . . . He was not seeking the brute, the animal man . . . What Verga's soul yearned for was the purely naïve human being." The futurists Lawrence admired and condemned on the same grounds. He admired their effort to liberate the artist from the old religious schemata that had denied man his own humanity; but he condemned their effort to substitute for them the new scientific schemata that also denied man his own humanity. "That is where the futurists are stupid," he said. "Instead of looking for the new human phenomenon, they will only look for the phenomena of the science of physics to be found in human beings." When Lawrence entered the dark domain of man's unconscious nature, it was to rediscover the free human individual whose very existence psychoanalysis and naturalism and futurism had variously forgotten.

Disenchanted though he was, then, with "the human people," passionate though he was for a people fit to colonize his New Jerusalem, Lawrence didn't always insist that characters in novels be heroes in the "legitimate" sense. Verga's Don Gesualdo, he noted with sympathetic interest, was "just an ordinary man" and, as such, wasn't "allowed to emerge in the old heroic sense, with swagger and nobility and head-and-shoulders taller than anything else." He may have denounced the democratic attempt to make every man his own hero, to substitute a psychological form of heroism for the physical form of it. But, he indicated elsewhere, the only authentic heroism was internal, not external, was moral, not physical. "How wicked the world has been to jeer at his physical appearance etc," he wrote in defense of Swinburne. "There was more powerful rushing flame of life in him than in all the heroes rolled together." In the particular was contained the universal: in the ordinary was contained the extraordinary.

In the real, in effect, was contained the ideal. Lawrence

may have felt a romancer's longing for all that was picturesque in life and nature, but he felt just as urgently the novelist's obligation to all that was grotesque. The Congregationalist fervor that inspired visions of the beautiful was accompanied by the Congregationalist conscience that condoned no evasions of the actual. "It never rains," he complained of Cooper's *Deerslayer*: ". . . it is never cold and muddy and dreary: no one has wet feet or toothache: no one ever feels filthy, when they can't wash for a week." Of course it was, he said in its defense, "a myth, not a realistic tale." Just the same, it wasn't "quite fair" to create a Heaven of the ideal that didn't have its source in the Hell of the real. "The root of all evil," he said, "is that we all want . . . this apparent heightening of life, this knowledge, this valley of many-coloured grass" and, what was still worse, "we want all this *without resistance*," without the resistance of the world's stubborn actuality. "The essential quality of poetry," Lawrence once wrote, "is that it makes a new effort of attention, and 'discovers' a new world within the known world." The essential quality of the novel he would define in the same basic terms: as the representational form of forms, it discovered the ideal in the real, the extraordinary in the ordinary, the new world in the old.

IV

Lawrence may have been eager, then, to preach and prophesy, to direct humanity to the site of a New Jerusalem; but this didn't mean that he endorsed an openly and aggressively didactic art. Since the universal was inherent in the particular, since what life meant was inherent in what life was, since, in other words, the form of life itself was dramatic, the form of the novel must be no less so. It should not mean but be. Multiform, not

uniform, fluid and fluctuating, not fixed or final, life made
no statements. Neither should the novel. For the sake of
an easy certitude or clarity, other modes of life and
thought asserted one cause, one sense or aspect of things,
at the expense of all others. But the novel refused this easy
way out, insisted on all or nothing at all. "Now here we see
the beauty and the great value of the novel," Lawrence
wrote. "Philosophy, religion, science, they are all of them
busy nailing things down, to get a stable equilibrium. . . .
But the novel, no." The novel did have of course to mean
something. It had to instruct or edify a fallen world. But
what it meant had to be just as strange and subtle as the
new "centrality" suggested by Einstein's theory of relativity. It should derive not from the relations of things to
some definable dogma or doctrine, but altogether from
their relations to each other. Like the form of life itself, in
short, the representational form of the novel was dramatic
form, was the form of the relations of all things to all other
things. "The novel is," said Lawrence, "the highest example of subtle inter-relatedness that man has discovered."

For the same reason, representational form was necessarily symbolic form. A dramatic universe, a universe that
announced its meaning in its own material, was in effect a
symbolic universe. An art that would represent it must be
no less so. Not of course symbolic in the artificial or the
literary sense. To be symbolic in this sense was to
rearrange reality, was to express not the world but only the
self or the self's idea of it. "We are such egoistic fools,"
Lawrence said. "We see only the *symbol* as a *subjective
expression:* as an expression of ourselves. . . . The old
symbols were each a word in a great attempt at formu-
lating the whole history of the soul of Man." *Lady
Chatterley's Lover* was, he acknowledged, a symbolic
novel, but not because he had personally engineered it.
"When I began *Lady C.,* . . ." he wrote, "I did not

deliberately work symbolically. But by the time the book was finished I realised what the unconscious symbolism was." Indeed, as functions of reality itself, symbols could be perceived or intuited but never planned or prepared. "No man can invent symbols," Lawrence declared. "He can invent an emblem . . . or metaphors: or images: but not symbols." If symbolic form was, then, like dramatic form, representational, it was because it rehearsed the very ambiguity of life itself. Like the dramatic image, the symbolic image suggested more than it stated, offered not one but many meanings. "You can't give a great symbol a 'meaning' . . ." Lawrence said. "Symbols are organic units of consciousness with a life of their own."

What this meant was that the novel's form should be internal and organic rather than external and mechanic. Since life submitted itself to no external forms, human or divine; since it constructed from its own rough and ready materials its own mysterious form, increate, internal, intrinsic to itself: the novel that would really represent it had no choice but do likewise. "The perfect statue is in the marble . . ." Lawrence wrote, as he began *The Rainbow* for the seventh time, "the thing is the getting it out clean." For Lawrence, accordingly, the novel's form was a feature not of the mind but of the feelings. "Life doesn't *start* with a form," he said with the hero of *Kangaroo*. "It starts with a new feeling, and ends with a form." To be like life, then, the novel had to let the feeling create the form, not the form the feeling. "The demon, when he's really there," said Lawrence, "makes his own form willy-nilly."

Lawrence didn't denounce the moral emphasis of the Russian novelists, therefore, in order to endorse the artistic emphasis of the French. Their formal perfection betrayed, he said, the same triumph of mental and mechanical over natural and organic form as the parables

of Tolstoi and Dostoevski. "This completeness, this con-
summateness . . . are conveyed in exquisite form . . ." he
wrote of this French kind of art. "But there is another
kind of poetry: the poetry of that which is at hand: the
immediate present. In the immediate present there is no
perfection, no consummation . . . Life, the ever-present,
knows no finality." The novel after Flaubert he accordingly condemned on the grounds that it didn't represent,
that the "exquisite finality" of its form wasn't correlative
with the dynamic form of life itself. It had "none of the
rhythm of a living thing . . ." he said. "There is an
unexpectedness in this such as does not come from their
carefully plotted and arranged developments." This wasn't
of course to invite a form of chaos, a chaos of form. "I tell
you," he wrote Edward Garnett *à propos Sons and Lovers*,
"it has got form—*form:* haven't I made it patiently, out of
sweat as well as blood." He eventually repudiated, however, this blood-and-sweat principle of composition. Evidently affected by Futurist notions of life and art, what he
hoped for in *The Rainbow* and *Women in Love* was a
form of fiction less patently constructed and hence more
faithful to the strange irregular rhythm of life. He was
increasingly out of patience, therefore, with all the mod-
ernist fussing over the artist's craft and technique. The
value of a novel wasn't interchangeable, he said, with the
studied elaborateness of its form. "We judge a work of art
by its effect on our sincere and vital emotion, and nothing
else. All the critical twiddle-twaddle about style and form,
all this pseudo-scientific classifying and analysing of books
in an imitation-botanical fashion, is mere impertinence."

In Lawrence's theory of fiction, accordingly, the stress
was all on the unconscious character of the artistic process.
Since life enacted itself dramatically, since it started not
with a form but a feeling and so evolved itself unconsciously, the novel that would be truly representational

should do no less. It should proceed unconsciously because life itself did. To write from the passional center of
one's being wasn't to write, as in Whitman and Tolstoi,
from a generalization, or, as in Flaubert and his followers,
from a principle of formal perfection. It was to write from
what Lawrence called "a strong root of life" and was thus
to establish contact with reality in its most naked and
irreducible form. "We can go wrong in our minds,"
Lawrence said. "But what our blood feels and believes and
says, is always true." If Hardy hadn't always sacrificed the
body of life to his theory of it, then, it was because his
sensuous or unconscious understanding of things was
usually greater than his mental or conscious understanding
of them. The artist had of course, Lawrence said, to have
some kind of operative or provisional metaphysic. "But,"
he added immediately, "the metaphysic must always
subserve the artistic purpose beyond the artist's conscious
aim." Where the metaphysic predominated, where the
novelist put his thumb in the scale to pull down the
balance in favor of his own conscious predilection, he
betrayed the dramatic form both of life and of art in
which all things were acknowledged and given free play.
Hence Lawrence's exhortation to trust the tale, not the
artist, to trust the artist's unconscious work, not his
conscious intention. "Oh, give me the novel! Let me hear
what the novel says. As for the novelist, he is usually a
dribbling liar."

To say that the artistic process should be a primarily
unconscious process was also to say that it should be a
primarily spontaneous one. The novel as Tolstoian pam-
phlet or parable, the novel as Flaubertian form or formula,
was by definition a planned performance; but the novel as
novel, the novel as an imitation of life's own unconscious
procedure, was by definition an unrehearsed performance.
He accordingly derided the conscientious labor on which

the professional novelist of the French school prided himself. He derided the Flaubert who said he " 'worked sixteen hours yesterday, today the whole day, and have at last finished one page" and the Thomas Mann who spoke of "an over-powering sense of responsibility for the choice of every word." He was willing to rewrite, he explained to Garnett, but not to revise: "I must go on producing, producing, and the stuff must come more and more to shape each year. But trim and garnish my stuff I cannot." For Lawrence, indeed, the artistic process wasn't distinguishable from the natural process itself. Like life's, like nature's, its motion or movement was from the particular to the universal, from the unconscious to the conscious. Heuristic, inductive, experimental, it was less an exposition than an exploration of the phenomenal world of men and things. Lawrence would later acknowledge a philosophy; but he insisted that this pseudo-philosophy, as he preferred to call it, was less the cause than the effect of his novels. The novels didn't come out of it; it came out of the novels. Such a claim would seem to apply more to books like *Sons and Lovers* and *The Rainbow* and *Women in Love* than to books like *Aaron's Rod* and *Kangaroo* and *The Plumed Serpent*, which were evidently written to rehearse some of his more undemocratic social and political notions. Even here, however, Lawrence wasn't out to transcend the novel's realism, to suspend the natural process it re-enacted. The laws that governed the novel being identical with the laws that governed life itself, his aim wasn't so much to assert his hypotheses as to test or tax them, to expose them, as F. R. Leavis has put it, "to something like the full test of reality." As things turned out, they didn't survive the novel's acid test. "There you have the greatness of the novel itself," Lawrence could say with a conviction born, doubtless, of his own experience. "It won't *let* you tell didactic lies, and

put them over." To the very end faithful to the novel as
the formalization of the inductive process in life and art,
Lawrence's books were written not to insist on what he
thought and felt but to *discover* what he could *legitimately* think and feel.

Indeed, as Lawrence conceived it, the novel was less a
species of art-experience than a species of life-experience.
Insofar as its process resembled the natural process itself,
the novel wasn't merely *about* life and experience. It *was*
life and experience. "The time has come to read Dostoevsky again," he angrily decided: "not as fiction, but as
life. I am so weary of the English way of reading nothing
but fiction in everything." He accordingly insisted that the
work of art be "cut close to the palpitating form of the
experience" instead of being "fingered by art into a grace
the experience does not warrant." It should be experience
rendered directly, not experience reformed or transformed
in the remote caverns of the artist's mind and imagination.
"I shall not *write* that third book: at least not for many
years," he wrote in 1923. "It's got to be lived out: not
thought out." If he abominated, then, the Flaubertian art
of Thomas Mann, it was because it was too much thought
out and not enough lived out, and so suggested a synthetic
experience instead of a real one. For him the novel was
truly representational only when the distinction between
art and life all but disappeared.

V

Lawrence could embrace the novel all the more readily
because he didn't find its realism irreconcilable with a
religious motive and mission in the world. On the
contrary, he found it positively necessary to the implemen-
tation of that motive and mission. To be the abstractionist
artist, to take liberties with reality, was, Lawrence decided,

to "make art out of antipathy to life." But to be the representational artist, to render the real without exaggeration or distortion, was to take life seriously, was to declare a religious respect and reverence for it. The "fair unrelenting realism" of Balzac he identified with a morally earnest relation to life; but the less rigorous realism of the English novelists he identified with an essentially frivolous one: "Can you find a grain of sentimentality in *Eugénie*? Can you find a touch of melodrama, or caricature, or flippancy? It is all in tremendous earnestness, more serious than all the profundities of German thinkers, more affecting than all English bathos." In the end, however, Lawrence found French novelists every bit as frivolous as English ones. In requiring a formal precision that life itself couldn't match, Flaubert and his school were just as guilty of falsifying life, of toy-making, as the humorists and sentimentalists of the English school. "Do you think," Lawrence asked, "that books should be sort of toys, nicely built up of observations and sensations, all finished and complete?—I don't." For him fidelity to life had moral as well as aesthetic implications: by being faithful to life in the formal sense, the novelist was faithful to it in the moral sense; by taking it seriously in the one sense, he took it seriously in the other. For Lawrence the realistic norms of the novel were necessarily religious ones as well.

This was first of all because the world the novel imitated was for him no moral void. It did make a sense of its own, did affirm a truth that the artist couldn't legitimately ignore or tamper with. There was, he insisted, "a *life* of the universe itself." There was such a thing, he believed, as an "inhuman, or non-human truth, that our fuzzy human emotions can't alter." "The wonder of Hardy's novels" was thus that they revealed "the vast, unexplored morality of life itself, what we call the immorality of nature." To be, then, the novelist, to represent the world and so disclose its "vast, unexplored morality," was to affirm and celebrate its sufficiency. But to be the moralist, to make the world the expression of some religious principle, was to betray a failure of belief in its sufficiency. As a novelist, as "a *true* artist," Tolstoi "*worshipped,*" Lawrence said, ". . . every manifestation of pure, spontaneous, passionate life." But as "a perverse moralist," he tried "to *insult* . . . the vividness of life." Hence the appropriateness for Lawrence of dramatic form, the form that issued no statement, that suffered things and their relations to make their own statement. It wasn't only that it imitated in this sense the ambiguous form of life itself. Expressing as it did the author's confidence that life had a "logic" of its own and hence didn't need the superimposition of the author's own "logic," dramatic form rehearsed his religious faith in life. To be the journalist instead of the dramatic artist, to make a "statement, without creation," was to be guilty, Lawrence said, of "a vulgarising of life."

Indeed, he accused the school of Flaubert and the French of the same crime against nature. By seeking a purity of form that life itself couldn't verify, it betrayed, he argued, less a fastidious artistic conscience than a fastidious distaste for life. The moral correlative of Flaubert's fixation with form was, Lawrence said, that he "stood away from life as from a leprosy." For his disciple Thomas Mann, he charged, "physical life is a disordered corruption, against which he can fight with only one weapon . . . his feeling for beauty, for perfection, for a certain fitness which . . . gives him an inner pleasure, however corrupt the stuff of life may be." If Lawrence insisted, then, on acknowledging "this vulgar world of accepted appearances," of stubbornly substantial actualities, it wasn't only because it was true or real in a way that the spiritual world alleged to exist behind it was not. It was also because to do so was to believe in this world

and this life. The idealist Christ of the New Testament
can die rejecting the world and opting for salvation in
another. But the Laurentian Christ of *The Man Who
Died* is "resurrected" "to find what an astonishing place
the phenomenal world is, far more marvellous than any
salvation or heaven." Hence Lawrence's emphasis on the
unconscious nature of the artistic process. The novelist as
Tolstoian moralist or Flaubertian formalist wrote from the
merely mental part of himself, from the part that harbored
his ideas and ideals and hence from the part that fed his
feelings of disgust and despair. But the novelist as
Laurentian artist wrote from the unconscious part of
himself, from the ineluctably naïve and sympathetic part
where ideas and ideals, disgust and despair, had no
dominion whatsoever. If Wells lacked "the subtle soul of
sympathy of a true artist," it was, Lawrence suggested,
because he rejected the unconscious or deeply religious
part of himself: ". . . he rigidly scorns all mysticism."

The Russian and the French novelists sinned, however,
not only by declaring their dissatisfaction with life but also
by declaring their superiority to it. To represent life, to
reveal its own forms and formulas, was to surrender oneself
to life's own means and ends; but to schematize life, to
reduce it to the terms of a form or formula not inherent in
its own matter, was to indulge the artist's own conceit.
Lawrence's quarrel with the form of tragedy wasn't just
that its form wasn't representational, wasn't coordinate
with the form of life itself. It was also that it expressed a
mean superiority to life instead of a sympathetic equality
with it. "You need not complain," he wrote the critic,
Carlo Linati, "that I don't subject the intensity of my
vision . . . to some vast and imposing rhythm—by which
you mean, isolate it on a stage, so that you can look down
on it like a god who has got a ticket to the show. I never
will: and you will never have that satisfaction from me.

Stick to Synge, Anatole France, Sophocles: they will never kick the footlights even. But whoever reads me will be in the thick of the scrimmage." Lawrence denounced the same vanity in the worshipers of formal symmetry and precision. The abstractionist painter who rearranged the universe instead of representing it betrayed, he said, just "another great uplift into self-importance." Similarly, the novelist who studied with Flaubert an artistic perfection acted on the assumption that he had "in him something finer than ever physical life revealed." Lawrence accordingly dissociated himself from the whole French vogue in art and literature. "To me," he said, "even Synge . . . is a bit too rounded off and, as it were, put on the shelf to be looked at. I can't bear art that you can walk around and admire." To make much of "books and genius" was indeed to write not as the democrat of life but as the aristocrat, as the member of an élite for whom, as for Flaubert and other devotees of pure form, the artistic experience was "an ecstasy granted only to the chosen few, the elect." For Lawrence the only proper posture of the artist as novelist was one of religious humility. It was to bear true and faithful witness not to the glory and the grandeur of the creator but to the glory and the grandeur of the creation itself.

It was just for this reason, among others, that Lawrence praised the principle of dramatic form. The dramatic artist who disappeared into or behind his own handiwork united himself in sympathy with men and things, but the omniscient author who took up a place beyond or above his handiwork disclosed a spiritual pride that didn't consist with the power to sympathize. He occupied, Lawrence wrote derisively, "that rather cheap seat in the gods where one sits with fellows like Anatole France and benignly looks down on the foibles, follies, and frenzies of so-called fellow-men." Lawrence didn't refuse the detachment of omniscient authorship, however, in order to accept the detachment of dramatic authorship. The austere self-denial of Flaubert and his disciples seemed to him no less exhibitionistic, no less a sign of authorial arrogance, than the florid self-assertion of Olympian authorship. "Self-effacement is quite as self-conscious, and perhaps even more conceited than letting oneself go," Lawrence said. "Maupassant's self-effacement becomes more blatant than Hugo's self-effusion."

If he rejected the impersonal form of the French, however, it was also because it revealed a failure of faith in the chances of life. By seeking in a purely aesthetic peace and perfection a peace and perfection that the Flaubertian novelist didn't look to find in life itself, it diffused, Lawrence believed, a spirit of pessimism. To be a Flaubert or a Thomas Mann, to crave for precision of form, was to say in effect that life had failed; but to be a D. H. Lawrence was to say no such thing. "We have learned our lesson," he said, "to be sufficiently aware of the fulsomeness of life." When the novelist wrote in the highly conscious manner of Thomas Mann, he wrote in a joyless spirit that was the correlative of his despair of life. But when he wrote in the unconscious fashion of a Lawrence, he wrote in a joyous spirit that was the correlative of his faith in life. His novels weren't the products, Lawrence emphasized, of the neurotic agonies of the Flauberts and the Manns. Issuing from "the underground of my consciousness," most of *The White Peacock* was written "five or six times," he said, "but . . . never as a task or a divine labour, or in the groans of parturition." To write unconsciously wasn't only to win access to the living reality and so assure the representational value of one's picture of life. It was also to free the writer to express his enthusiasm for, his sympathy and solidarity with, that living reality.

The same moral logic that governed Lawrence's registration of life also governed his registration of character. If he insisted on rendering his people in terms of the unconscious sexual and physical realities, it wasn't only on the representational grounds that the subsurface of man's unconscious being was more true than the surface of his social one. It was also on the moral grounds that man's unconscious existence was *superior* to his social one, that in his unconscious reality he was more sympathetically in contact with his fellowmen than in his social reality. To define characters in social terms was to emphasize what separated them, was to arrest the flow of sympathy between them: "Class makes a gulf, across which all the best human flow is lost." But to define them in sexual-physical terms was "to restore into life . . . the natural warm flow of common sympathy between man and man, man and woman." It was, moreover, to reaffirm the dignity and freedom of the human creature. It was bad enough that as merely social creatures, Galsworthy's people should lack reality, truth-to-life. But as social creatures, they also lacked virtue, lacked authentic goodness and freedom and innocence. "When one reads Mr. Galsworthy's books," Lawrence complained, "it seems as if there were not on earth one single human individual. They are all these social beings . . . There is not a free soul among them."

If Lawrence cherished the novel, then, it was precisely because it did represent things. As representational form, it wasn't only an imitation of life; it was also a creation of it. It wasn't only a description of life; it was also an affirmation of it. It expressed, as such, a fundamental faith in the essential form of life itself. His longings for New Jerusalems may have made him push against the limits of life, against the limits of the novel. But since his New Jerusalems were of this world rather than the next, since they could only be redeemed from the unredeemed stuff of this one, his religious longings made him just as passionate to embrace the limits of life and the limits of the novel. If he thought the novel worth writing, it was after all because he thought this life worth living. It was because the novel was for him "the one bright book of life."

6 *Virginia Woolf:*
Fire in the Mist

Virginia Woolf was by no means the profoundest philosopher of the novel but she was easily the most knowing, the
most knowledgeable. An indefatigable reader and reviewer
and publisher of books, she was the professional student of
fiction in a way that James and Conrad, Joyce and
Lawrence, never were. Their theories of the novel were
essentially the products of their practice and of the
pressures of their practice. They knew it from the inside, as
it were. As the practicing novelist, Virginia Woolf did,
too, of course. But she also knew it from the outside.
Steeped in every form of prose and poetry, conversant, like
Hardy, with the narrative and dramatic masterpieces of
the past, she was able to see and place the novel in the
perspective of literary history. Indeed, like Hardy himself,
she could even think, sometimes, of adjusting the novel to
the lofty standards of the ancient masterpieces. In the end,
however, she didn't love her Sophocles and Shakespeare in
order to assert with old-fashioned Hardy the novel's
continuity with the older forms of fiction or to assert with
him its inferiority to them. It was rather to assert with
James and Conrad, Joyce and Lawrence, the novel's

Virginia Woolf, 1882–1941. (*The Bettmann Archive*)

uniqueness as a literary form. It was to assert with them its
equality with and even its superiority to the traditional
forms of fiction.

                                   I

  The first and fundamental condition of its speciality
was, she recognized, that it sought to *represent* life, to
create an image of life as indistinguishable from life itself
as possible. "We glide into the novel," she said, "with far
less effort and less break with our surroundings than into
any other form of imaginative literature." If this was so, it
was because it acted upon epistemological assumptions
that sharply differentiated it from the traditional forms of
fiction. For the novel, reality was a creation not of the
universal but of the particular, not of some theory that
expressed and explained the whole of existence but of the
objective data and detail by means of which existence
expressed and explained itself. "Directly we begin . . . to
lay down laws we perish," Mrs. Woolf said. Ideally,
therefore, the novelist declined to play the philosopher.
Ideally, he presupposed with Laurence Sterne "no universal scale of values." Writers like George Eliot and
Meredith and Hardy were only "imperfect novelists,"
Virginia Woolf believed, because they demanded "qualities of thought and of poetry . . . incompatible with
fiction at its most perfect."
  If the novelist wasn't licensed to play the philosopher,
neither was he licensed to play the poet. The philosopher
brought to the world an intellect too powerful, too
egocentric or eccentric, to do it justice; but the poet
brought to it an imagination too powerful, too egocentric
or eccentric, to do it justice. The defect of Dickens was
thus for Mrs. Woolf "the exuberance of his genius," the
hyperactive imagination that made his picture of life

either smaller or larger than life itself. The excellence of
George Eliot, on the other hand, was just the modesty of
her genius, her refusal to indulge "that romantic intensity
which is connected with a sense of one's own individuality,
unsated and unsubdued, cutting its shape sharply upon the
background of the world." For Mrs. Woolf, indeed, what
distinguished the form of the novel from the more
traditional form of the drama was that where the play
would intensify reality, the novel would render it on its
own sober scale. In the play ("the little contracted play"),
"the emotion [is] concentrated, generalised, heightened,"
she said; but in the novel ("the long leisurely accumulated
novel"), "the emotion is all split up, dissipated and then
woven together." The defections of writers like Dickens
and Meredith from the novel's representational norm she
accordingly ascribed to their infatuation with the theater.
"The emphasis, the caricature of these innumerable scenes
. . . descend from the stage," she wrote in disparagement
of Dickens. "Was he, perhaps," she asked of Meredith, "a
dramatist born out of due time—an Elizabethan sometimes, and sometimes . . . a dramatist of the Restoration?
Like a dramatist, he flouts probability, disdains coherency,
and lives from one high moment to the next." The world
didn't exist after all to serve the novelist, to serve the
needs of his intellect or imagination. The novelist existed
to serve the world, to express that world more fully than
he expressed himself.

The novelist had, then, to be less the passionate poet or
philosopher of things than the dispassionate observer of
them. The rise of the novel was in fact identified by
Virginia Woolf with the developing habit of observation,
with the emergence of a purely empirical response to
reality. What direction would fiction take after Sidney's
Arcadia? she asked. "Will it fix its gaze upon Greece and
prince and princesses . . . Or will it look closely and

carefully at what is actually before it?" It had of course
elected to look closely and carefully at what was actually
before it. Women had proven themselves better novelists
than poets, Mrs. Woolf believed, because, "living as she
did in the common sitting-room, surrounded by people, a
woman was trained to use her mind in observation and
upon the analysis of character. She was trained to be a
novelist and not to be a poet." Not the intellect of the
philosopher nor the imagination of the poet was the
novelist's *modus operandi*, then, but the more disinterested senses and sensations which sufficed the empirical
observer of things. "He can no more cease to receive
impressions," Virginia Woolf wrote, "than a fish in
mid-ocean can cease to let the water rush through his
gills." The problem of Scott and Jane Austen was just that
they refused, she said, "to gratify those senses which are
stimulated so briskly by the moderns; the senses of sight,
of sound, of touch."

The novelist, however, could hardly be the observer
where the world itself offered him little or nothing to
observe. He could hardly objectify life where life hadn't
already objectified itself. For Virginia Woolf, therefore,
the novelist's reality was by definition a social reality, a
reality that materialized itself in the tangible forms of
social codes and customs. When the artist represented life,
when he held his mirror close to the surface of things, what
he found reflected wasn't man in the universe but man in
society, wasn't man in his invisible and unverifiable
relations to God or Fate but man in his entirely visible and
verifiable relations to his fellowmen. "If as novelist you
wish to test man in all his relationships," Mrs. Woolf
declared, "the proper antagonist is man; his ordeal is in
society, not solitude." The novelist had of course to be
born and bred in a time and place rich enough in social
facts and phenomena to serve his need. Like the English

novelist, he had to find himself surrounded by a clearly and densely constituted social life. He couldn't be denied, like poor Sinclair Lewis, "the richness of an old civilisation—the swarm of ideas upon which the art of Mr. Wells has battened, the solidity of custom which has nourished the art of Mr. Bennett." The novel was so dependent, Mrs. Woolf considered, on the nice distinctions and discriminations of a fully developed social reality that with their disappearance in the classless society of the future, the form itself might very well become extinct. "Very likely that will be the end of the novel, as we know it."

The same rage for representation that committed the novelist to the social reality also committed him to the contemporary reality. Novelists, said Mrs. Woolf, produced "long books about modern life" for the very good reason that modern life was the only life they could really know, observe, particularize. Indeed, what set the romancer apart from the novelist was that he would flee the present for the past and so liberate his imagination from the oppression of more facts than he could handle: "Where Scott will go back a hundred years to get the effect of distance, Mrs. Radcliffe will go back three hundred. With one stroke, she frees herself from a host of disagreeables and enjoys her freedom lavishly." It was thus the mark of the novelist in E. M. Forster that he asked for no such freedom. "The colour and constitution of the year 1905," Mrs. Woolf observed "affect[ed] him far more than any year in the calendar could affect the romantic Meredith or the poetic Hardy."

If the novelist addressed himself to the life of his own day, however, it was also because reality as he conceived it was the particular reality, the poor perishable reality, that changed with every time and tide, and not the rock of ages, the general or universal reality, that knew no change from generation to generation. Mrs. Woolf's quarrel with

Arnold Bennett was just that he wasn't contemporary enough, was that he didn't see his time and place in a way that disclosed its specific and special reality. "Owing to one of those little deviations which the human spirit seems to make from time to time," she said, "Mr. Bennett has come down with his magnificent apparatus for catching life just an inch or two on the wrong side . . . Whether we call it life or spirit, truth or reality, this, the essential thing, has moved off, or on, and refuses to be contained any longer in such ill-fitting vestments as we provide." The novelist had accordingly to express, as no other artist did, his own particular personality or point of view. To register the reality that changed with every time and place, he had necessarily to depend upon the witness of his own unique sense and sensibility. He couldn't safely imitate anyone else, couldn't spend "his time moulding and remoulding what has been supplied him by the efforts of original genius perhaps a generation or two ago." He had, said Mrs. Woolf, to be original, had to bring, as George Moore had done, "a new mind into the world . . . a new way of feeling and seeing." For that matter, it wasn't even enough that he imitate no one else. Since reality changed within as well as without the individual, the novelist wasn't even free to imitate himself. "I will go on adventuring, changing . . . refusing to be stamped and stereotyped," Virginia Woolf declared. "The thing is to free one's self: to let it find its dimensions, not to be impeded." The novel's prosperity was therefore utterly dependent, she insisted, on its freedom from censorship and convention, from all those laws that would restrict it to this subject matter or that, to this technique or another. The novel could only represent life if it was free to change as much and as often as life itself did. The novel had by definition to be novel. " 'The proper stuff of fiction' does not exist," said Mrs. Woolf; "everything is the proper stuff of fiction . . . And

if we can imagine the art of fiction come alive . . . she
would undoubtedly bid us break her and bully her . . . for
so her youth is renewed and her sovereignty assured."

The novel's formal realism derived, Mrs. Woolf intimated, from just such epistemological and methodological
assumptions as these. Since, for one thing, reality, as the
novelist understood it, was a function of things, not
theories, of particulars, not universals, his power to
represent ultimately rested on solidity of specification, on
his readiness to particularize life in the same minute way
that life particularized itself. "Of all writers," Virginia
Woolf declared, "the novelist has his hands fullest of
facts." Indeed, the novel had declared its independence of
the drama in part at least because it had proposed to
particularize reality where the drama had insisted on
generalizing it. "Here, in the play," said Mrs. Woolf, "we
recognise the general; here, in the novel, the particular."
"In the *Electra* or in the *Antigone*" she noted, "we are
impressed by . . . heroism itself, by fidelity itself." But "in
six pages of Proust we can find more complicated and
varied emotions than in the whole of the *Electra*." If
Meredith was a novelist, then, it was only in a very
problematical sense. "He creates," Mrs. Woolf observed
"not the living men and women who justify modern
fiction, but superb conceptions who have more of the
general than of the particular in them."

It followed from the novel's infatuation with facts that
it was better off with too little style than too much. The
development of the novel was indeed specifically associated in Mrs. Woolf's mind with the development of prose
itself. "To express the facts of life rather than the poetry,"
she said, the novel had necessarily to await "the democratic art of prose," its willingness to "go anywhere," to
"lick up with its long glutinous tongue the most minute

fragments of fact" and insinuate itself "into crannies and crevices which poetry [could] never reach." This wasn't of course to say that poetry was forbidden the prose novel. It was only to say that the poetry most proper to it derived less from the words themselves than from the things the words referred to. "Exquisite and individual as his poetry is," Mrs. Woolf said of Sterne, "there is another poetry which is more natural to the novel . . . It is the poetry of situation rather than of language." Recognizing that the language native and natural to the novel was a largely referential and discursive one, she would indeed contend that a novelist could write a perfectly undistinguished prose without compromising himself or his form. "Great novelists who are going to fill seventy volumes write after all in pages, not in sentences," she wrote in defense of Scott's allegedly "execrable" style. For the same reason that it was better off with too little style than too much, the novel was better off with too little architecture than too much. Since its work in the world was to particularize reality, not universalize it, it could no more legitimately sacrifice life to art than it could sacrifice it to philosophy or poetry. Mrs. Woolf was therefore skeptical of the formulations of comedy and tragedy, of their attempt to make either this or that a reality that was neither one thing nor another. "It is impossible to say," she wrote in praise of Chekhov's short stories, " 'this is comic,' or 'that is tragic.' " She was even more skeptical of the formulations of allegory, of its attempts to reduce the richness and complexity of life to the terms of a single idea or ideology. She disapproved of Goldsmith the dramatist for the reason that the allegorical names he gave his characters "seem to allow but one quality apiece." "Trained in the finer discriminations of fiction," his observation did work, she granted, "much more cunningly than the names suggest," but even as the author of *The Vicar of Wakefield* he was too often tempted to make his people "come back at the tug of the string to illustrate the moral."

Mrs. Woolf accordingly rejected the premise that plot was the first principle of fiction. Plot-making, she declared in effect, was inconsistent with the novel's whole effort of representation. It rearranged reality, made it more rational and schematic than it was, insisted on a pattern or design that had no authority whatsoever in life and nature. The Scotts and Jane Austens could legitimately improvise stories, she suggested, because they felt sure that the distinct configuration of the plot corresponded in some way to a configuration in life itself. But modern novelists couldn't manage their confidence, their certitude. "They cannot tell stories," she said, "because they do not believe the stories are true. They cannot generalise." "What delights me is the confusion," says Bernard, the artist in *The Waves*. ". . . Of story, of design I do not see a trace." To go on inventing plots after the fashion of Thomas Hardy was, then, to refuse to "observe the probabilities, and keep close to reality." Much more tonic was the practice of Chekhov who refused to manufacture plots and so make life nicer and neater than it was. "Once the eye is used to [his] shades," Mrs. Woolf remarked, "half the 'conclusions' of fiction fade into thin air . . . The general tidying up of the last chapter, the marriage, the death, the statement of values . . . so heavily underlined, become of the most rudimentary kind. Nothing is solved, we feel; nothing is rightly held together."

It was a passion for characters, not a passion for plots, that made the novel different from all other forms of fiction. "It is to express character—not to preach doctrines . . ." Mrs. Woolf declared, "that the form of the novels . . . has been evolved." Defoe's merit, she said, was that he saw Moll Flanders as "a woman on her own

account and not only material for a succession of adventures"; Turgenev's was that he saw his books "as a
succession of emotions radiating from some character"
and not "as a succession of events." For Virginia Woolf,
indeed, character was the natural counteragent to all those
forms of abstraction that would confound the novel's
endeavor to represent. The greatest novelists, she said,
"have brought us to see whatever they wish us to see
through some character. Otherwise, they would not be
novelists; but poets, historians, or pamphleteers." In the
novelist who was either more or less than a novelist,
accordingly, characters became casualties of the poet's
passion or the thinker's theory. Meredith, said Mrs.
Woolf, was "among the poets who identify the character
with the passion or with the idea; who symbolize and make
abstract." In the novelist who was every inch the novelist,
the complexity of the character triumphed over the
simplicity of the doctrine. "If he thinks he thinks in the
round. An idea at once dresses itself up in flesh and blood
and becomes a human being."

The sign of the novel, then, was that its characters were
representations, not abstractions. In the little, austere
play, the human creature necessarily appeared as "flat and
crude as a face painted on a playing card." But in the more
liberal and generous accommodations of the novel, the
human creature became "flesh and blood, nerves and
temperament." Congreve reminded us, said Mrs. Woolf,
that the play couldn't satisfy "the desire for certain
subtleties," that it couldn't produce "the imponderable
suggestions which come together on silent feet in fiction."
This was first of all because the novel was free to record, as
the play was not, the influence of time on the formation of
character. Unique with the novel, Mrs. Woolf recognized,
was its power to follow the lives of many people "over a
long stretch of time" and so "create many-sided characters

. . . who change with the years, as the living change."
Unique, too, with the novel was its power to render the
influence of place or space on the formation of character,
to show character in the context of those natural and
social conditions that were most responsible for its specific
identity. Not the least of Forster's credentials as a novelist,
Virginia Woolf said, was that he saw "his people in close
contact with their surroundings."

For a close and careful notation of the human creature,
however, the novelist had to specify the internal conditions that made men what they were. Thoughts and
feelings were just as much a part of life as words and
deeds, houses and clothing, classes and customs. Indeed,
said Mrs. Woolf, they were a great deal more. To read
George Eliot after Jane Austen was to realize, she said,
that the record of what men thought and felt *included* the
record of what they did and said. It was to realize "not
only that the working of the mind is interesting but that
we shall get a much truer and subtler understanding of
what is actually said and done if we so observe it." The
novelist was less than faithful, then, to the representational genius of his form when he arbitrarily restricted
himself to the theatrical conventions of plot and dialogue,
action and speech. The play "lets slip between its meshes,"
Mrs. Woolf reflected, "half the things that [the author]
wants to say. He cannot compress into dialogue all the
comment . . . that he wants to give." The novelist only
came into his own when he transcended the playwright,
when he claimed the historian's privilege of analyzing and
dissecting, of narrating and reporting. The lesson of
George Eliot was, she said, that "people can say very little
directly. Much more can be said for them or about them
by the writer himself."

The novel also insisted on the priority of character over
plot, however, for the reason that the one registered the

ordinary and the other the extraordinary. Plots had a habit of exaggerating life, of making it more heroic and spectacular than it really was. Conrad's novels had become classics, Mrs. Woolf observed, "by means of qualities which the simple story of adventure . . . has no claim to possess." James's novels had arrived at the same high estate by the same modest means: "Crises cannot be precipitated by any of the old devices which Dickens and George Eliot used. Murders, rapes, seductions, sudden deaths have no power over this high, aloof world." It wasn't just a matter, however, of shifting fiction's center of gravity from plot to character. It was also a matter of shifting it from the heroic character to the unheroic one. Reality had changed in the course of time. "A middle class had come into existence," Virginia Woolf explained, "able to read and anxious to read not only about the loves of princes and princesses, but about themselves and the details of their humdrum lives." Under the old feudal and aristocratic dispensation of things, the Elizabethan poets and dramatists could freely indulge their affection for "figures seen sublimely in outline or in heroic conflict." But under the new bourgeois and democratic dispensation, the passionate consummations of love and war were neither possible nor desirable. "There is no violence in private life," Mrs. Woolf declared; "we are polite, tolerant, agreeable . . . War even is conducted by companies and committees rather than by individuals." Hence, she pointed out, the obsolescence for modern minds of so much Elizabethan drama. Our reality was "based upon the life and death of some knight called Smith, who succeeded his father in the family business . . . did much for the poor of Liverpool, and died last Wednesday of pneumonia"; but in the ardent fires of the Elizabethan imagination the Smiths were "all changed to dukes, [and the] Liverpools to fabulous islands and palaces in Genoa."

Hence, too, for Mrs. Woolf, the instant obsolescence of modern verse drama: it "is always about Xenocrates and not about Mr. Robinson," she complained; "it is about Thessaly and not about Charing Cross Road."

If, then, the novel had declared its independence of the traditional forms of fiction, if it had "worked itself free and made itself distinct from its companions," it was, she said, because it had chosen to embrace not Xenocrates but Smith and Mr. Robinson, not Thessaly but Liverpool and Charing Cross Road. Which way would the novel go after Sidney's *Arcadia*? "Will it keep to simple lines and great masses and the vast landscapes of the epic? . . . [Or] will it take for its heroes . . . ordinary people of low birth and . . . deal with the normal course of daily human life?" It had of course opted to go its own way. What dissociated it from romance was just in fact that it refused to continue the old heroic conventions. To enter the world of the Scotts and Stevensons was to discover that "the dustman has become a Lord." But to enter the world of the novel was to encounter the reality of the "common human experience." The measure of Jane Austen's feeling for her form was thus that she allowed within its precincts "no tragedy and no heroism": she was content, said Mrs. Woolf, "to write of the trivialities of day to day existence," to chronicle "a ball in a country town; a few couples meeting and taking hands in an assembly room . . . and for catastrophe, a boy being snubbed by one young lady and kindly treated by another."

For all that she knew and respected the novel's historic origins, Virginia Woolf was hardly willing, however, to leave it as it was. Its form was ineluctably representational, but it couldn't go on being representational in the same old way. A new reality called for new ways of representing it. An altered world called for an altered novel. The novelist could only reveal life where life had already revealed itself; but under the troubled and troublesome conditions of modern times, life no longer revealed itself in readily recognizable objective forms. Under an older dispensation, life and character could be defined according to the terms of generally accepted religious or philosophical systems of value. But these systems had since deteriorated: reality had lost its old moral and intellectual coherence. Scott and Jane Austen could still rejoice, said Mrs. Woolf, in "the same natural conviction that life is of a certain quality," but modern novelists couldn't claim their certitude, their confidence: "They cannot generalise. They depend on their senses and emotions." Such indeed was the current confusion of values that they couldn't even depend on the authority of their senses and emotions. "Feelings which used to come single and separate do so no longer," Mrs. Woolf lamented. "Beauty is part ugliness; amusement part disgust; pleasure part pain." Hence the special significance for her of Dostoevski and the Russians. They seemed readier than Dickens and the English, she said, to admit the new contrasts and ambiguities, to show "the elements of the soul . . . not separately in scenes of humour or scenes of passion as our slower English minds conceive them, but streaked, involved, inextricably confused." To the charge that she hadn't created characters that survived, she accordingly responded with what she called "the old post-Dostoevsky argument," with the argument "that character is dissipated into shreds now." Under the circumstances the reader had to expect and accept, she said, "the spasmodic, the obscure, the fragmentary."

If the disappearance of the old moral and intellectual unity had left the novelist without valid ways and means of defining things, so, too, had the disappearance of the old social unity. It did take an old civilization, a civilization rich in ancient custom and tradition, to set a novelist

in motion, but, said Mrs. Woolf, the social codes of this
civilization, like its old religious and philosophical codes,
had long lost their force, their reality, and could no longer
supply the novelist with objective correlatives for the
mystery of existence. There flourished at present, she said,
"no code of manners which writers and readers accept as a
prelude to the more exciting intercourse of friendship."
Readers and writers were accordingly asked to accept, for
the time being, "a season of failures and fragments."
"Where so much strength is spent on finding a way of
telling the truth," she said, "the truth itself is bound to
reach us in rather an exhausted and chaotic condition."
Hence, once again, her admiration for Dostoevski and the
Russians. Rejecting the old social divisions equally with
the old moral divisions, they had refused to render the
human condition in the bankrupt terms of social caste and
custom. The English novelist might still be obliged to
recognize the reality of social distinctions, but, she liked to
think, "no such restraints were laid on Dostoevski." For
Mrs. Woolf indeed, the forms of the external physical
world were no more valid than the forms of the external
social world. Novelists had traditionally registered life and
character in the language of objective facts, in the
language of houses and streets, hats and buttons and coats.
But, she maintained, the data of the physical environment,
like the data of the social environment, had lost their
value as signs of life and so could serve no longer the
representational ends of the novel. Hence her distrust of
Bennett and Galsworthy and Wells. "They have given us a
house," she protested, "in the hope that we may be able to
deduce the human beings who live there." For her as for
the Russian novelists she praised, houses and people
weren't interchangeable; for her as for them, "novels
[were] in the first place about people, and only in the
second about the houses they live in."

When she insisted on a psychological fiction, then,
Virginia Woolf wasn't only saying that the inner world of
man's notions and emotions was more important than the
outer world of his words and deeds. She was also saying
that it was more important than the outer world of his
environment. Reality had changed. It was conterminous
no longer with moral and philosophical systems, with
social classes and customs, with the physical objects that
surrounded man or with which he surrounded himself. It
was conterminous, now, with those careless motions of the
mind where doctrines and classes, houses and clothing,
had all but no existence. Life was, said Mrs. Woolf, "a
luminous halo, a semi-transparent envelope surrounding us
from the beginning of consciousness to the end." This
being the case, it was "the task of the novelist to convey
this varying, this unknown and uncircumscribed spirit . . .
with as little mixture of the alien and external as possible."
In the absence of all external keys and codes, life itself of
course became infinitely more problematical, more difficult to assess and measure, than it had ever been before.
The external reality of things and theories Mrs. Woolf
connected with all that was substantial and sure, the
internal reality of consciousness with all that was fluid and
fluctuating. To assume with Defoe a world of solid objects
or with Scott and Jane Austen a world of solid values was
to occupy a friendly and familiar place. But to consider
with the Russians the "perplexed liquid" of the human
psyche was to discover a mysterious place where things and
theories had no standing and all was "streaked, involved,
inextricably confused." It was the record of just such an
unconditioned and unconditionable reality, however, that
the novel had always proposed as the first aim and end of
its realism. If Virginia Woolf called for radical innovations
in the form of fiction, if she exhorted novelists to abandon
the old external emphasis of the traditional English novel

and enter with her the stream of consciousness, it wasn't to make the novel less representational but to make it more so. It wasn't to reject the novel but to revise and rehabilitate it.

II

In the end, however, Virginia Woolf's quarrel was with the novel itself, with the limits of the representational enterprise itself. Her first perception may have been that its realism was the condition of its special power. But her second perception was that that same realism was also the condition of its special weakness. It made the novel different, all right, from the traditional forms of fiction, made it readier than the poem and the play to imitate life. But it also made it all too different, all too less ready than poem or play to appraise and interpret life. "The novel, it is agreed, can follow life; it can amass details. But can it also select? Can it symbolize? Can it give us an epitome as well as an inventory?" Virginia Woolf was sure that it could, that it should. She called therefore for the same reaction against the purely representational that had already revolutionized the art of painting. The novelist, she said, "has been concerning himself unduly with inessentials . . . has been worrying himself to achieve infantile realisms." "Is it not possible," she asked, with the Neo-Impressionists in mind, "that some writer will come along and do in words what these men have done in paint?" For the artist in prose as well as for the artist in paint, it wasn't enough to reflect life; he had also to reflect upon it. It wasn't enough that he observe and imitate the world; he had also to analyze and simplify it.

Mrs. Woolf called accordingly for a total revision of the novel's representational ends and means. She challenged, to begin with, the old assumption that the novelist was primarily the scientist of life and letters, that he had no business playing the poet or philosopher. "Of the men who go to make up the perfect novelist . . ." she wrote in disparagement of Dickens, "two—the poet and the philosopher—failed to come when [he] called them." The glory of the Sternes and the Peacocks, on the other hand, was that they stood further back from life than Dickens did and so could apply to it the clarifying disciplines of the poet and philosopher. "It is with . . . pleasure," she said, "that we accept Peacock's version of the world, which ignores so much, simplifies so much." "We are looking out at life in general," she wrote of Sterne. ". . . his genius is rich enough to let him sacrifice some of the qualities that are native to the character of the novel." The novelist of the future would take, she hoped, this nonrepresentational direction. "His effort will be to generalize," she said. Purposing to give "as poetry does, the outline rather than the detail," he would be less preoccupied with facts and observations and more with "the wider questions which the poet tries to solve—of our destiny and the meaning of life."

She accordingly questioned the novel's long-standing commitment to solidity of specification, to those proliferations of facts and figures that paralyzed the power to generalize and simplify. Less mimetic and more analytic, the novel of the future would "make little use," Mrs. Woolf predicted, "of the marvellous fact-recording power, which is one of the attributes of fiction." It would emulate, she said, not the "Russian" Dostoevski who "would say that everything matters" but the "French" Turgenev who would "clear the truth of the unessential"; not Bennett and Galsworthy and Wells with their old-fashioned realism but the much-maligned Meredith with his poet's passion for abstraction: ". . . he will represent the scene merely by a ring on a finger and a plume passing the window. But into the ring and plume he puts such passion and character . . . that we seem to be in possession of all the details as if a painstaking realist had described each one of them separately . . . That is the way, as one trusts at such moments, that the art of fiction will develop."

For Mrs. Woolf, then, the novel of the future would be the product of an active intelligence or imagination. It would receive its impulse not from the world as it acted upon the mere sensations of the observer, but from the world as it was acted upon by the creative mind of the poet or philosopher. "We have been letting ourselves bask in appearances," Virginia Woolf maintained. "All this representation of the movement of life has sapped our imaginative power." Forster's failure was thus that he gave us "a greater accumulation of facts than the imagination is able to deal with." But the triumph of Hardy and Emily Brontë was that they freed "life from its dependence on facts," was that they felt some "wild spirit of poetry which saw . . . that no reading of life [could] possibly outdo the strangeness of life itself." Indeed, they claimed for the novelist a freedom to invent, to make or imagine in the lordly tradition of the ancient poets and dramatists, that the sober novel with its concern for truth, its concern to be taken seriously as science or history, had resisted from the very beginning. "The novel had to justify its existence by telling a true story and preaching a sound moral," she remarked in her essay on Defoe. But the Hardys and Brontës recognized no such limitation. "She could tear up all that we know human beings by," said Mrs. Woolf of Emily Brontë, "and fill these unrecognisable transparences with such a gust of life that they transcend reality." "We have been freed from the cramp and pettiness imposed by life," she wrote of Hardy's novels. "Our imaginations have been stretched and heightened." On the verge of her own most creative performance, therefore, she meditated on novels that owed less to fact than to vision. "The approach will be entirely different this time," she promised herself: "no scaffolding; scarcely a brick to be seen; all crepuscular, but the heart, the passion, humour, everything as bright as fire in the mist."

As Virginia Woolf conceived him, then, the novelist of the future would make more liberal concessions to the ideal and the beautiful than his predecessors had done. As novelist, he was necessarily committed to a close and conscientious notation of the familiar reality around him. But such a reality wasn't necessarily interchangeable, she contended, with squalor and meanness. "Ugliness is not the whole truth," she said; "there is an element of beauty in the world." Her quarrel with the traditional realism of the novel was indeed that it made the world *less* beautiful than it was, that it regarded truth itself as by its very nature disagreeable. Defoe's fiction was founded, she said, "upon a knowledge of what is most persistent, though not most seductive, in human nature." Because Maupassant's world was a world "in which one can believe with one's eyes and one's nose and one's senses," it was also a world "which secretes perpetually a little drop of bitterness." What's more, the facts of the psychological novelist weren't a bit more edifying than the facts of Defoe and Maupassant. She considered unacceptable the proposition "that truth is always good; even when it is the truth of the psychoanalyst and not the truth of imagination." The gracious truth of the imagination was no less true, she argued, than the truth of the senses and sensations.

Hence her reluctance to believe that the novel had to be "about the old familiar things; what we do, week in, week out, between breakfast and bedtime." Just as the ideal and the beautiful were no less true than the real and the actual, so the mysterious and the marvelous were no less true than the trivial and the ordinary. The sober reality of Smith and Liverpool wasn't after all the very last word in reality. "We know indeed," said Virginia Woolf, "that this reality is a chameleon quality, the fantastic becoming . . . often the closest to the truth, the sober the furthest from it." She accordingly honored Meredith's determination "to destroy the conventional form of the novel," his refusal "to preserve the sober reality of Trollope and Jane Austen." It was of course true that life itself had become somewhat less spectacular in the course of time and history, that the external reality had been diminished by science and democracy and middle class manners. But, said Mrs. Woolf, this external reality wasn't the only reality. To enter the realm of the mind was to rediscover the beautiful, the marvelous, the extraordinary. "When life sank down for a moment," she said, "the range of experience seemed limitless." "We carry with us the wonders we seek without us," she felt with Sir Thomas Browne; "there is all Africa and her prodigies in us." In the end, however, her appetite for marvels and miracles wasn't appeased by the milder mysteries of the human psyche. The inner space of the mind was, no less than the outer space of the world, a very ordinary space. She accordingly affiliated herself with the Sternes and the Peacocks whose fictions scorned the facts of the psychologist equally with the facts of the sociologist. "I want fun. I want fantasy," she said. She wanted what she called "a writer's holiday," a holiday from the novel. After the hard representational labors of *Mrs. Dalloway* and *To the Lighthouse*, she wanted to write *Orlando*, to create a fictitious world as removed as possible from the commonplace world of Stephen Smith and Mr. Robinson.

If she was willing, then, to abandon the richly consti- tuted social world dear to the traditional novel, it wasn't only because it could no longer reflect reality itself. It was also because in its very solidity and specificity, it prevented the poet's beauty, the philosopher's truth. Turgenev could ask the profoundest questions of heaven and earth but only for the reason that he was "never, as in England he might have been, merely the brilliant historian of manners." Not men and women in their ordinary relations to each other but men and women in their extraordinary relations to God or Fate or the Universe would be, Mrs. Woolf declared, the care and concern of the new novel. "It will resemble poetry in this," she said, "that it will give not only or mainly people's relations to each other . . . as the novel has hitherto done, but . . . the relation of the mind to general ideas." Turgenev's merit was thus that his people were "profoundly conscious of their relation to things outside themselves"; Tolstoi's that there was always at the center of his book some character who "never ceases to ask . . . what is the meaning of it, and what should be our aims." For the sake of poetry and philosophy, Virginia Woolf would even exclude the physical world itself. To be too much under its spell was to put the novelist at the mercy of more facts than he could master. "The solidity, the likeness to life," had the effect, she said, "of obscuring and blotting out the light of the conception." But to enter the inner world of consciousness, to show the human creature in his "soliloquy in solitude," was to find the very forms of truth and beauty. Novelists trusted, Mrs. Woolf complained, "that, if only the egg is real and the kettle boils, stars and nightingales will somehow be thrown in by the imagination of the reader. And therefore all that side of the mind which is exposed in solitude they ignore. They ignore its thoughts, its rhapsodies, its dreams." If the novel of the future was to generalize and simplify life, it had perforce to become, as the novel of the past and the present was not, the psychological novel.

Before she was through, however, Mrs. Woolf had her

second thoughts. She wasn't at all sure in the end that the inner world of motive and psychology was any more the repository of beauty and truth than the outer world of houses and clothing. Facts were facts and weren't the less so because they were psychological rather than sociological. The effect of Proust's elaborate examination of "the infinite range and complexity of human sensibility" was, she reflected, that "we lose the sense of outline." To turn from the sociological to the psychological novel was to jump, then, from the frying pan into the fire. It was to exchange one set of facts for another, one convention of lifelikeness for another. To achieve the condition of poetry or drama, the new novelist had accordingly to set aside, said Mrs. Woolf, something of his interest in the minutiae of the mind. Since his effort would be to give us once again "the sense of outline," his characters would have to have, she decided, "a dramatic power which the minutely realized characters of contemporary fiction often sacrifice in the interests of psychology."

If character was to be particularized neither from the outside nor the inside, however, what was to become of character itself? What was to become of the carefully individualized character which had always constituted the novel's very first principle? In the nonrepresentational novel of the future, Mrs. Woolf implied, character, like life itself, would be simplified and even caricatured. Because Mrs. Browning's *Aurora Leigh* was a poem as well as a novel, it ignored, she said, "the slighter, the subtler, the more hidden shades of emotion by which a novelist builds up touch by touch a character in prose." "Snipped off and summed up with something of the exaggeration of a caricaturist," its characters had, she noted half enviously, "a heightened and symbolical significance which prose with its gradual approach cannot rival." In the novel that aspired to the abstractionism of poetry and drama, character, she intimated, would be similarly "snipped off and summed up." It would aim, as she herself had aimed in *The Waves* and *The Years*, "to cut the characters deep in a phrase," "to give in a very few strokes the essentials of a person's character." It was indeed a question for her whether in the novel-to-come character as such would exist at all. To achieve the outline rather than the detail, the novel had to sacrifice the particular to the universal, the reality of the individual character to the necessities of a higher or greater reality. The condition of Turgenev's poetry was just, she said, that his people composed "one subtle and profound type rather than several distinct and highly individualized men and women." She accordingly refused to believe that the novel was "more intimately and humbly attached to the service of human beings than the other arts," that Henry James should be condemned for "coercing [his characters] into a plan which we call with vague resentment 'artificial.'" In a novel that would pass beyond the limits of the novel, it wouldn't be the characters that counted, but the pattern or design into which the characters fell. It was as no mere character-monger, certainly, that Virginia Woolf conceived herself. The poetry of *Jacob's Room* was a product, she said, of its freedom from the tyranny of character: ". . . it will be highly praised in some places for 'beauty'; will be crabbed by people who want human character." She was surprised and disconcerted that a reviewer of *The Waves* "should praise my characters when I meant to have none."

Calling as she did for less life and more poetry, Virginia Woolf also called for less matter and more art. If the novel was to achieve the thought, the dream, the rhapsody, it had to pass the crude material of life and nature through the purgatorial fires of a conscientious artistic process. "The accuracy of representation, the looseness and simplicity of its method, its denial of artifice and convention, its immense power to imitate the surface reality—all the qualities that make a novel the most popular form of literature—also make it . . ." Mrs. Woolf observed, "turn stale and perish on our hands." The novel had to be more than an art of representation, therefore. It had also to be an art of abstraction. It had to provide the structure, the sense, that life itself didn't have. "Stridently, clamorously, life is forever pleading that she is the proper end of fiction . . ." she declared. "She does not add, however, that she is grossly impure; and that the side she flaunts uppermost is often, for the novelist, of no value whatever." She accordingly questioned Forster's premise that fiction was "a parasite which draws sustenance from life and must in gratitude resemble life or perish." A better and braver novel would instead believe, she said, that "tumult is vile; confusion is hateful; everything in a work of art should be mastered and ordered."

It wasn't, then, the novel's continuity with life but its discontinuity with it that Virginia Woolf preferred to emphasize. Like any other work of art, the novel had to consist not with life's tumultuous "logic" but with its own self-created logic. It had to be self-sufficient, to be sufficient in itself. Bennett and Wells and Galsworthy, she protested, "were never interested . . . in the book in itself. They were interested in something outside. Their books . . . required that the reader should finish them, actively and practically, for himself." In the hands of artists like Sterne and Jane Austen, on the other hand, the novel didn't need or ask the world outside to complete it: it was complete in itself. In spite of its ancient obligation to life and experience, then, it was to art and literature that Virginia Woolf would obligate the novel. "Write daily; write freely," she said; "but let us always compare what we have written with what the great writers have written." Her objection to Lawrence was that he wasn't "interested in literature as literature . . . he echoes nobody, continues no tradition, is unaware of the past." She accordingly favored the highly conscious tradition of the continental novel, not the unconscious tradition of the native English novel. "In France and Russia they take fiction seriously. Flaubert spends a month seeking a phrase to describe a cabbage. Tolstoy writes *War and Peace* seven times over." The artistic act, as she understood it, was neither an easy nor a joyous one. The main thing in writing a novel, she said, "is to feel not that you can write it, but that . . . it's to be pulled through only in a breathless anguish."

If the novel was to compete with poetry and drama, however, it hadn't only to provide for more structure than the realistic novel normally provided for. It had also to provide for more style. The crisis in modern fiction Mrs. Woolf in fact defined as in part at least a stylistic crisis. "With the whole wealth of the English language at the back of them," she wrote of her contemporaries, "they timidly pass about from hand to hand . . . only the meanest copper coins." The development of the novel as a special form of fiction was bound up, it's true, with the development of a purely practical and referential prose language. But such a language she connected with the novel in its infancy and immaturity: she refused to believe that "in poetry, in drama, words may excite and stimulate and deepen . . . but [that] in fiction they must first and foremost hold themselves at the service of the teapot and the pug dog." Indeed, she ascribed the drabness of its language to its historic preoccupation with a merely factual and ordinary reality. "The lack of metaphor, the plainness of the language" in the novel of Defoe and Trollope and Maupassant were necessary by-products, she suggested, of a "perfunctory fact-recording." When the writer sought the outline rather than the detail, however, he abandoned the barren language of an unreconstructed realism and attempted the richness and complexity of the idiom of poetry. De Quincey had "turned from the neat precise speech of his time," had turned to "the weighing of cadences, the consideration of pauses, the effect of repetitions and consonances and assonances," just for the reason, Mrs. Woolf believed, that he would remove us "to a distance in which the near fades and detail is extinguished." She accordingly revered those writers who sought to restore the many-splendored language the novel had traditionally rejected. "Meredith underrated," she noted in her diary. "I like his effort to escape plain prose." The virtue of fantastics like Sterne and Peacock was, she said, that they "write often as poets write, for the sake of the beauty of the sentence . . . and so stimulate us to wish for poetry in the novel."

In her impatience with the novel, with the limits and limitations of its representational form, Virginia Woolf wasn't even sure that there was such a thing as a novel at all. "We have only to remember the comparative youth of the novel . . ." she said, "to realize the folly of any summary." When she did recognize it as a unique and distinct literary form, it was often to reject it outright. In the middle of *Orlando* she confessed she was "glad to be quit this time of writing 'a novel'" and hoped "never to be accused of it again." Even *To the Lighthouse* she was reluctant to think of as a novel. "I will invent a new name for my books to supplant 'novel,'" she declared. "A new —— by Virginia Woolf. But what? Elegy?"

III

At the very last, however, Virginia Woolf's effort wasn't to destroy the novel. It was to reform it. It wasn't to sacrifice the necessities of its formal realism to the higher necessities of poetry and drama. It was to adapt them to these higher necessities. She wanted the heightened reality of poetry and drama all right, but she wanted only so much of it as the novel could take without ceasing to be the novel. The fiction of the future was accordingly summoned to hold the mirror far enough from life to suggest its poetry but close enough to keep its prose. "It will give the relations of man to nature, to fate; his imagination; his dreams," Mrs. Woolf predicted. "But it will also give the sneer, the contrast, the question, the closeness and complexity of life." The great Elizabethans had exalted the spirit with their dukes and grandees, with their fabulous islands and their castles in Genoa. But they had done so by excluding the grubby world of the Smiths and the Liverpools. "If it is to keep us on the alert through five acts or thirty-two chapters," Virginia Woolf decided, "[literature] must somehow be based on Smith, have one toe touching Liverpool, take off into whatever heights it pleases from reality." The novel of the future had accordingly to occupy "a station somewhere in mid-air, whence Smith and Liverpool can be seen to the best advantage." "It is the panorama of life, seen not from the roof, but from the third story window that delights me," she said with the hero of *The Waves*.

What this meant was that the novelist had to hold the mirror far enough from life to register the universal but close enough to register the particular. For Virginia Woolf *the* "reality," the essential or the quintessential thing, wasn't separable from the reality itself. Something did lurk in or behind the physical appearances of things, but that something couldn't be sundered from the appearances themselves. It was "something abstract," she suggested, "but residing in the downs or sky." No matter how abstractionist the novel aspired to become, then, it couldn't lawfully divide the universal from the particular, the outline from the detail. It had to combine them. Mrs.

Woolf did sometimes suggest that poetry in the novel could best be achieved by excluding the facts altogether; but she considered in the end that the only legitimate poetry was a poetry that coped and came to terms with them. "The poets succeed by simplifying: practically everything is left out," she noted. "I want to put practically everything in: yet to saturate." When, as she phrased it elsewhere, the novelist "subdued his army of facts" and "brought them all under the same laws of perspective," they worked "upon our minds as poetry works upon them." She accordingly celebrated those writers who had proved that the novelist and the poet, the historian of things and the philosopher of them, could peacefully co-exist. "Many novelists do the one," she pointed out; "many do the other—we have the photograph and the poem. But few combine the fact and the vision." Emily Brontë was, she suggested, one of the happy few. As poet, "she could free life from its dependence on facts," but as "novelist as well as poet . . . she must face the fact of other existences, grapple with the mechanism of external things, build up, in recognisable shape, farms and houses." Forster, on the other hand, didn't quite make it: he gave us, Mrs. Woolf said, "an almost photographic picture on one side of the page; on the other . . . the same view transformed and radiant with eternal fires." For that matter, she wasn't at all sure that she herself had managed the magic of uniting the prose and the poetry of things. "After abstaining from the novel of fact all these years . . ." she wrote after *The Waves*, "I find myself infinitely delighting in facts for a change . . . I feel now and then the tug to vision, but resist it." What she wanted, she said of *The Years*, was "facts as well as the vision."

Just as that poetry was best which fused the fact and the vision, so that poetry was best which fused the objective and subjective worlds. Mrs. Woolf may have rebuked

Bennett and Wells and Galsworthy for making so much of
the external life of objects and so little of the internal life
of dreams. But she also rebuked the Henry James for
whom the outer life was only an extension of the inner. "If
London is primarily a point of view, if the whole field of
human activity is only a prospect and a pageant, then . . .
what," she asked, "is the aim of the spectator, what is the
purpose of his hoard?" She concluded, certainly, that an
exclusively psychological fiction was no more legitimate
than an exclusively sociological one. The lesson of *Orlando* and *The Years* wasn't only that there was "a good
deal of gold—more than I'd thought—in externality," but
that the office of the novelist was, precisely, to reconcile
the externality and internality of life. "I see," she said,
"that there are four? dimensions: all to be produced, in
human life . . . I; and the not I; and the outer and the
inner."

In her desire for a prose that was also a poetry, then,
Virginia Woolf may have envied the Elizabethans their
splendid imaginations, their hunger for heroics. But she
recognized, too, that just as the novel had to find the
poetry of life in its prose, so it had to find the spirit of the
extraordinary in the facts of the ordinary. It had to take
"the usual and [make] it blossom into the extraordinary."
Indeed, insofar as it discovered the universal in the
particular, it made the trivial blossom into the important.
"The most common actions . . ." Mrs. Woolf said with
Montaigne, "can be enhanced and lit up by the association of the mind." Ibsen's merit was thus that, like Defoe,
he could make "common objects beautiful," could make
us feel "that all the forests and nightingales in the world
cannot be so romantic as a room with bookcases and
upholstered furniture." The common characters of novels
had of course to undergo the same magic transformations
as the common objects. The problem of the modern

novelist, said Mrs. Woolf, was that he had "to preserve the beauty and romance of the heroic together with . . . character-drawing and likeness to life." In imperfect novelists like Hardy and Meredith, "poetry seems to mean something impersonal, generalized, hostile to the idiosyncrasy of character, so that the two suffer if brought into touch." But in perfect novelists like Melville and Emily Brontë, the claims of the extraordinary and the ordinary were beautifully blended. In the characters of *Moby Dick* and *Wuthering Heights*, she said, "we feel that something beyond, which is not human yet does not destroy their humanity."

If the novel couldn't legitimately engage the extraordinary in character, neither could it legitimately engage the extraordinary in event. Virginia Woolf coveted "the explosive emotional effect of the drama," its capacity for great moments. But she recognized, too, that the novel's proper strategy wasn't to isolate the great moments from the trivial ones but to make the trivial ones great. "Some of the most emotional scenes in fiction are the quietest," she observed. "We have been wrought upon by nine hundred and ninety-nine little touches; the thousandth, when it comes, is as slight as the others, but the effect is prodigious." In a supreme novelist like Turgenev, accordingly, the ordinary and the extraordinary were so perfectly harmonized, it was impossible to say where the one ended and the other began. In Turgenev, she said, "the scene has a size out of all proportion to its length. It expands in the mind." Indeed, the virtue of the *art* of the novelist was exactly that it converted the ordinary into the extraordinary. Like Turgenev's, Jane Austen's art made her world infinitely larger and more important than the mere stuff of which it was made: "What she offers is, apparently, a trifle, yet is composed of something that expands in the reader's mind and endows with the most enduring form of life

scenes which are outwardly trivial." The novel was for
Mrs. Woolf the magic place where the ordinary and the
extraordinary intersected.

It was also the magic place where the true and the
beautiful intersected. She may have wanted more beauty
than the realistic novel was usually willing to offer but she
also wanted only so much beauty as consisted with its
character as novel. The defect of a novelist like Hardy was
that he didn't achieve the marriage of truth and beauty.
"The fate of a writer who was at once poet and realist,"
she said, was that "first one gift would have its way with
him and then another." The fate of a Meredith was even
more serious. It wasn't only that he wouldn't marry truth
and beauty in the novel but that he would even willfully
divorce them. Where Gissing's passion was for an ugliness
that didn't acknowledge the beauty of things, Meredith's
was for a beauty that didn't acknowledge the ugliness of
things. It was thus the superiority of Tolstoi and Melville
and Emily Brontë that they hadn't given all to beauty.
"The perfect novelist . . ." said Mrs. Woolf, "has the
power of expressing it in a manner which is not harmful to
the other qualities of the novel." Indeed, she wasn't
altogether sure that she had herself successfully negotiated
the narrow straits of truth and beauty. *Jacob's Room* was,
she feared, "a graceful fantasy, without much bearing
upon real life." *Mrs. Dalloway*, she promised, would be
"less lyrical."

She may have called, then, for less life and more art but
the claims of life and art required, she recognized, like
those of truth and beauty, the most delicate adjustment.
The novel had to satisfy the demand for artistic proportion without denying the equally urgent demand for
likeness-to-life. "It is the gift of style, arrangement, construction," she wrote, "to put us at a distance from the
special life . . . while it is the gift of the novel to bring us

into close touch with life. . . . The most complete novelist
must be the novelist who can balance the two powers so
that the one enhances the other." If it was possible, then,
to give too much to beauty, it was also possible, like "most
French writers," to give too much to art. Where Cervantes
gave us, Mrs. Woolf observed, "deep, atmospheric, living
people casting shadows solid, tinted as in life," the French
gave us "a pinch of essential dust instead, much more
pungent and effective, but not nearly so surrounding and
spacious." The office of the artist in the novel was after all
to combine life and art, the photograph and the poem, not
sacrifice the one to the other. In fiction, she granted, the
government of art was "much weaker than in poetry or in
drama because fiction runs so close to life the two are
always coming into collision." But Jane Austen had proven
to her satisfaction that the novel could gratify the
demands both of art and of life, "that this architectural
quality can be possessed by a novelist" without "chilling
the interest."

Virginia Woolf accordingly animadverted upon the
kind of symbolist form that would superimpose itself upon
the substance of the fiction. The novelist had, she said, to
combine the image and the symbol in the same way that
he had to combine life and art, truth and beauty, the fact
and the vision. The trouble with Forster was that he failed
"to connect the actual thing with the meaning of the
thing" so that we came to "doubt both things—the real
and the symbolical." It was the beauty of Turgenev, on
the other hand, that in him as in Ibsen the image hadn't
"ceased to be itself by becoming something else." Because
facts were symbols to poet-novelists like Hardy and
Melville and Emily Brontë, their books gave us "a more
overwhelming and passionate experience . . . than any
that Turgenev offers us. And yet what Turgenev offers us
not only often affects us as poetry, but his books are

perhaps more completely satisfying than the others." It
was his kind of poetry at any rate—something intermedi-
ate between the image and the symbol—that Virginia
Woolf herself aspired to. "What interests me . . ." she
wrote of *The Waves*, "was the freedom and boldness with
which my imagination picked up, used and tossed aside all
the images, symbols which I had prepared," was the way
she used them "not in set pieces . . . coherently, but
simply as images, never making them work out; only
suggest." If the novel of the future was to be more
"arranged" than the novel of the past, it was to be so
without seeming to be so. Novelists had the license, said
Mrs. Woolf, as playwrights didn't, "of modelling their
meaning with an infinity of slight touches."

For all her dedication, then, to the revival of style,
Virginia Woolf was just as skeptical of the arrangements
of the stylist as of the arrangements of the formalist. The
novel had to have beauty of style as well as of structure;
but the beauty should be of a kind that included rather
than excluded the facts of life. It should be capable, Mrs.
Woolf said, "of rising high from the ground . . . and of
keeping at the same time in touch with the amusements
and idiosyncrasies of human character in daily life." There
were admittedly dangers in trying to bring together the
poetry and the prose of language. "Memory supplies but
too many instances of discomfort, of anguish," she wrote,
"when in the midst of sober prose suddenly the tempera-
ture rises . . . we go up with a lurch, come down with a
bang." But there were instances, too, she said, when there
was "no such sense . . . of something unfused, unwrought,
incongruous." *Tristram Shandy* was "a book full of
poetry," she observed, "but we never notice it" because it
was "poetry changing easily and naturally into prose, prose
into poetry." "The objection to the purple patch . . ."
she decided, "is not that it is purple but that it is a patch."

For Mrs. Woolf, indeed, form and style should exist in the novel not for their own sake but for the sake of the feeling behind them. Structure a novel had to have, but it had to be a reflex of the novelist's emotion and not a substitute for it. She was accordingly doubtful of the school of James and Lubbock, of their concept of a visible form and technique. "The 'book itself,' " she declared, "is not form which you see, but emotion which you feel." It was important "to insist," she said, "among all this talk of methods, that both in writing and in reading it is the emotion that must come first." James's *The Wings of the Dove* made so much of method itself, she said, that he lost "the power to feel the crisis." What was true of structure in the novel was also true of style. "A sight, an emotion," Mrs. Woolf declared, "creates this wave in the mind, long before it makes words to get it." George Moore was more the writer than the novelist, she accordingly judged: "the phrase comes to him before the emotion." She couldn't be sure in fact that she wasn't herself more the writer than the novelist. "One must write from deep feeling, said Dostoevsky. And do I? Or do I fabricate with words, loving them as I do?" The function of the novel was to unite form and feeling in the same way that it united image and symbol, the fact and the vision. To this extent the novelist united the conscious writer and the unconscious one. On the one hand he had to write, not live; on the other, he had to live, not write. To *register* the crisis he had to be the wide-awake and conscientious artist in the tradition of Flaubert and his followers. But to *feel* the crisis, he had also to let himself go, to take his chances. By "emotion recollected in tranquillity," Virginia Woolf proposed, Wordsworth "meant that the writer needs to become unconscious before he can create." For all "his prodigious dexterity," she said of James, his procedure was a lot more unconscious than the legend suggested: "the theory of a

conscious artist taking out his little grain of matter and
working it into the finished fabric is another of our critical
fables."

For all that she desired for the future a more abstractionist novel, then, it was an abstractionist novel that
didn't break entirely with the representational novel of the
past. What she wanted after all was a fiction that
combined the prose and the poetry, the realistic virtues of
the traditional novel and the abstractionist virtues of old
poetry and drama. She wanted to revise the novel, not
obliterate it.

IV

If Virginia Woolf couldn't reject the novel outright, it
was for the reason that, exactly as novel, it had a crucial
moral and social mission to perform in the world. By
virtue of the realism of its form, it expressed in the writer
and inspired in the reader a moral relation to life, a
humane and sympathetic relation to it. Insofar as it
represented the world, insofar as it acted to increase "the
stock of our knowledge," it aroused a consciousness of and
delectation in the innumerable forms of life and experience that existed outside the narrow limits of our own
immediate life and experience. "The process of discovery
goes on perpetually," she wrote of the novel's work.
"Always more of life is being reclaimed and recognized."
To this extent, to the extent that it was a form of
knowledge or experience, the novel had the power, she
said, of "fertilizing and refreshing our entire being." "We
get from their novels," she wrote of Defoe and Trollope
and Maupassant, "the same sort of refreshment and
delight that we get from seeing something actually happen
in the street below." It wasn't just a sympathetic knowledge of the facts of life that the novel was asked to

propagate, however. It was, more especially, a sympathetic knowledge of the form of life. The prohibition against plot-making was more than a representational matter. It was also a moral one. To tell stories or spin yarns wasn't only to insist on a design in the universe for which the universe itself could produce no warrant. It was also, by that very token, to "manipulate the evidence so as to produce something fitting, decorous, agreeable to our vanity." It was to gratify not a noble passion for real truth or knowledge of the world, but a more primitive passion for entertainment or amusement. "Writing was then story telling to amuse people sitting round the fire . . ." Virginia Woolf wrote of *Don Quixote*, "the jolly, fanciful, delightful tale is told to them, as to grown up children." If the novel constituted, then, an advance in seriousness and sobriety over the fiction of the past, it was because it proposed to create characters instead of telling tales. Because Scott's men and women were only the servants of his stories, they couldn't be taken seriously as grown-up people by grown-up people. Compared with Tolstoi's and Stendhal's and Proust's, Scott's people were "merely bundles of humours . . . who serve to beguile our dull hours and charm our sick ones, and are packed off to the nursery when the working day returns." By making characters instead of manufacturing plots, the novel in effect had declared its determination to take itself and the world more seriously than fiction had done in the past.

For the sake of the same real truth and knowledge of the world, a truth and knowledge that brought the reader into sympathetic contact with it, the novelist was exhorted to be at once personal and impersonal. When he brought "a new mind into the world," when he felt and registered things from the point of view of his own particular personality, he not only guaranteed the representational vitality of his picture of things. He also guaranteed its moral vitality. Since the world for Mrs. Woolf was all inclusion and confusion, the novel's moral resonance could only be the effort and effect of the novelist himself, of the organizing sense or sensibility he brought to bear upon that world. This didn't make him, however, the licensed egocentric or eccentric. It didn't give him *carte blanche* to do with the world what he would. Reality was the form neither of the world nor of the self but of the relationship between them and hence, to insist too strenuously on the novelist's personality, on his power to reduce the vast and incoherent substance of things, wasn't only to fail to represent life. It was to fail to honor it. When he made the world in his own image, the novelist merely celebrated the self; but when he made it in its own image, he celebrated the world itself. "Centred in a self which . . . never embraces or creates what is outside itself," Joyce's *Ulysses* gave us the "sense of being . . . confined and shut in, rather than enlarged and set free." But no such failure of sympathy infected the work of George Eliot. "What were the loves and sorrows of a snuffy old clergyman, dreaming over his whisky, to the fiery egotism of Jane Eyre . . ." Mrs. Woolf asked? She accordingly blessed "the flood of memory and humour which [George Eliot] pours so spontaneously into one figure, one scene after another, until the whole fabric of ancient rural England is revived." The same natural reverence, the same faith that life was too sacred to be left to the mercy of every writer's will or whim, informed the work of the Russian novelists. Their virtue was, said Mrs. Woolf, that they "allowed human life in all its width and depth, with every shade of feeling and subtlety of thought, to flow into their pages without the distortion of personal eccentricity or mannerism. Life was too serious to be juggled with. It was too important to be manipulated."

It was of course their defect as well as their virtue. Mrs.

Woolf had mixed feelings about the loose and baggy monsters of the great Victorian and Russian masters, about the large inclusiveness that their passion for representation led them to. She was momentarily seduced by the message of Meredith who, refusing to believe that life was too important to be manipulated, had insisted that "sheer realism [was] at best the breeder of the dungfly." But her reservations about Meredith were eventually much more powerful than her reservations about Tolstoi and Dostoevski. "Sheer romance breeds an insect more diaphanous [than sheer realism]," she wrote, "but it tends perhaps to be even more heartless than the dungfly." The Meredithian abstractionism that registered a mere conceit of the world betrayed in effect an antipathy for things; but the Russian representationalism that registered the world on its own ample scale expressed a generous sympathy with them. By creating the world in his own image the novelist united us with himself; but by creating it in its own image the novelist united us with the world. It wasn't enough that he bring a new mind into the world. He had also to bring a mind so gracious in the range of its affirmations and affections that it united itself with the world. Joyce's *Ulysses* had failed, said Mrs. Woolf, "because of the comparative poverty of the writer's mind." But George Eliot and the Russians had succeeded because of the comparative richness of theirs, George Eliot because hers was "so large and deeply human," the Russians because theirs was so "comprehensive and compassionate."

A certain limit was set, then, on the novelist's power to practise poetry or philosophy. When he simplified things, reduced them to the state of his own private theory or theorem, he not only excluded more life than he included and so misrepresented it; in so doing, he also rejected more than he embraced and so failed to express that reverence for all the forms of life which was inseparable from representation. "I think it a blasphemy," she wrote of the Lawrence cult, "this fitting of Carswells into a Lawrence system. So much more reverent to leave them alone: nothing else to reverence except the Carswellism of Carswell. . . . What a discovery that would be—a system that did not shut out." No such thing existed, however, a system that didn't shut out, and so Virginia Woolf was all for Marcel Proust who, having more sensibility than philosophy, was readier to sympathize than to systematize. "We are never told," she said, "as the English novelists so frequently tell us, that one way is right and the other wrong. . . . The mind of Proust lies open with the sympathy of a poet and the detachment of a scientist to everything that it has the power to feel." "If we look for direction to help us put them in their places in the universe," she noted of his characters, "we find it negatively in an absence of direction—perhaps sympathy is of more value than interference, understanding than judgment." She reached the same conclusion about the Russian novelists. By entering with Proust the regions of the soul or psyche, by leaving alone the outer world of facts and things, they hadn't only discovered the fount of life itself and thus the power to represent. They had also discovered the place where dogma and doctrine had no standing, where good and evil had no existence, where nothing need be condemned and all could be condoned. "The old divisions melt into each other. Men are at the same time villains and saints; their acts are at once beautiful and despicable."

For the same reason that the novelist was forbidden to sacrifice life to the terms of a moral formula, he was also forbidden to sacrifice it to the terms of an artistic formula. To superimpose upon reality a pattern or design that was the reflex of the writer's own ego, of his mind or

imagination, was in effect to betray reality. But to let that
reality declare its own pattern or design was to express
confidence in it, was to believe with the Russians that it
was too important to be juggled with. On the eve of
writing *The Years*, Virginia Woolf could thus confess that
she didn't want "to strain to make a pattern just yet," that
she wanted instead "this more humane existence . . . the
width and amusement of human life." For that matter, to
develop a special method or technique and to make much
of it exposed the novelist to the same moral danger of
feeling and recording more self than world. If Joyce made
us feel "neither jovial nor magnanimous," it was due, Mrs.
Woolf suggested, "to some limitation imposed by the
method as well as by the mind."

The novelist was invited to particularize life, then,
instead of generalizing it, not only because the particular
was a condition of the novel's representational form but
also because it was a condition of its "finer discriminations," of its more humane and sympathetic regard for life.
Because Scott and Jane Austen approached things from
the standpoint of certain large general ideas, their picture
of life lacked sensitiveness: "shades and subtleties accumu-
late and they ignore them." The same was true of
Meredith, said Mrs. Woolf. She may have envied him his
aristocratic contempt for particulars, his eagerness to
sacrifice, for beauty's sake, "the solidity which is the result
of knowing the day of the week, how the ladies are
dressed, and by what series of credible events the great
crisis was accomplished." But she wondered in the end if
he hadn't sacrificed "something of greater importance
than mere solidity," if he hadn't sacrificed the sympathy
that was the concomitant of the solidity. "A touch of
realism—or is it a touch of something more akin to
sympathy?—would," she decided, "have kept the Meredith hero from being the honourable but tedious gentle-

man that . . . we have always found him." To generalize
was to be insensitive and unsympathetic to human life and
character; to particularize was to be sensitive and sympathetic to them.

To particularize life and character was in fact to declare
a specifically democratic affection for them. By recording
reality in the terms of its most trivial data and detail, the
novelist not only represented life but affirmed a fraternal
feeling for it. By virtue of the "democratic prose" that
included so much and excluded so little, the novelist
cherished and memorialized precisely what the aristocratic
poet had despised and rejected. "In an age of utilitarian
prose like our own," wrote Mrs. Woolf, "we know exactly
how people spend the hours between breakfast and bed
. . . [But] poetry ignores these slighter shades." Indeed,
the novelist justified existence, declared his faith in its
ultimate sufficiency, not only by recording the ordinary
but by making the ordinary extraordinary, by making
"common actions dignified and common objects beautiful." It was in his affinity for common people, however,
that the novelist best indicated his radical sympathy with
life. By registering the lives of the ordinary middle class
men and women of modern times instead of the lives of
the high-born lovers and warriors of ancient times, he not
only established the representational authority of his
version of life. He also established his democratic rapport
with these ordinary lives. The world of the anti-novelist
like Meredith was "an aristocratic world, strictly bounded,
thinly populated, a little hard-hearted, and not to be
entered by the poor, the vulgar, the stupid, or that very
common and interesting individual who is a mixture of all
three." But the world of the faithful novelist like George
Eliot was something else again. "No satirist," breathing
instead "the melancholy virtue of tolerance," she made us
share the lives of her ordinary folk "not in a spirit of

condescension or of curiosity, but in a spirit of sympathy."
The novelist's world wasn't of course heroic in the usual
sense. But because its heroism was moral rather than
physical, it wasn't therefore less satisfactory, less satisfying.
The secular and scientific wisdom that had "dried the
melancholy mediaeval mists; drained the swamp and stood
glass and stone upon it" had also, Mrs. Woolf believed,
"equipped our brains and bodies with such an armoury of
weapons that merely to see the flash and thrust of limbs
engaged in the conduct of daily life is better than the old
pageant of armies drawn out in battle array upon the
plain."

If she thought the novelist should render things in
psychological rather than in social terms, then, it wasn't
only on the representational grounds that the psychological realities were more genuinely signs of life than the
social realities of class and custom. It was also on the
moral and social grounds that a psychological rendering of
things stimulated the flow of democratic sympathy between man and man in a way that a sociological rendering
of them didn't. At the surface social level, all men were
fatally different, were forcibly divided from each other;
but at the profounder level of the soul or psyche, all men
were one, were at one with each other. At such a level of
reality, all the old divisions, social as well as moral and
philosophical, simply melted away. Because he was under
a special pressure to recognize the social barriers of upper
and middle and lower classes, the English novelist was
inclined, said Mrs. Woolf, "to satire rather than to
compassion." But the lucky Russian novelist was under no
such pressure. "It is all the same to him whether you are
noble or simple . . . The soul is not restrained by barriers.
It overflows, it floods, it mingles with the souls of others."
Without the English accent on social distinctions and
discriminations, Russian fiction was free, she said, to put

the emphasis "upon the immensity of the soul and upon the brotherhood of man."

In her anxiety to moralize certain features of the novel's landscape, Virginia Woolf was sometimes forced into positions that did her heart more credit than her head. Thus, it wasn't only the external social universe that was morally bankrupt. The external physical universe was, too. It was materialistic. The psychological wasn't: it was spiritual. Wells and Bennett and Galsworthy were accordingly denounced not just because the physical reality they reproduced, the reality of hotels and railway carriages, was no longer true or real, but also because it was a reflex of their own moral coarseness, of their crass materialism. "It is because they are concerned not with the spirit but with the body," she said of them, "that they have disappointed us, and left us with the feeling that the sooner English fiction turns its back upon them . . . the better for its soul." It should turn, instead, she considered, to the Russian novelists who were more concerned with spirit than with body. Refusing "to inform us whether we are in an hotel, a flat, or hired lodging," they had made "the soul . . . the chief character in [their] fiction." "If we are sick of our own materialism," Mrs. Woolf declared, "the least considerable of their novelists has by right of birth a natural reverence for the human spirit." Even ribald James Joyce could, at the end of such a funny train of reasoning as this, be called spiritual. "In contrast with those whom we have called materialists," she solemnly reported, "Mr. Joyce is spiritual; he is concerned at all costs to reveal the flickerings of that innermost flame." Such an opinion, however, she had trouble defending even to herself. The mind, it seemed, at least as Mr. Joyce beheld it, was meaner than she thought. A psychological realism, it seemed, wasn't more spiritual than a sociological one.

Something more was required of the novel of course

than sheer representation. It had to interpret and evaluate the world as well as represent it. If it was asked, however, to relax the rigor of its realism, to admit the intensities of poetry and philosophy, it wasn't just for art's sake, for the novel's sake. It was for the sake of the larger society and civilization the novel existed to serve. For very modern Virginia Woolf no less than for very Victorian Matthew Arnold literature had a practical social function to fulfill. Indeed, she went Arnold one better. With the deterioration of the old religious and philosophic systems that had hitherto sustained mankind, poetry, Arnold believed, would serve the purpose philosophy and religion had served in the past. As Wordsworth's "breath and finer spirit of all knowledge," poetry would provide, as religion and philosophy no longer did, "an ever surer and surer stay" against the riot and confusion of experience. Performing the office that priests and prophets had performed in the past, poets would mediate between mankind and the increasing incoherence of the world around him. As Virginia Woolf saw it, however, Arnold's poets hadn't been equal to the task; their poetry hadn't provided that surer and surer stay. Chaucer and Shakespeare and even Browning had been able to cope with the trivial and the grotesque; but, Mrs. Woolf complained, "it is October 1931, and for a long time now poetry has shirked contact with . . . life." Even when the poets *would* accommodate the mean and mixed realities that defined the modern experience, Mrs. Woolf wondered whether they *could*, whether the very nature of their medium didn't forbid it. When poetry was asked, she said, to express the confused conditions and values of modern life, "to express this discord, this incongruity, this sneer . . . she [couldn't] move quickly enough, simply enough, or broadly enough to do it," and Mrs. Woolf concluded "that the emotions here . . . imputed to the modern mind submit more

readily to prose than to poetry." "Poetry with her rhythms,
her poetic diction, her strong flavour of tradition," she
decided, "is too far from us to-day to do for us what she
did for our parents. Prose perhaps is the instrument best
fitted to the complexity and difficulty of modern life."

Not the poet, then, but the novelist was to be the priest
and prophet of this and future times. Not the poem but
the prose novel was to supply that surer and surer stay
against the forces of confusion and dismay. By making
men and women know the life they lived, the experience
they experienced, it would act, as poetry and drama had
acted in the past, to liberate them from the contagion of
their life and experience. It would accept and discharge
the same moral and social obligations that poetry and
drama had accepted and discharged in the past. If she
asked it to reform itself without abolishing itself, to
attempt the nonrepresentational without diminishing its
power to represent, it wasn't simply to magnify the novel
itself. It was to magnify life. For Virginia Woolf no less
than for James and Conrad, Joyce and Lawrence, the faith
of the novel was that it justified, as the epic poem had
done in the past, the ways of "God," the ways of a world
without God, to men.

7 Epilegomena:
The Single Vision

If Hardy and James, Conrad and Joyce, Lawrence and Virginia Woolf were involved in a common enterprise, they didn't always know it. Conrad revered his James, Lawrence his Hardy. The range of Mrs. Woolf's affections would eventually include both James and Hardy. Otherwise, however, they treated each other with scant courtesy and little charity. " 'Tess of the d'Urbervilles' is vile," James announced. "The pretence of sexuality is only equalled by the absence of it, and the abomination of the language by the author's reputation for style." Hardy, for his part, was no admirer of this magisterial American. James had, he decided, "a ponderously warm manner of saying nothing in infinite sentences." Their mutual incomprehensions were as nothing, however, compared to those of Joyce and Lawrence later. For the Hellenistic Irishman *Lady Chatterley's Lover* was detestable, was "a piece of propaganda in favour of something which, outside of D. H. L.'s country at any rate, makes all the propaganda for itself." But for the Hebraistic Englishman the great *Ulysses* was not less detestable: "What a stupid *olla podrida* of the Bible and so forth James Joyce is: just stewed-up fragments of quotation in the sauce of a would-be-dirty mind. Such effort! such exertion! *sforzato davvero!"* While they were busy despising each other Virginia Woolf was busily despising them both. *The Rainbow* she reviled as the product of "a private indecency press," *Ulysses* as "the book of a self taught working man . . . egotistic, insistent, raw, striking, and ultimately nauseating." These mutual aversions had of course their reasons and explanations. They registered serious differences, at certain crucial points, in their conceptions of life and art. At the very last, however, they came more from the surface than from the center of their convictions. The varieties and variations of their practice notwithstanding, what united their theories of life and literature was eventually more remarkable than what separated them.

Hardy of course excepted, they were united first and foremost by their faith in the novel. Scornful of those narrative and dramatic masterpieces of the past to which antediluvian Hardy would keep his fictions faithful, they recognized in the novel an entirely new development in the world, a giant step forward in the artistic exploration of life and nature. As the literary expression of science, of a purely empirical way of seeing and knowing things, it sought, they said, to *represent*, to behold the world with a fidelity and sobriety hitherto unattempted in literature. "The only reason for the existence of a novel," they said with James, "is that it does attempt to represent life." For the traditional makers of fiction with their roots in a mystical sense of things, reality was an attestation of the universal, of a power that lay outside the natural and the human. But for the novelist as for the scientist and historian, it was an attestation of the particular, of those human forms and natural phenomena which were the work of the world itself. Accordingly, it wasn't for the novelist to read reality in the light of some general theory or theorem. Like the scientist, he "proceeded by a sense for facts," by a feeling for "the things of this earth." Like him, he consulted what Conrad called "the aspects of the visible world," what James called "the packed and constituted . . . world before him." Even more essentially, he consulted the packed and constituted *social* world before him. Since life objectified itself most objectively of all in the constituents of social life, the novelist cherished them, said James, as of "the element exposable to the closest verification."

The novelist was to this extent committed to the life of a particular time and place. Reality wasn't for him, as it was for the traditional tellers of tales, the general or noumenal reality that transcended the limits of time and space. It was the particular or phenomenal reality created and conditioned by that time and space. "Inspiration," Conrad said, "comes from the earth, which has a past, a history, a future, not from the cold and immutable heaven." "The day of the absolute is over," Lawrence said after him. "Everything is true in its own time, place, circumstance, and untrue outside of its own place, time, circumstance." It was to his own circumstance, however, that the novelist was more especially committed. The life of his own time and place was surely the only life he could really observe, know, establish, was the only life that could supply him with a copious fund of particular objects. Oppressed by the surge and pressure of the contemporary scene, by the sheer profusion of its facts and values, the artist of the epic and romance could seek an imaginative freedom in the unverified and unverifiable life of the past. But the novelist, eager to represent, to receive and report a fully particularized reality, refused such a freedom. His fate, his happy fate, said James, was to engage "the palpable present *intimate*." It was to live, said Mrs. Woolf, "very close to the life of [his] time."

It was indeed to live very close to his own life, to the palpable present of his own intimate experience in and of the world. When all was said and done, his own history was the only history he could wholly vouch for, was the only history he could fully know and authenticate. Conrad liked to think that his fictions owed nothing whatsoever to invention, that they were entirely the products of his own ascertainable life and experience. *"J'ai vécu tout cela,"* he was fond of saying. What's more, he sometimes claimed, like Lawrence later, that his fictions rearranged the original experience as little as possible, that, like *Heart of Darkness*, they were "experience pushed a little (and only very little) beyond the actual facts of the case." It was Joyce who insisted most fanatically, however, on the actual facts of the case, on the necessary interdependence of the novelist's life and art. For him as for Conrad, the novel could represent life, could shun the "make-believe" of epic and romance, only to the extent that it came from a life or from lives that had actually been lived. Joyce indeed pursued this principle with a zeal unknown to Conrad and doubtless undesired. When he hadn't already lived or observed the experience he proposed to record, he was prepared to arrange it, would ruthlessly maneuver himself, his family, his friends, into the necessary life-situations. Though Lawrence never went this far, he acted in effect on the same essential principle of composition. A novel, he too believed, should be lived out before it was written out.

Lived out: not thought out. It wasn't the novelist's part to play the philosopher, to reduce the richness of experience itself to the poverty of a single theme or thesis. For him as for James, that novelist was most faithful to his representational calling who approached life and art with no preconceptions of any kind. If Conrad wrathfully refused to be identified with the Tolstois and the Dostoevskis, it was accordingly because they offended not the Polish nationalist but the English novelist, had subjected the large and various nature of life to the narrow necessities of "a Byzantine theological conception." No Pole certainly, Lawrence felt the same revulsion exactly. "People are not fallen angels, they are merely people," he said with Conrad. "But Dostoevsky used them all as theological or religious units, they are all terms of divinity." Conrad and Lawrence were indeed as hard on scientists as on seers and for the same urgent reasons. Like the idealist, Russian or otherwise, the scientist would sacrifice the complexity of existence to the tyranny of a simple explanation. The novelist characteristically liked to boast, therefore, that he was no philosopher in the formal sense. "I don't want 'a philosophy' in the least," Virginia Woolf declared after reading Lawrence's letters. But so, too, declared not only James and Conrad but Lawrence himself when he insisted that "this pseudo-philosophy of mine . . . [was] deduced from the novels and poems, not the reverse." So, too, for that matter, did "philosophical" Hardy. "Positive views on the Whence and the Wherefore of things," he argued, "have never been advanced by this pen as a consistent philosophy." For him as for his fellows in the novel, the phenomenal universe the philosophers rejected as "vain" was more enduring and significant than the powerful abstractions they superimposed upon it.

It was more enduring and significant, certainly, than the abstractions of the literary philosophers. A dogma wasn't less a dogma because it was literary rather than moral or scientific. It wasn't less reductive of life, wasn't less destructive of representation. Hence the contempt of the pure novelist for the ancient forms of tragedy and comedy. Hardy could ask the world and the novel to consist with these strict and simplifying conventions. But for James and Conrad, for Joyce and Lawrence and Virginia Woolf,

life was neither tragic nor comic but a mysterious mixture
of the two ("a tragi-comical adventure" in the phrase of
Conrad's Marlow) and hence the novel that would represent it must be neither one nor the other. It must slip, said
Conrad, "between frank laughter and unabashed tears."
"How difficult," as Mrs. Woolf would put it, "not to go
making 'reality' this and that, whereas it is one thing." For
the same reason that he condemned the tragic poet, the
novelist also condemned the lyric poet. For if the philosopher would submit the world as object to the claims of a
wholly subjective idea, the lyric poet would submit it to
the claims of a wholly subjective vision. More infatuated
with self than with world, with the state of his own feelings
than with the status of the world's objects, the versifier
seemed indeed to the novelist the supreme egotist of life
and letters. For Hardy and Lawrence, the legitimacy of the
poet might not be questionable, but for James and
Conrad and Mrs. Woolf as well as for Joyce, the "sumptu-
ous exaggerations to which the poets rose" derived, they
were sure, from their "leading haughty and elaborate
lives." When young Dedalus stated that narrative and
dramatic form had advanced beyond the lyric, he was
hardly expressing a prejudice peculiar to Joyce. He was
expressing the conviction of every committed novelist that
the poet's procedure was more self-centered, less objective
and responsible, than his own.

It was neither as poet nor philosopher, then, that the
novelist offered himself, but as the scientist. "A single-
minded observer and conscientious interpreter of reality,"
Conrad called him. Like the scientist, he proposed less to
think and imagine things than to see and observe them.
Scorning with Conrad "the pride of fanciful invention,"
scorning with James "those artistic perversions that come
. . . from a powerful imagination," the novelist proposed
with the scientist to rely on those humble senses and

sensations which recorded more faithfully than the poet's fancy and the philosopher's wisdom the world as physical object, "the mighty world of eye and ear." He had always written, Conrad was certain, "with an absolute truth to my sensations (which are the basis of art in literature)." "He is a very bold man," Joyce too declared, "who dares to alter . . . whatever he has seen and heard." For the novelist, indeed, the world was more palpable to the eye than to the ear, was more provable as something seen than as something heard. Not for Conrad alone was the novelist summoned "to make you *see*." "No theory is kind to us," James said too, "that cheats us of *seeing*."

In effect, then, the novelist read and rendered reality neither in the passionate spirit of the poet nor in the "interested" spirit of the philosopher but in the entirely dispassionate and disinterested spirit of the scientist. Like him he practised the skepticism that Conrad described as "the way of art and salvation." Instead of "calling down his inspiration ready-made from some heaven of perfections of which he knows nothing," the novelist, Conrad said, "mature[d] the strength of his imagination amongst the things of this earth." He had accordingly to write not from a Dionysiac state of mind or being, not from an abnormal state of exaltation or exasperation, but from an Apollonian state, from the perfectly normal state, that saw things steadily and saw them whole. Like the classical artist cherished by Joyce, he had to write from a sense of security and satisfaction. "Even before the most seductive reveries," as Conrad put it, "I have remained mindful of that sobriety of interior life . . . in which alone the naked form of truth . . . can be rendered without shame." Even the Lawrence whose "insecure, unsatisfied, impatient temper" Joyce and Conrad alike would have execrated did himself come out on the side of the same saving sanity and sobriety. "For God's sake, mistrust and beware of these states of exaltation and ecstasy," he said. ". . . there is no real truth in ecstasy."

This wasn't, however, to say that the novelist suppressed the self. On the contrary, he existed to express the self. One man's time and space wasn't after all another's. The reality that changed from time to time and from place to place also changed from person to person. For the novelist as for the scientist, therefore, there was no truth that didn't derive from the individual's unique understanding or experience of it. For him as for the scientist, the only defense against the poet's dream and the philosopher's doctrine, against all that would come between the writer and "the naked form of truth," was that he spurned the help of all convention and tradition and precedent and approached the world with nothing but his own sole sense and sensibility to guide him. To be a novelist, said James, was to reveal "a particular mind, different from others." It was to express, said Lawrence, "the naïve individual," the individual whose uniqueness hadn't been corrupted by social and moral and political convention. "If any man on earth more than another needs to be true to himself as he hopes to be saved," Conrad said, "it is certainly the writer of fiction." When Joyce's young artist-hero denied the claims of folk and family, church and state ("non serviam"), when he vowed to express his own individual nature fully and freely and without shame ("I shall express myself as I am"), there's therefore no reason to believe he wasn't speaking for Joyce himself. He was only affirming in its most uncompromising and outrageous form the "egomaniac aesthetic" by which all novelists proposed to live and work. "What can a man know," as Joyce would put it, "but what passes inside his own head?"

In a very special sense, then, the novelist had to be original. In a very special sense the novel had to be novel. "Before all, *imitate no one!!*" Conrad said with emphasis.

"We have to hate our immediate predecessors," Lawrence
said after him, "to get free from their authority." Indeed,
the novelist couldn't legitimately imitate himself, even.
The volatile reality that changed *from* individual to
individual also changed *within* the individual. Like Conrad and Lawrence, therefore, Virginia Woolf insisted on
the novelist's freedom to change from time to time, from
novel to novel. "I have . . . forced myself to break every
mould," she said, "and find a fresh form of being . . . for
everything I feel or think." Such a freedom as this involved
had of course its liabilities, its terrors. To be the single-
minded interpreter of reality, to expect "nothing from
gods or men," to explore the immense darkness of the
universe with nothing but the frail bark of the self or soul
to guide and sustain him, was a task not lightly undertaken
or easily borne. "I am frightened when I remember that I
have to drag it all out of myself." So Conrad confessed and
so, too, did Joyce and Lawrence after him. For all its
terrors, however, the novelist's fearful freedom was the
sole condition of his power to represent life. If one thing
united James and Hardy, Joyce and Conrad, Lawrence and
Mrs. Woolf, more than another, it was their contempt for
every form of censorship and convention that would
restrict the novelist's freedom of choice to this subject or
that, to one technique or another. As Conrad put it,
"liberty of imagination should be the most precious possession of a novelist." As Virginia Woolf put it, "nothing
—no 'method,' no experiment, even of the wildest—is
forbidden." For the novelist as for the scientist, the right
to explore and experiment, to follow the wayward ways of
the individual soul, was the indispensable precondition of
his effort in the world.

It was out of such a sense of the world and of his
relation to it that the novelist's sense of his form derived.
If he was to circumvent the *a priori* assumptions of priests

and philosophers, poets and politicians, if he was to represent a world that represented itself in its own material appearances, he had perforce to particularize things in the same copious way that life itself did. Since what life meant was inherent in the sum and substance of its objects, "solidity of specification" was for all novelists as well as for Henry James the "very essence of the novelist's art." "The value," said Conrad, "is in the detail." Hence the special character of the novel's language. It wasn't meant, like the language of poetry, to transfigure or disfigure the things of this world. It was meant, like the language of science, to define these things without exaggeration or distortion. The emergence of the novel was indeed coeval, Virginia Woolf suggested, with the emergence of a scientific knowledge and description, with the emergence of a referential prose that made such a knowledge and description possible. The modern novelist did call, it's true, for style, for "poetry," for an idiom more sensitive to the subtlety of things, than the plain prose of Defoe, say, or Smollett. But his motive was to make the language of the novel more rather than less representational, more rather than less capable of capturing the particularities that composed existence. Like James, he would make life condense "into audible or into visible reality." Like Conrad, he would make "the whole scene and all the details leap up before the eye" and so "make you *see*" the physical *appearances* that described reality itself. To rejoice in "artistic writing," in style for the sake of style, was to defeat the whole purpose of representation. In the long run, said James in effect, it was better to have too little style than too much.

For the same reason it was better to "have too little architecture than too much." The novel had to have a pattern, a design, a figure in its carpet; but the pattern, the design, the figure, had to be as enigmatic and elusive as it was in life itself. It wasn't the novel's business, James said, "to alter and arrange the things that surround us." It was to register, rather, "the strange irregular rhythm of life." Hence the novelist's detestation of parable and allegory. Evoking the metaphysical ideas of the priest and the philosopher instead of the physical facts of the scientist and historian, they authorized a more arbitrary rearrangement of things than was compatible with representation. "If allegory ever establishes a fact," said James, reciting Poe's objection to Bunyan's *Pilgrim's Progress*, "it is by dint of overturning a fiction." "One wants *experience* revealed, not allegory," Lawrence declared, and hence for him Dostoevski's novels were "only parables . . . like Christ's 'Sower went forth to sow,' and Bunyan's *Pilgrim's Progress*." At the very last, indeed, Lawrence would demand even less architecture than James did. He didn't propose to deliver the novel from the Procrustean bed of Dostoevski's moral logic in order, like James, like Conrad and Joyce, to place it in the Procrustean bed of Flaubert's formal logic. Such French arrangements were too carefully plotted, such modelings of life too emphatic and arbitrary, he argued, to capture the strange irregular rhythm of life. For all that she was charmed by James and repelled by Lawrence, Virginia Woolf herself had the same misgivings. "One of his most remarkable qualities," she wrote of Lawrence, was that "one never catches [him] . . . 'arranging,' " but one of James's least remarkable qualities, she thought, was that one did catch him arranging, was that he sacrificed "the interest and importance of his subject" to "a symmetry which [was] dear to him."

For the modern novelist, accordingly, the presence of a plot in a novel was a "nefarious" presence. Like parable and allegory, it made life more schematic than it was; like them it insisted on a form that had no authority in nature. As ancient Hardy saw it of course, such a consummation

was a consummation devoutly to be wished. Convinced
that novels needed more architecture rather than less, he
couldn't understand the new motives that would banish
plots altogether and with them all simplicities and symmetries of form. "They've changed everything now," he
groaned after reading Aldous Huxley. "We used to think
there was a beginning and a middle and an end. We
believed in the Aristotelian theory. Now one of those
stories came to an end with a woman going out of the
room." But for none of Hardy's juniors in the novel could
his grief have been meaningful. If James was dear to
Conrad, if Chekhov was dear to Mrs. Woolf, it was
precisely because they didn't believe in the Aristotelian
theory, didn't permit themselves the factitious climaxes
and resolutions of the Aristotelian plot. Lawrence was
indeed acceptable to Mrs. Woolf only because his fictions
had very little to do, she said, "with any of the usual
resting places, eminences, and consummations of the usual
novel."

"Novelists differ from the rest of the world because . . .
they feel that there is something permanently interesting
in character in itself." For the new novelist as here for Mrs.
Woolf, the novel's special genius wasn't the simplification
of the plot with its intimation of a Fate or Universal
Motive, but the complication of the character with its
intimation of particular fates, particular motives. The
novelist's love of reality derived, James decided, from "his
extreme interest in character." "That is where I think the
novel differs fundamentally from drama," Lawrence said
with him. "The novel is concerned with human beings,
and the drama is concerned with events." More especially,
the novel was concerned with human beings as the
products of their environment, of their natural and social
conditions. From the novelist's point of view as from the
social scientist's, men were the creatures of their physical

circumstances, not of some metaphysical system of good and evil. "Mankind generally is neither guilty nor innocent," Conrad declared. "It simply is." For every novelist as for Mrs. Woolf, the sign of the novel was thus that it saw its people "much at the mercy of those conditions which change with the years."

When all was said and done, then, the world of the novelist was a perfectly ordinary one. Conceivable no longer as a gigantic drama of good and evil, as "a theorem of divine power and love and universality," it had ceased to be the spectacular place, the arena of sinners and saints, it had seemed to metaphysical philosophy and ecclesiastical authority. Predicating with the scientist a wholly terrestrial existence, the novelist restricted reality to what was measureable or verifiable, to what was known or could be known. The world as he knew it wasn't, like that of the epic and romance, a world affected, or deflected, by the miraculous interventions of the divine, the supernatural. Like the scientist's, it was governed by wholly natural laws, by the laws that obtained under the conditions of time and space. "Fiction," said Conrad, "is history, human history, or it is nothing." Indeed, for Conrad and Lawrence alike, death itself wasn't properly the concern of the true novelist. Unknown, unknowable, one of those hours and spots over the edge of time and space, it didn't qualify as life, didn't qualify as a *fact*. "Life is the fact, the everything," Lawrence said with Conrad before him: "Death is only the 'To be concluded' at the end of the volume."

If the novelist wasn't licensed to summon the supernatural, neither was he licensed to summon the superhuman. The same secular dispensation that denied the existence of gods also denied the existence of heroes. Like the natural world, the social world itself had diminished in the course of time. A new middle class society had come into being hostile to the old feudal values of love and war. "The brood of men now, in towns and cities, is not of fierce passion," the youthful Joyce observed. "The ordinary person is calmer, smoother, more self-contained than he used to be," said Mrs. Woolf. For them as for Conrad, accordingly, "most of the working truths on this earth [were] humble, not heroic." An ancestral literature of epic and romance, saga and tragedy, could celebrate in its high-born protagonists the aristocratic passions of love and war. But the new literature of the novel defined in its Emmas and Pamelas and Robinson Crusoes the more domestic passions of a pious and practical middle class. Its study wasn't the exceptional case but the average one, wasn't the sublime figure of the feudal imagination but the less remarkable and more ambiguous figure of the modern imagination. What made Turgenev so purely the novelist was, said James, that his heroes were "never heroes in the literal sense of the word . . . their function [was] to be conspicuous as failures." Hence, once again, the prohibition against plots. It wasn't only that they made life more systematic than it was; it was also that they made it more amazing. To enter the realm of character and psychology was to encounter a world we could know, but to enter the realm of plot and action was to encounter a surprising world out of all relation to our own. "It was only on the stage," reflected Conrad's Razumov, "that the unusual was outwardly acknowledged." "A writer should never write about the extraordinary," Joyce said. "That is for the journalist."

Not beauty, then, but truth, truth in the exact and exacting sense of science, was the novel's only province. In his passion for beauty, for artistic transcendence, the poet came, Conrad charged, "to despise truth itself as something too cold, too blunt for his purpose." But not the novelist. "Truth alone," Conrad said, "is the justification of any fiction which makes the least claim to the quality of art." It wasn't for the novelist to entertain the world, to console or inspire it. That was for lyric and epic and tragical poets. As scientist, the novelist's only aim and aspiration was to bring the reader into the somber presence of the truth. For just about every novelist, accordingly, "a literature of entertainment" was an abomination. Joyce despised it, his brother recalled, as "the province of men of letters . . . who toyed with literature." "Even the greatest men," Lawrence protested, "spend most of their time making marvellous fine toys. Like *Pickwick* or *Two on a Tower*." The novel's vast importance, its superiority to every other form of fiction, was thus that as representation, it took itself seriously and took the world seriously. "The successive generations still demand artlessly to be amazed, moved and amused," Conrad complained; but the novel was meant, he would insist, "for a humanity which has outgrown the stage of fairy tales, realistic, romantic or even epic."

II

So far the assumptions of modern novelists didn't differ radically from those of the founding fathers of the form. Like Defoe and Richardson, Fielding and Smollett, they took it for granted that the novel's special care in the world was to represent, was to represent a reality that was by definition external and objective. From the turn of the century on, however, they became increasingly dissatisfied with this largely exterior emphasis. Reality, they perceived, had changed. It was less matter now than spirit, less world than experience, less the visible universe that man inhabited than the invisible universe that inhabited him. They called accordingly for a revolution not against representation as such but against the exclusively physical reality the

realistic novel had long agreed to represent. With an
urgency that increased from James to Mrs. Woolf, they
called for a psychological fiction.

This new departure was first of all evident in the revolt
against the standard novel of plot and dialogue. For a
traditionalist like Hardy, life could still be rendered best in
the external codes of what men did and what men said.
But for the novelists who succeeded him, life was irreducibly thought and feeling and events as such were only
accidents. As Conrad saw it, the task of the novelist was
"to create human souls . . . and not to create events that
are properly speaking *accidents* only." As James saw it, it
was to register "moral and intellectual and spiritual life,
and not the everlasting vulgar chapters of accidents . . .
which rise from the mere surface of things." It was the
externality of French naturalism, however, that the new
novelist opposed most strenuously. Conrad could still
respect its feeling for the external aspects of life. Alphonse
Daudet "saw only the surface of things . . ." he could say,
"for the reason that most things have nothing but a
surface." For Conrad's contemporaries, however, the external aspects no longer sufficed. "My real world," said
Lawrence, "is the world of my inner soul . . . The outer
world is there to be endured, it is not real—neither the
outer life." For Virginia Woolf, too, the real world was
the world inside, not the world outside. For her as for
Lawrence, the novelist's concern should be the inner soul
and not the clothing and upholstery with which it found
itself surrounded. Hence her pleasure in Tolstoi and
Dostoevski, her displeasure with Bennett and Wells. "If
we wished to tell the story of a General's love-affair . . ."
she lamented, "we should begin with his house; we should
solidify his surroundings. Only when all was ready should
we attempt to deal with the General himself."

It was the external world of social objects, however, that

the modern novelist was most disposed to call in question. For all his lordly assurance that the forms of social life were coordinate with the forms of life itself, even Henry James could doubt their continuing validity as terms of representation. The increasing uniformity of the urban experience was already effacing, he noted, "those inherent oppositions from type to type" upon which the novelist so crucially depended. His misgivings, however, were only momentary. Not so Thomas Hardy's. The social norms were never for him the vital signs of life they were for James. If he fled the urban life of London, it was because its social substance obscured rather than revealed the essential reality of life and character. It had the effect, he said, of "making the exteriors of men their screen rather than their index." Nor was this perception Hardy's alone. Even more violently, it was Lawrence's and Mrs. Woolf's. When they attacked the Edwardian realists, it was on the identical grounds that they had mistaken the social reality for reality itself. "There is a constant pressure upon an English novelist to recognise these [social] barriers," Virginia Woolf complained. ". . . he is inclined . . . to scrutiny of society rather than understanding of individuals themselves." "In all his books," Lawrence complained of Galsworthy, as he had also complained of Wells, "I have not been able to discover one real individual—nothing but social individuals." The wealth of social classes and categories that had seemed to James and Conrad the English novelist's great good fortune thus seemed to Mrs. Woolf his great misfortune. The wealth of social custom and ceremony that James and Conrad had come to England to find Lawrence left England to lose. A more total rejection of their most cherished assumption that life was social or it was nothing can hardly be imagined than Lawrence's angry admonition to deny the reality of the social appearance. "The world, the social world," as he put it bitterly, "can offer little or nothing any more."

The modern novelist had, then, to find a new language, a new vocabulary, for reality. He had perforce to be or become the psychological novelist. Such a prospect wasn't of course to Hardy's liking. He feared a subjective notation of reality just as much as he feared an objective notation of it. In this, however, he stood alone. "We forget," said Virginia Woolf, "that we spend much time sleeping, dreaming, thinking, reading, alone; we are not entirely occupied in personal relations." The novelist who would capture life itself had accordingly to give much less to sociology and much more to psychology. "If we want life itself," she grudgingly acknowledged after reading *Ulysses*, "here, surely we have it." One man's psychology wasn't, it's true, another's. The life of the mind as Joyce conceived it was detestable to Lawrence and the life of the mind as both Joyce and Lawrence conceived it was equally detestable to Mrs. Woolf. For the time being at least, however, they were united in the recognition that reality had abandoned the visible forms of the external world and entered the invisible forms of the internal world. If the novel was to represent at all, it had to represent a new reality. It had to turn its finely polished looking glass from the outer universe of physical and social facts to the inner universe of thoughts and feelings.

In the last analysis, however, the modern novelist called for a great deal more than a mere revision of the novel's realism. He called, more startlingly, for a rejection of it. The great shift in emphasis from the external to the internal not only involved a radical change in the substance of the novel. It also involved a radical change in the form of the novel. It wasn't only necessary to record the inside of life, to record it as a reflex of the character's consciousness. It was also necessary to record it *from* the inside, to record it as a reflex of the author's consciousness. The world outside, the world as seen from the outside, didn't after all explain itself. It needed the explaining, the explanations, which could only come from the world inside, from seeing the world from the inside. "I am getting weary, and wearier, of the outside world," Lawrence said. "I want the world from the inside, not from the outside." "We want to be rid of realism," said Mrs. Woolf, "to penetrate without its help into the regions beneath it." To this extent, the same dissatisfaction with an exclusively external universe that produced the demand for a psychological fiction also produced the demand for a nonrepresentational fiction. It wasn't enough, it seemed, to reflect reality; it was also necessary to reflect upon it. It wasn't enough to repeat reality; it was also necessary to create it.

The novelist's first perception may have been, then, that his form could be too analytic, too abstract, too philosophical; but his second perception was that it wasn't analytic, abstract, philosophical, enough. He hadn't rejoiced in the collapse of the old universals in order to rejoice in the absence of all universals. A truth did inhabit the earth that was "little susceptible of change," said Joyce. "There is a *principle* in the universe," said Lawrence, "towards which man turns religiously—a *life* of the universe itself." The novel had accordingly to offer less life and more philosophy, less perception and more conception. Joyce declared his contempt for "a young generation which has cast away belief and thrown precision after it, for which Balzac is a great intellect and every sampler who chooses to wander amid his own shapeless hells and heavens a Dante without the unfortunate prejudices of Dante." "It was the greatest pity in the world," Lawrence declared with him, "when philosophy and fiction got split. They used to be one, right

from the days of myth. Then they went and parted . . . So
the novel went sloppy, and philosophy went abstract-dry.
The two should come together again—in the novel." In
this context Hardy's longing for "abstract imaginings" was
hardly eccentric. No less than Joyce and Lawrence, he
would have the novel "distinguish truths which are temporary from truths which are eternal."

If the modern novel was increasingly skeptical, then, of
the external universe of physical and social objects, it
wasn't only because it was no longer reflective of life itself.
It was also because it resisted the effort to distinguish the
essence from the appearance, the universal from the
particular. It resisted, in its overwhelming materiality and
particularity, the simplifications of the philosophic mind.
It wasn't Hardy alone who condemned a realistic art with
its "presentation of mountains, cities, clothes, furniture,
plate, jewels, and other real and sham-real appurtenances."
"We must establish ourselves in the absolute truth,"
Lawrence said too, "and scorn this filthily contemptible
world of actuality." Seeking the outline rather than the
detail, the novel of the future would tell us, Virginia
Woolf predicted, "very little about the houses, incomes,
occupations of its characters; it [would] have little kinship
with the sociological novel or the novel of environment."

Hence the necessary emphasis on life as psychology. •
The inner reality of the mind wasn't only closer to life
itself than the outer reality of the world. It was inherently
more philosophical, more abstract, more capable of pro-
viding for a moral assessment of experience. Characters of
"cultivated consciousness" would register and transmit,
James believed, a clearer understanding of their lives and
of life than the primitive creatures of the naturalistic
novel. "The person capable of feeling in the given case
more than another . . ." he said, "is the only sort of
person on whom we can count not to betray . . . the value

and beauty of the thing." As Hardy and Lawrence saw it, however, a subjective system of establishing life and character was just as trivial as an objective one. The universal was an aspect, they argued, not of the cultivated consciousness but of the uncultivated unconsciousness. When Lawrence quit England for Sicily and Mexico, accordingly, it was to find the same "rule of ancient instinct" that made Hardy quit London for Wessex. It was to find the agents of "some greater, inhuman will,"—people in whom still lurked "the tremendous unknown forces of life." If Lawrence detested the psychological novel, however, it was also because it obliterated the record of man's intellectual life. "A novel is supposed to be a mere record of emotion-adventures, flounderings in feelings," he wrote angrily in *Kangaroo*. "We insist that a novel is, or should be, also a thought-adventure." Novelists and their characters should be free, that is, to be "philosophers," to think and talk about the mysteries of things and so disclose their secrets. At the very end, indeed, Virginia Woolf herself could think so, too. For her as for Lawrence, the psychological data of Proust and Joyce were no more revelatory of "the true and the enduring" than the sociological data of Bennett and Wells. Character immersed in the expanding stream of consciousness was no less immersed in life, was no less prevented from standing back and measuring it, than character immersed in the steady-state of kitchens and kettles, classes and crowds. "We still find ourselves distressingly near the surface," she decided after reading Dorothy Richardson, ". . . never, or only for a tantalizing second, in the reality which underlies these appearances." Like Lawrence, accordingly, she wanted characters freer to descant upon "our destiny and the meaning of life."

It was indeed to reinstate the poetry as well as the philosophy of existence that the modern novelist proposed to work. As representation, the novel's primary obligation was to truth, was to all that was demonstrably real and probable in the life of things. But it didn't follow that it was therefore condemned to squalor and ugliness, that it could have no commerce at all with the good and the beautiful. There wasn't, James insisted, "a bit more luminosity in treating of low life and of primitive man than of those whom civilization has kneaded to a finer paste." It wasn't necessarily true, Virginia Woolf insisted with him, "that to be born the son of a butcher is a blessing and to be unable to read a virtue . . . that what we call 'life' and 'reality' are somehow connected with ignorance and brutality." Her quarrel with Joyce and Lawrence was just that their sense of the real was "neither jovial nor magnanimous," that their *Ulysses* and their *Lady Chatterley*s didn't make what James had called "an eloquent plea for the ideal." In point of fact, however, it was Lawrence, precisely, who agitated most strenuously for the ideal, for a more joyous and generous conception of what was comprehended by "reality" and "realism." A novel shouldn't be just a *criticism* of life, he contended; it should also be a *creation* of it. It should be, he argued with the ardor of a James or Mrs. Woolf, "a life in itself, far better than the vulgar thing people *call* life." The novelist had of course to register the rhythm of destroying, had to reveal the horror of what did actually exist. This was what it was to be the scientist of life and letters. But he had also to register the "rhythm of creating," had to create the charm of all those lovely gracious things that were yet to enter the circle of existence. This was what it was to be the poet or prophet of life and letters. Lawrence was hardly satisfied, then, with the author of *Under Western Eyes*: "Conrad should always do the beautiful, magic atmospheres. What on earth turned him to Razumov?" He was satisfied even less with the rigorous author of *Ulysses*, "the dirtiest, most indecent, obscene thing ever written." If the novel was to have a future, he said, it had to *create* a future, had "to present us with . . . a whole line of new emotion . . . Instead of snivelling about what is and has been . . . it's got to break a way through."

The Laurentian indignation wasn't entirely mistaken. Joyce was a rather strict interpreter of the novel's contract to the truth and nothing but the truth. James and Conrad were prepared to rejoice in the terms of this contract, in the novel's commitment to the prosy particularities of life, but they would hardly have been prepared for the "pebbles and rubbish and broken matches" Joyce found the world to contain, not to mention the "unreflecting admissions and unregarded trifles" he found the human mind to contain. Life, it seemed, was a meaner, more trivial, affair than they had dreamed of in their philosophies. For all the severity of his sense of things, however, not even Joyce was deaf to the siren songs of the beautiful. Like James he was offended by a certain moral brutality he found in the writing of the French. Like Lawrence he was offended by a certain moral brutality he found in the writing of the Russians. A continental conception of life and art may account for the austerities of *Stephen Hero* and *Dubliners* and even *Portrait of the Artist*, but it hardly accounts for the genialities, for the jovialities, of *Ulysses* and *Finnegans Wake*. Stephen may be guilty of "snivelling about what is and has been," but as the "good man" Joyce intended his hero to be, Leopold does "break a way through," does offer us "a whole line of new emotion." For Joyce no less than for Lawrence, the novelist had more to do in the world than repeat the conditions of the current reality; he had also to create the conditions of a new one. Like Stephen Dedalus, he must "forge in the smithy of [his] soul the *uncreated* conscience of [his] race." Like him he must embrace not with Yeats "the loveliness which has long faded from the world," but with Lawrence and however differently, "the loveliness which has not yet come into the world." At a time when the prestige of the French novel was at its zenith and that of the English at its nadir, a reaction was evidently taking place. That reaction is least remarkable in Conrad, say, and most remarkable in Lawrence, but it is general all over England and reflects a growing sense that what pertained to the ideal and the beautiful was no less in the novelist's interest that what pertained to the real and the true. In this context, the demands old Hardy made on the novel weren't simply the aberrations of his provincial genius. When he questioned "any system of inversion that should attach more importance to the delineation of man's appetites than to the delineation of his aspirations, affections, or humors," his reasons and language may have been old-fashioned but his argument wasn't. Like James and Joyce, like Lawrence and Mrs. Woolf, he was protesting the French infatuation with merely sensual and material values to the neglect of all ideal and imagined ones.

The novelist's first conviction may have been, then, that he must be more the observer of things than the poet or philosopher. But his second conviction was that he must be more the poet or philosopher. Since the world outside offered in or of itself neither truth nor beauty, it behooved the novelist to regard it from the inside and with all the rich resources of the heart and mind. The trouble with Howells, James decided, was that he could "write solely of what his fleshly eyes have seen." "We have sat receptive and watched," Mrs. Woolf complained of her contemporaries, "with our eyes rather than with our minds, as we do at the cinema, what passes on the screen in front of us." Not the mere sensations of the scientific observer but the imagination of the poet and the intellect of the philosopher were thus the keys to life and art. The failure of Flaubert, said James, was that he mistook his "innumerable marvels of observation" for "the underlying moral unity of what is called a 'purpose.' " "Since every novelist who amounts to anything has a philosophy—even Balzac," Lawrence declared, "any novel of importance has a purpose." It was Joyce and Mrs. Woolf, however, who were most emphatic on the place of the philosopher in life and literature, the Joyce who insisted that "it must be asked concerning every artist how he is in relation to the highest knowledge," the Mrs. Woolf who insisted that he apply to the world "the generalizing and simplifying power of a strict and logical imagination." They called indeed for a degree of abstraction in the novel that James and Conrad would have wondered at. The generalizing and simplifying power that James deplored in the fictions of Meredith and Hardy Joyce and Mrs. Woolf to some extent admired. "Any book about the philosopher is worth reading," Joyce could write in Meredith's praise, "unless we have given ourselves over deliberately to the excellent foppery of the world." It was his virtue, not his defect, wrote Mrs. Woolf in Hardy's praise, that he gave us "a vision of the world and of man's lot as they revealed themselves to a powerful imagination."

The novelist's first instinct, then, may have been to sacrifice self to world, subject to object, but his second was to sacrifice world to self, object to subject. As long as the external reality made its own sense, then a French impersonality, a Flaubertian suppression of the self, was mandatory. But with the collapsing confidence in that external reality, the dynamic self, the marked personality or point of view of the novelist, had to come into play. "The affair of the painter," said James, "is not the immediate, it is the reflected field of life, the realm not of application, but of *appreciation*." Lawrence spoke even

more urgently for the claims of reflection and appreciation. "We never know that we ourselves are anything," he
protested, "we think there are only the objects we shine
upon." Hence, once again, the prophetic soul of Thomas
Hardy. A novel wasn't "the thing," he insisted with them,
but "a view of the thing." "The seer should watch," he
stated, "that pattern among general things which his
idiosyncrasy moves him to observe."

The novelist accordingly passed from feeling he
couldn't have too many facts at his disposal to feeling he
could have much too many. The same solidity of specification that was the condition of his power to represent life
was also the condition of his powerlessness to simplify it.
Hence, while Joyce and Conrad could fret about the
shortage of facts, James and Hardy and Virginia Woolf
could fret about the superfluity of them, James reviling the
"fluid puddings" of Tolstoi and Dostoevski, Hardy and
Mrs. Woolf the same fluid puddings of Dreiser and
Bennett and Wells. A less representational novel, a novel
more abstract and analytic, would give us, Mrs. Woolf
accordingly promised, less detail and more outline, less
facts and more structure. Facts were of the outside of life,
were what appeared when life was seen from the outside;
but structure was of the inside of life, was what appeared
when life was seen from the inside. From the point of view
of representation it was better to have too little architecture than too much, but from the point of view of
abstraction it was better to have too much architecture
than too little. The trouble with naturalistic novels, James
and Hardy could thus agree, was that they were all matter
and no form, all fact and no structure. Bennett's *Clay-
hanger*, James protested, was a case "of a compositional
office absolutely discharged by mere multiplication ... of
the facts." "One prefers—expects—some sort of structure,"
Hardy wrote of Dreiser, "not a mere heap of bricks."

If the novelist's first inclination, then, was to subordinate the claims of design to the necessity of character, his second was to subordinate the claims of character to the necessity of design. He may have insisted at the first that the pattern of the novel be a function of the characters and their behavior, but he insisted in the end that the characters and their behavior should be functions of the pattern. Reality derived, he said in effect, not from particular characters in their relations to each other but from particular characters in their relation to a fate above or beyond, behind or beneath, them. "I am tired of this insistence on the *personal* element . . ." Lawrence declared. "I want . . . relations based upon some unanimous accord in truth or belief." "We long for some more impersonal relationship," said Mrs. Woolf to the same effect. "We long for ideas, for dreams, for imaginations, for poetry." The accent of the modern novel had accordingly to fall not on character as such but on some force or form in the universe that transcended and included the particularity of character. "In a book you should love the idea and be scrupulously faithful to your conception of life. There lies the honour of the writer, not in the fidelity to his personages." So said Conrad but so, one way or another, said James and Joyce, Lawrence and Mrs. Woolf. The fascination of Ibsen's theater came, the youthful Joyce observed, not from the characters themselves but from a "naked drama" that was independent of the characters. "Don't look for the development of [*The Rainbow*] to follow the lines of certain characters," Lawrence said to the same purpose: ". . . the characters fall into the form of some other rhythmic form." Against this background, once again, Hardy's readiness to sacrifice his people to the ancient gods of comedy and tragedy isn't quite the oddity it appears. Neither James nor Conrad could have understood his nostalgia for comic and tragic plots, but Joyce and Lawrence and Virginia Woolf at least would have understood the moral and artistic motive behind it, the passionate desire to submit the particularity of the character to the universality of the design.

It's a question, indeed, whether in his ardor for abstraction, for symmetries of form and structure, the modern novelist wouldn't have liked to do away with character altogether. What he wanted wasn't character particularized, individualized, as the expression of its sociological or psychological conditions. What he wanted was character generalized, universalized, as the expression of larger forces that transcended the conditions of its particularity. He wasn't interested, Lawrence said, in the "old stable *ego*—of the character," in character defined from the "stable" point of view of purely human moral and social and psychological codes. He was only interested, he said, in those "allotropic states," in those unconscious states of mind or being, in which the old stable ego, in which the old human categories, dissolved and disappeared altogether. "I am most sick of this divinity-of-man business. People are *not important*: I insist on it. It doesn't matter what Stavrogin does, nor whether he lives or dies." Joyce's allotropic states weren't Lawrence's of course, but they were just as allotropic and were designed no less than his to abolish the old stable ego of the character. In the daytime world of *Ulysses*, the background of the Homeric epic notwithstanding, the characters would retain something of their old stable egos; but in the nighttime world of *Finnegans Wake* they would lose these identities in the larger dimensions of archetypal dream and myth. "Time and the river and the mountain are the real heroes of my book," Joyce would write of it. The same impulse to universalize, to make the human creature either more or less than human, was felt by Virginia Woolf. In *The Waves*, she said, as Lawrence and Joyce had said before her, she would have no characters at all, would abolish their old stable egos. "I don't want a Lavinia or a Penelope: I want 'she.' " When Lawrence denounced novels that were about "people, people and nothing but people: *ad nauseam*," he was by no means expressing a sentiment eccentric with himself. It was an aspect of a new passion that would make the old novel either more or less than wholly representational.

If it was true, then, that the novelist couldn't celebrate the extraordinary at the expense of the ordinary, it was also true that he couldn't celebrate the ordinary at the expense of the extraordinary. To insist that the world was an apparition of the particular, of people, people and nothing but people, was to insist that it was a perfectly ordinary world; but to insist that it was an apparition of the universal, of a pattern external to and greater than its merely human population, was to insist that it was a rather remarkable place after all. Character as character mightn't be important or interesting, but character as the expression of the universal, of a deity or demon that was more than merely human, was something else again. "They may be bores," as Joyce said of Ibsen's people, "but the drama in which they live and move is invariably powerful." Hence when writers as various and indeed as apparently incompatible as Hardy and Lawrence, Joyce and Mrs. Woolf, proposed to abolish the old stable ego of the character, to dissolve it in the larger sense of the novel as a whole, it wasn't only to revive and renew the reality of the universal. It was, by that very token, to revive and renew the reality of the miraculous. It was Lawrence of course who wished most devoutly for just such a consummation. Like the Cézanne who painted the human-ness out of his human figures, he was anxious to evoke "the vast, uncomprehended and incomprehensible morality of nature or of life itself, surpassing human consciousness." But Joyce attempted not much less when he sought in *Finnegans Wake* to make his figures functions of "time and the river and the mountain," when he sought to make them functions of such "tremendous unknown forces" as were embodied in myth and psychology and anthropology. And Virginia Woolf attempted not much less when she sought in *The Waves* to convey "the idea of some continuous stream, not solely of human thought," when she sought to create, that is, not only the stream of consciousness located in men but the stream of consciousness in which men were located. In this context, once again, Hardy's practice was prophetic. By making his people the principals of tragic processes, he denied with Joyce and Lawrence and Mrs. Woolf that the human character was everything, that it played no part in a larger dream or drama. Like them he refused to believe in a world from which all prospect and possibility of the marvelous were banished forever.

Certainly, the modern novelist refused to take it for granted that he was bound to the ordinary in life and character. Joyce could reject the legitimate hero of traditional literature, could rejoice in the bourgeois hero of Ibsen's theater; but his contemporaries were increasingly discontented with the meager people who crept about in the prosy pages of the realistic novel. For Mrs. Woolf the Stephen Smiths and Mrs. Gapes were hardly enough. For Lawrence the Bovarys and Malavoglias were hardly enough. One way or another they would rediscover the aristocratic character, the aristocratic character in the figurative and even the literal sense. The role of heroes in modern novels was, James conceded, to be conspicuous as failures, but they could also be, he liked to think, conspicuous as successes, could be aristocrats in spirit if not in fact and so claim something of the qualities of the Hamlets and Lears. Virginia Woolf felt the same immortal longings. Not for her Gissing's clerks and other miscellaneous victims of life. For her too as for James, for her even more than for James, the Hamlets and Lears, the masters of life, the aristocratic creatures capable of descanting on its meaning or mystery. "Your excellence as a subject arises largely from your noble birth . . ." she wrote Vita Sackville-West who sat for the hero or heroine of *Orlando*, "and the opportunity thus given for florid descriptive passages in great abundance." It was Hardy and Lawrence, however, who objected most of all to the novel's fixation with anti-heroes. James and Mrs. Woolf would have heroes and heroines all right but since their heroism would be moral or psychological, not physical or external, they would be heroic only in the problematic sense, only in the sense in which it was possible for all human beings to be heroic. Hardy and Lawrence, however, would insist on heroes and heroines in the "legitimate" sense of the term, in the more literal and unambiguous sense of it. Hardy's quarrel with the novel was just that it refused to accommodate creatures on the aristocratic scale of tragedy. Less sympathetic to tragedy, Lawrence's quarrel with it was that it refused to accommodate creatures on the aristocratic scale of Carlyle, those exceptional individuals who felt and fought for the universe itself. "I am so sick," he said, "of those modern inspired young heroes with weak, rhubarby guts. Why do young men never conceive a hero with a bit of fighting spunk?"

If the external terms of social and physical forms seemed to Hardy and Lawrence inadequate, then, it wasn't only because they lacked reality. It was also because they lacked mystery and glamour. The English world of social custom and ceremony was dear to James and Conrad because it was so ordinary, so human, and so set limits on the total range of experience. But it was abhorrent to Hardy and Lawrence precisely because it was so ordinary, so human, precisely because it did exclude all that was strange and surprising in the spectrum of experience. Lawrence wanted as ardently as Hardy himself "another domain for the imagination to expatiate in." "I know, from the Egyptian and Assyrian sculpture—what we are after," he said. "We want to realise the tremendous *non-human* quality of life." Hence for him as for Hardy the powerful appeal of the natural cosmos, the nonhuman world of heath and hill, of bird, beast and flower. Such a cosmos mattered to Conrad only insofar as it affected man or was affected by him. Like the sea in Fenimore Cooper, it was, said Conrad, "a factor in the problem of existence, and, for all its greatness, it [was] always in touch with the men . . ." For Lawrence as for Hardy, however, its greatness was precisely that it wasn't in touch with men, was that it evoked "something supernatural, which is not of human life." To presuppose with James and Conrad a reality wholly social and human, wholly known and knowable, was to find acceptable a perfectly ordinary reality; but to presuppose with Hardy and Lawrence a vast surrounding universe that transcended man and his society, that was by definition nonhuman and even superhuman, was to reaffirm the existence of a magic in the world.

For the modern novelist, however, the magic was within man as well as without him. If he entered the internal world of mind and motive it wasn't only because it was more real than the external world of fact and matter. It was also because it was more remarkable. The uncharted seas of the human consciousness were just as full of surprises, James proposed, as the islands of the Spanish Main. Once the self shed its attachments to the outer world, Virginia Woolf said with him, it "was free for the strangest adventures." For Hardy and for Lawrence, however, not quite strange enough. For them a psychological notation of reality was no less commonplace than a

sociological one. " 'Did I feel a twinge in my little toe, or
didn't I?' asks every character of Mr. Joyce or of Miss
Richardson or M. Proust," Lawrence wrote indignantly.
The adventures James and Virginia Woolf sought in the
brightly lit chambers of consciousness Lawrence accordingly sought in the deeper darker caverns of unconsciousness, in what he called, fittingly enough, the *fantasia* of
the unconscious. If, like Hardy, he explored the primitive
in people and places, people and places still governed by
"a rule of ancient instinct," it wasn't only to rediscover
elemental states of being in which what was apparently
local should be really universal. It was also to discover
elemental states of being in which what was apparently
ordinary should be really extraordinary. For that matter
the Joyce he despised would himself turn to more and
more unconscious, more and more fantastic, conditions of
being. "Why all this fuss and bother about the mystery of
the unconscious?" Joyce once asked. "What about the
mystery of the conscious?" But for him in the end as for
Lawrence, the subconscious could seem the last frontier of
the mystery of things. Not for Virginia Woolf, however.
She may have come, like Lawrence, to doubt the marvel of
man's conscious nature but she didn't therefore elect the
more dreadful marvels of his unconscious nature. In her
passion for poetry, for philosophy, she would have less
Proust and more Peacock, less Freud and more fantasy.
"Fantasticality," she decided, "does a good deal better
than sham psychology." Neither the world outside nor the
world inside was after all as extraordinary as the mind that
beheld it from the inside and brought to bear upon it its
own strange store of eccentricity.

The modern novelist put his representational form
under a new pressure, then. If he didn't ask it to register *a*
heightened or intensified reality, he asked it to heighten or
intensify *the* reality. In either case he called for less

representation and more abstraction, less mimesis and more poesis. He may even have felt the influence of the great abstractionists and expressionists who were already revolutionizing the art of painting in Paris and Munich. Even when he didn't himself paint, as Lawrence did, he often surrounded himself or found himself surrounded, like Joyce in Paris and Virginia Woolf in London, by people who did. "Sculpture never quite satisfies me," Lawrence could say. "It is not sufficiently abstracted. One resents the bulk, it frustrates the clarity of conception." "Now undoubtedly we are under the dominion of painting," Mrs. Woolf observed. "Were all modern paintings to be destroyed, a critic of the twenty-fifth century would be able to deduce from the works of Proust alone the existence of Matisse, Cézanne, Derain, and Picasso."

III

In the end, however, the novelist wouldn't give all to abstraction. He would have his cake and eat it. He would have abstraction and representation too. The reality he proposed to render was after all a measure neither of the particular nor of the universal, neither of the substance nor of the idea. It was a measure of their interdependence. A unity, a universal, did animate the world, but it wasn't distinguishable from the sensuous shapes it took in time and space. "The final mystery is one mystery," Lawrence said. "But the manifestations are many." "Beauty is a white light," Joyce was told, but a white light, he replied, "made up of seven colours." For the novelist, accordingly, there was no necessary incompatibility between the effort of representation and the effort of abstraction. As James conceived it, the novelist's special work in the world was "to render the look of things, the look that conveys their meaning." It was to find, Conrad said, "the truth, manifold and one, underlying its every aspect," was "to find in its forms, in its colours, in its light . . . the very truth of their existence." Hence the novelist's stress on *seeing*, on making things vividly visible. To make the reader *see* in the sense of physically apprehending things was to make him *see* in the sense of morally comprehending them. In the particular was contained the universal; in the appearance was contained the reality.

This wasn't to say, however, that life was coordinate with the sum of its particulars. It was rather to say that it was coordinate with the form of their relations. In life all things were relative to all other things and were only real, were only true, in their relations to all other things. As James defined it, reality was a function of "the relations life throws up at every hour and on every spot." As Lawrence defined it, it was "the rapid momentaneous association of things," was "everything . . . in its own rapid, fluid relationship with the rest of things." For James, a phenomenon found "its extension and consummation only in the rest of life." For Lawrence, "nothing [was] true, or good, or right, except in its own living relatedness . . . to the things that [were] in the stream with it." Thus for them the novel's special beauty. Like life itself, it defined the universal as a derivation not of things in themselves, not of their relations to some ultimate theme or theory, but purely of their relations to each other. "In proportion as it lives," James said of the novel, "will it be found . . . that in each of the parts there is something of each of the other parts." "In a novel," Lawrence said after him, "everything is relative to everything else, if that novel is art at all."

For the new novelist as for the old, then, a universal did exist, a principle of unity or harmony; but for the new novelist this unity or harmony was a condition neither of the world's idea on the one hand nor of its substance on the other. It was a condition of its form or process and, more specifically, of its dramatic form or process. A universe that declared its meaning in its own material, that defined its reality by the relations of phenomena to each other, was necessarily a dramatic universe, was necessarily what Conrad had called "a spectacular universe." Hence for the modern the currency of the dramatic principle. Bunyan's form was too abstract: it sacrificed the substance to the idea. Defoe's was too representational: it sacrificed the idea to the substance. But the form of drama was something else again. It expressed the formal relation between the idea and the substance that obtained in life itself and so satisfied at once the claims of abstraction and representation. This didn't of course mean that the novelist's idea or his subject didn't matter. It only meant that his idea or subject as such was less important than the dramatic form of their relation. The novelist had to have a subject but what counted wasn't the subject in itself but the treatment of it, the manner of its unfolding. It was a means to an end, not an end in itself. It served the novelist as a reason or occasion for the creation of a form. Such, too, was the status of his conceit, his conception. He had to have one, but what counted wasn't the conceit or conception in itself but the treatment of it, the manner of its unfolding. For novelists as various as James and Hardy, Conrad and Joyce, it wasn't valuable in itself. It was tentative, provisional, a *modus operandi*. For Conrad, the form didn't exist for the sake of the idea, the idea existed for the sake of the form, and so he could say with Marlow that "the meaning of an episode was not inside like a kernel but outside, enveloping the tale which brought it out only as a glow brings out a haze." Even a writer as aggressively ideological as Lawrence could at times suggest that the ideology was a means to an end rather than an end in itself. Every novelist had to have a metaphysic, he said, but it was an operative metaphysic and, as such, "must always subserve the artistic purpose beyond the artist's conscious aim." What was important wasn't the idea but the contest with its opposite and hence, like the novelist's subject matter, it supplied a reason or occasion for the creation of a form. "Of all the art forms," as Lawrence put it, "the novel most of all demands the trembling and oscillating of the balance." If the novel was mimetic, then, it was so in a very special sense. Insofar as it imitated not life's substance but its form, it was less mimetic than analogical. It wasn't Nature itself but a model of it. It achieved representation, as James said, "not by the addition of items . . . but by the art of figuring synthetically."

For the same reason that he insisted on the form of drama, the modern novelist also insisted on the form of symbol. To the extent that the universe was dramatic, to the extent that its meaning embodied itself in its own material things and their relations, it was also a symbolic universe. Not, however, symbolic in the literary sense, in the sense of something created or invented from without. Joyce rejected as "literary talk" the proposition that by "claritas" Aquinas had meant "symbolism or idealism, the supreme quality of beauty being a light from some other world . . . the reality of which it [the thing] was but the symbol." In the same spirit Conrad and Lawrence alike denounced as "a literary proceeding" the artificial symbolism whose genesis wasn't the world as thing but only the self or will of the artist. Like Joyce, what they had in mind was a natural symbolism. If it seemed to Conrad that "all the great creations of literature [were] symbolic," if it seemed to Lawrence that "all art [was] *au fond* symbolic," it was for the reason, and in the same way, that nature itself was *au fond* symbolic.

The form that united the world, that was the sole
condition of its universality, was, in other words, artistic
form. Insofar as life was dramatic or symbolic, insofar as it
joined the particular and the universal, the thing and the
meaning of the thing, it was itself an artistic phenomenon,
a work of art. Like Coleridge's poem, it contained within
itself the reasons why it should be so. In nature, as in a
perfect poem, to recall what Joyce had felt with Saint
Augustine, nothing was accidental or unintended. There
was accordingly no necessary disrelation between life and
art, between the aim of the realist with his interest in life
for life's sake and the aim of the aesthete with his interest
in art for art's sake. Since Nature imitated Art, since it was,
like a work of art, its own excuse for being, then making
the novel as formally perfect as a good poem or drama,
making it contain all the reasons why it should be so and
reducing all explanations to the explanation of everything
by everything else, wasn't a going from nature but a going
to it. "The supreme cry of Art for Art, itself, loses the
exciting ring of its apparent immorality . . . It has ceased
to be a cry, and is heard only as a whisper, often incomprehensible, but at times and faintly encouraging." So
said Conrad but so, too, in effect, said James and Joyce,
Lawrence and Virginia Woolf. When the novelist studied,
in the spirit of aestheticism, in the spirit of Pater and his
followers, not the idea or the substance of life but the very
form of it, he achieved at once the particular and the
universal, the representation and the abstraction.

The art of the novelist was accordingly the art of the
suggestive, the complex, the ambiguous. A meaning did
invade the earth but since it was of the form of things
rather than of their idea or substance, it was a meaning
that necessarily remained a mystery. To enter a work of art
whose form was faithful to the form of life itself wasn't, we
recall Joyce maintaining, to look for a meaning. It was to

discover in phenomena, in "present things," a meaning which remained "unuttered." This was surely what Conrad had in mind when he declared of Galsworthy's *To Let* that it escaped "from the particular into the universal by the sheer force of its inner life," when he declared of Proust's work that "it appeals to our sense of wonder and gains our assent by its veiled greatness." To imitate the idea or the substance, the universal or the particular, was to capture a part of life only; but to imitate the form was to capture the whole living thing. It was to account at once for the idea and the substance, the universal and the particular. It was to make the novel more abstract, more philosophical, as it were, without making it less novelistic, less representational.

In the same way that the form of the world combined universal and particular, it also combined truth and beauty. Just as it authorized no final separation between meaning and being, so it authorized no final separation between the real and the ideal. It wasn't for the novelist to sacrifice truth to beauty or beauty to truth and so make life either more or less beautiful than it was. That was for romancers and tragedians on the one hand, for naturalists and satirists on the other. It was rather to show that in art as in life, the ideal was inherent in the real, the beautiful was inherent in the true. Sharing the despair of the romantic artist, Joyce's demoralized Stephen could "consider the two worlds as aliens one to another"; but inspired by the lesson of Ibsen, by his more vigorously "classical" art, he would discover the possibility of reconciling the real and the ideal, "the world of his experience and the world of his dreams." If the modern novelist did demand more poetry and less prose, it wasn't, accordingly, the easy kind of poetry that shirked the prose of things. "The romantic feeling of reality" was acceptable, Conrad said, but only insofar as it admitted "the knowledge of truth," only insofar as it was disciplined by "a recognition of the hard facts of existence." "Beauty is the most perverse of spirits," as Virginia Woolf expressed it. ". . . she must pass through ugliness or lie down with disorder before she can rise in her own person."

The art of the novelist was to this extent the art of overcoming difficulties. For James the message of George Sand was that "no mistakes and no pains [were] too great to be, in the air of art, triumphantly convertible." For Joyce the message of Aquinas was that under the laws that governed the perception and creation of beauty, "even the most hideous object may be said to be beautiful." In novels and novelists who were less than perfect the conversion of truth to beauty hadn't taken place. Fenimore Cooper had produced "some of the loveliest, most glamorous pictures in all literature," Lawrence noted; but "alas, without the cruel iron of reality." In his *Salammbô* and *Saint-Antoine*, James complained, Flaubert had satisfied "his hunger for style and history and poetry" but at the expense of his "power to catch [life] in the fact." In such a consummate novelist as Turgenev, on the other hand, the difficult marriage of truth and beauty had been fully achieved. "The element of poetry in him is constant," James remarked, "and yet reality stares through it without the loss of a wrinkle." "On one and the same page," Virginia Woolf observed, "we have irony and passion; the poetic and the commonplace; a tap drips and a nightingale sings. And yet, though the scene is made up of contrasts, it remains the same scene." For all that he condemned a Jamesian prosaic, for all that he admired a Meredithian poetic, even Hardy could reluctantly acknowledge that in a novel the poetry of life must function as a condition of its prose. "It is remarkable," he wrote of James, "that a writer who has no grain of poetry, or humour, or spontaneity . . . can yet be a good novelist.

Meredith has some poetry, and yet I can read James when I can not look at Meredith." For Hardy no less than for the others, after all, the business of the novelist, like that of the poet, was "to find beauty in ugliness." For him as for them it was to create the romance of the real. It was indeed to create the reality of romance. The same paradoxical logic that insisted on the interdependence of art and nature also insisted on the interdependence of romance and reality. Since the novelist imitated neither an idea nor a substance but a form or process, it didn't really matter whether he idealized the real or realized the ideal, whether he made the true beautiful or the beautiful true. It amounted in the end to the same thing. In a novel that was truly a novel, what belonged to romance could hardly be set apart from what belonged to reality itself, the same laws of form applying to the one as to the other. To render the form of life rather than its idea or substance was inevitably to discover the essential oneness of truth and beauty.

It was also to discover the essential oneness of the ordinary and the extraordinary. The law that affirmed the radical community of the real and the ideal also affirmed the radical community of the ordinary and the extraordinary. Not for the novelist, accordingly, the easy way out of romance, of "golden hair and promiscuous felony." The graver task appointed him was to make the ordinary extraordinary, was to convert "bread and butter and commonplace" into something rich and strange. Like D'Annunzio, it was to demonstrate, James said, that "quality and dignity of looming larger which a great feeling on the painter's part ever gives to small things." The art of the novelist was once again, in other words, the art of overcoming difficulties. It was, said James, "to convert the very substance of the commonplace . . . into matter of literature." It was to convert, said Joyce, "the

bread of everyday life into something that has a permanent artistic life of its own." When the novelist *expressed*
or *presented* things fully, when he rehearsed the dramatic
form of life in which all things were related to and
revealed by each other, then the unimportant became
important, the trivial became great. Any subject loomed
large, as James phrased it, "from the moment one is ridden
by the law of entire expression." Any subject loomed large,
as Joyce phrased it, from the moment it was treated with
the "slow elaborative patience of the art of satisfaction."
Flaubert's greatness was thus, James said, that "the
familiar . . . under his touch, took on character, importance, extension." Ibsen's greatness, as Joyce saw it, was no
different. "When Rubel and Irene meet in *When We
Dead Awaken* . . ." he observed, "their most trivial word
is more dramatic than all the magical verses of *Othello*."
In his rage for New Jerusalems, Lawrence did rail, it's true,
against just such a realism, against a realism that condemned the novelist to "the souls of quite commonplace
people." But even he would submit to the limits set by life
and art. For him in the end as for James and Joyce, the
only legitimate form of heroism was moral, the only
legitimate form of the extraordinary one that had its
source in the ordinary. "Wells need not scoff at the little
fellow's feelings when he is stirred to the full depth of his
soul," he wrote in defense of the battered hero of
Tono-Bungay. "Everybody is great at some time or other."
In the unheroic was contained the heroic; in the ordinary
was contained the extraordinary. Indeed, it worked the
other way around, too. In the heroic was contained the
unheroic, in the extraordinary was contained the ordinary.
For Hardy, the novelist's business was to show "the
grandeur underlying the sorriest things," but it was also to
show "the sorriness underlying the grandest things." For
Conrad, it was to make familiar things surprising, but it

was also "to make unfamiliar things credible." For Joyce, it was to make human things divine, but it was also to make divine things human. By imitating the dramatic form of life itself, the form that revealed the subtle interrelatedness of everything, the novelist not only made the ordinary extraordinary in Wordsworthian fashion. He also made the extraordinary ordinary in Coleridgean fashion. He asserted in effect the unitary nature of the ordinary and the extraordinary as well as the unitary nature of the particular and the universal, the real and the ideal.

The novelist of the future had to be the poet as well as the novelist, then, but without displacing the novelist. He had to bring into play the powerful resources of the imagination but without nullifying the scientific observer, the true and faithful witness of the world's irrefutable reality. The imagination existed after all not to abolish the world outside, the world as object, but to establish and reveal it. "The face of nature and civilization . . . will yield its secrets only to a really *grasping* imagination," James wrote. "The reality of substantial bodies," Lawrence wrote after him, "can only be perceived by the imagination." "The romantic feeling of reality" constituted, Conrad decided, "a point of view from which the very shadows of life appear endowed with an internal glow." That novelist therefore was supreme who was at once and together the poet and the scientist, the man who felt things and the man who saw them. James's Balzac was "of imagination on one side all compact . . . on the other an insatiable reporter of the immediate, the material, the current combination." In Virginia Woolf's Turgenev, "the interpreter [was] never allowed to mount unchecked into the realms of imagination; again the observer pulls him back and reminds him of the other truth, the truth of fact."

The novelist was a novelist, it seemed indeed, not because he was the poet-philosopher on the one hand or the empirical scientist on the other, but because he was the artist, a category of creature that included and reconciled them. Since the world was more remarkable as a form than as an idea or substance, since its wholeness was more artistic than philosophical or scientific, it was more available to the artistic temperament than to the philosophic or scientific one. Registering life as idea or as substance, the philosopher and scientist registered a part of it only, but registering it as a form that combined the idea and the substance, the moral and the material, the novelist registered the whole thing. In his ideal character, the novelist indeed claimed a unity of being that was the subjective correlative of the same unity of being he found in the world itself. Since the great life he imitated was all things to all men, since the great novel that imitated it was all things to all men, then the novelist had himself to be all things to all men. Seeking as the maker of the one bright book of life to capture *everything*, he had in effect to *be* everything, to unite in himself the same polarities that were united in the world itself. "If there is one gift more essential to a novelist than another," Virginia Woolf declared, "it is the power of combination—the single vision." It was the power, she said, of persuading "a difficult family of gifts . . . to live in harmony together: satire and sympathy; fantasy and fact, poetry and a prim moral sense." It was just such a power, just such a single vision, that Conrad found and praised in the person of Turgenev. "Every gift has been heaped on his cradle," Conrad wrote, "absolute sanity and the deepest sensibility, the clearest vision and the quickest responsiveness . . . an exquisite perception of the visible world and an unerring instinct for . . . the essential in the life of men and women . . . and all that in perfect measure." It was Lawrence, however, who celebrated in the most exalted terms of all the unity and universality of the novelist's genius. "I absolutely flatly deny," he said, "that I am a soul, or a body, or a mind, or an intelligence, or a brain, or a nervous system, or a bunch of glands, or any of the rest of these bits of me. The whole is greater than the part. . . . For this reason I am a novelist. And being a novelist, I consider myself superior to the saint, the scientist, the philosopher, and the poet, who are all great masters of different bits of man alive, but never get the whole hog." No wonder, then, that the novelist should demand of himself so many things that would seem at first at war with one another: consciousness and unconsciousness; passion and dispassion; a feeling for the world outside and a feeling for the world inside. It behooved the novelist, as it behooved no other artist, to be and harmonize the "different bits of man alive." It behooved him to be the godlike consciousness, the unified and unifying consciousness, that had otherwise disappeared from off the earth. The novel itself might describe a world without saints or heroes, but, as Conrad put it, "in every sphere of human perplexities and emotions, there are more greatnesses than one—not counting here the greatness of the artist himself." "In every great novel, who is the hero all the time?" Lawrence asked with him. "Not any of the characters, but some unnamed and nameless flame behind them all." In a world without heroes he was the only hero left. In a world without gods he was the only god left.

In effect, then, the novel formalized the unity of self and world, subject and object, in the same way that it formalized the unity of idea and substance, universal and particular. Reality was a function neither of the world outside, the thing seen, nor of the world inside, the seer. It was a function, Virginia Woolf suggested, of "the thing seen and the seer inextricably mixed." So, too, said

Lawrence. If he inveighed against a Flaubertian impersonality, if he insisted on the novel as the act of the naïve or
unconscious individual, it wasn't to celebrate self at the
expense of world but to reassert their unity and continuity.
With the collapse of the free individual, he contended,
there was a split between the subjective and objective
worlds, between seer and thing seen: ". . . we get the I
which is staring out of the window at the reality which is
not itself." But with the restoration of "the primal integral
I, which is for the most part a living *continuum* of all the
rest of living things," the split was healed and the essential
community of self and world was reestablished. Hence his
dissatisfaction with both the psychological novel and the
sociological novel. Ideally, he thought, the novel should
combine George Eliot who had "started putting all the
action inside" and Henry Fielding with whom "it had
been outside." "I can't help thinking there ought to be a
bit of both," Lawrence said. To this conclusion, too, came
Mrs. Woolf. Early elated by her discovery of the new
inner reality of self and consciousness, she was later elated
by her rediscovery of the old outer reality of world and
object. "The discovery of this book . . ." she wrote of
The Years, "is the combination of the external and the
internal." "I have discovered," she said, "that there must
be contrast: one strata or layer can't be developed
intensively, as I did I expect in *The Waves*, without harm
to the others." The modern novelist would ask for more
psychology, for less sociology and physiology, but, given
the ultimate identity of outer and inner, he wouldn't ask
for the one without the other.

The same law that called for the amalgamation of the
psychological and the sociological, of the life inside and
the life outside, also called, even more importantly, for the
amalgamation of the representational and the nonrepresentational, of life from the outside and life from the

inside. The novelist had to exercise the power of his personality, had to see and register the world from the inside of his own consciousness, but this was to define the world outside, not deny it. Maupassant's merit, Conrad said, was that he acted to express neither self nor world but their unity, their formal community: "his subtlety, his humour, his grimness, though no doubt they are his own, are never presented otherwise but as belonging to our life, as found in nature." The merit of a Van Gogh painting, said Lawrence to the same effect, was that it expressed neither the seer nor the thing seen but their unity, their formal community, "the vivid relation between himself, as man, and the sunflower, as sunflower, at that quick moment of time." Hence once again for the novelist the supreme necessity of dramatic form. When life was rendered not as idea or substance but as the form of drama, the identity of subject and object, of creator and creation, became no less apparent than the identity of the universal and the particular, "the artist, like the God of the creation, remain[ing] within or behind or beyond or above his handiwork." If the art of the novel was necessarily ambiguous, it was indeed because it rehearsed this mysterious interdependence of the seer and the thing seen. Just as a logic should be there but without seeming to be, so should a personality be there but without seeming to be. The novelist must work, James said, "behind the veil—inscrutably, as it were, and with the 'fun' of secret harmonies." He must work, Conrad said, as "a figure behind the veil; a suspected rather than a seen presence."

For the sake of a new abstractionism, a new purity or clarity of conception, then, the modern novelist may have sought less life and more art, less fact and more architecture. But rather than sacrifice one value to the other, he elected in the end to adjust and combine them. Where the pure abstractionist would achieve the design at the expense of the detail, the novelist, the artist of the difficult, would achieve at once and together the maximum of detail and the maximum of design. Just as subject and object, universal and particular, composed in life itself one single unbroken circuit, so in the novel should world and vision, fact and structure. As James defined it, "the whole business [was] too divorced on the one side from observation and perception, and on the other from the art and taste." The novelist had, like Balzac, he said, to unite "quantity and intensity"; he had, like Howells, to unite "extreme elaboration" and "studied compactness." The same great synthesis of the one and the many Virginia Woolf conceived, too. For her as for James the supreme sign of the novelist was that he connected the fact and the vision, was that he accomplished at once "immense breadth and immense intensity." He could make his facts aspire to the condition of symbols but without denying or destroying their primary facticity. He could give his characters the special power that symbols suggested but without obliterating their first existence as characters. In ultimate novelists like Melville and Emily Brontë, she said, "we get a vision of presence outside the human beings, of a meaning that they stand for, without ceasing to be themselves." This, too, was Lawrence's emphasis. The novelist's aim should be, he said, to reconcile his power to individuate the character and his power to generalize it. He may have campaigned against the character-novel in the old sense, may have sought to abolish the old stable ego of the character and make it instead the agent of certain physic or nonhuman forces, but this wasn't, he insisted, to dehumanize the character. It was rather to renew its humanity. It was to rediscover, like Giovanni Verga, "the purely naïve human being."

The modern novelist may have felt, then, the impact of

the new abstractionism in modern painting and sculpture, but if he did so, it affected his art in a very special and limited sense only. Joyce dismissed Proust as "analytic still life." Lawrence scorned the stylizations of Braque and Matisse, was unsympathetic to all schematizations of reality that went beyond the stage of Cézanne. A danger was involved, Mrs. Woolf noted after *Jacob's Room*, in "breaking with complete representation. One flies into the air. Next time, I mean to stick closer to facts." By definition the most representational of all literary forms, the body of the novel rejected at last a transplant so foreign to its nature as the rather complete abstractionism envisioned by the new sculptors and painters. Though the modern novel did betray a special interest in form, it wasn't an artificial or a manufactured one. What it wanted was a form that matched the form of life itself. By imitating not the idea or the substance of life but its essential form, it would create an image or model of life that united the virtues of abstraction and representation.

IV

If the modern novelist couldn't reject altogether the representational form that had been basic to the novel from the beginning, it was because it wasn't after all morally uneventful. As Conrad, Joyce and Lawrence saw it, the world wasn't without moral import. A unity did invest it, though a unity that referred to a form, not an idea. The meaning of things wasn't semantic like the surface grammar of a sentence and therefore analyzable and paraphrasable. It was formal or syntactic like the deep grammar of a sentence and therefore unanalyzable, unparaphrasable. So far, then, as the novel represented this world, so far as its form or grammar imitated the deep form or grammar peculiar to life itself, it too was an artistic phenomenon that was its own moral end. More than an indifferent mode of describing things, the novel's realism expressed in itself a moral value that inhered in nature and to this extent the novel could be said to be moral without striving to be moral. Conrad could have meant no less when he declared that a work of art should be written "with no didactic purpose, but with a moral intention." And Joyce could have meant no less when he said that it should be written with no moral purpose but with a moral effect, when he said with Conrad that it shouldn't *intend* to "instruct, elevate, amuse" without inferring that it needn't *produce* the same essential moral effect: "I do not say that drama may not fulfill any or all of these functions." ·

Writers like James and Mrs. Woolf could sometimes suggest, it's true, a wholly different construction of things. "All inclusion and confusion," the world didn't always seem to them its own good reason for being. As they saw it, "the 'moral' sense of a work of art" couldn't depend on the world it represented. It could only depend on "the kind and the degree of the artist's prime sensibility." Representation as such, they said, couldn't be a value in itself but only a way of expressing value. Even they, however, could intimate that it was a great deal more, that the novel's meaning was something more than an effect of the author's prime sensibility. The medium itself was the message; the novel itself was the meaning. As representation, it reflected or rehearsed the great grammar, the deep form or structure, that made the universe its own moral cause.

To this extent the novel was a form of faith. It expressed. a radical and ineradicable belief in natural and human existence, in the essential virtue of its form and process. In life all things were related not to any Idea outside the boundaries of time and space but to all other things inside

these boundaries. Life didn't have to be justified from
without; it justified itself from within. To represent,
therefore, wasn't just to *register* the relatedness of all
things. It was to *rejoice* in their relatedness. When the
artist took a religious or metaphysical view of the world,
when he described it as a form or formula that acted upon
it from outside, he was guilty in effect of betrayal, of
denying that in the here and the now it was possible to
reconcile the universal and the particular, the ideal and
the real. But when he took an empirical or novelistic view
of the world, when he described it as the incarnation of its
own internal form or formula, he declared his faith, his
conviction, that in the here and the now the universal and
the particular, the ideal and the real, could indeed be
reconciled. Hence for so many the inacceptability of
artists as apparently dissimilar as romantic poets and tragic
dramatists and Russian novelists. Idealists all who saw the
world as the scene of a catastrophic conflict between
Heaven and Earth, the dream and the reality, they
betrayed a failure of faith in the essential harmony deep
down things. In the classical poet, Joyce said, "the sane
and joyful spirit issue[d] forth and achieve[d] imperishable
perfection, nature assisting with her goodwill and thanks,"
but in the romantic poet was revealed "an insecure,
unsatisfied, impatient temper which [saw] no fit abode
here for its ideals" and so created a perishable perfection
with no authority in nature. It was on much the same
grounds that Conrad and Lawrence attacked the tragic
emotion of the Russian novelist. We had, as Lawrence put
it, "to go back, a long way, before the idealist conceptions
began, before Plato, before the tragic idea of life arose."
We had "to reestablish the great relationships which the
grand idealists, with their underlying pessimism, their
belief that life is nothing but futile conflict . . . destroyed
for us." It wasn't for the novelist to make men see and

justify the world in the light of their ideas or ideals. It was to make men see and justify the world in its own strong and satisfactory light. It was, as Conrad said, to "compel men entranced by the sight of distant goals to glance for a moment at the surrounding vision of form and colour."

As representation, then, the novel was a form of optimism. Its assumption wasn't the pessimistic one that the mystery of things, their truth or beauty, was outside nature and hence beyond man's power to perceive and achieve, but the optimistic one that it was inside nature and therefore well within his power to perceive and achieve. The one unpardonable sin of the novelist was thus the sin of doubt or despair. Like the James who couldn't forgive Zola and his followers for being "intense pessimists," Lawrence couldn't forgive Wells for being such "a terrible pessimist," for arousing "a bitter little struggle with one's heart of faith—in the ultimate goodness of things." Neither could he forgive Conrad "for being so sad and for giving in" nor Joyce for accepting, like Flaubert and Ibsen, the fatal imperfection of things. For Conrad and Joyce no less than for James and Lawrence, however, sanguinity, the zest of life, the pursuit of • happiness, was a precondition of the novelist's calling. Conrad didn't think his tales were "gloomy, or even very tragic, that is not with a pessimistic intention." The world was, he insisted, "a spectacle for awe, love, adoration, or hate, if you like, but . . . never for despair." So, too, thought Joyce in effect. If romantic artists were anathema to him, it was because they had no belief that man could find the link between the real and the ideal and so "expressed the most utter of pessimisms." "His faith in life," said Joyce's brother, "sustained him with the joyous certainty that in spite of the squalor that surrounded him, life had some not ignoble meaning."

If the novelist embraced the form of drama, then, it

wasn't only because it was identical with the form of life itself. It was also because it expressed and inspired a radical satisfaction with the form of life. To bring the world down to an abstraction was to sacrifice life to art, being to meaning. It was to celebrate not *the* moral and artistic unity that informed the world itself but *a* factitious moral and artistic unity wilfully superimposed upon it from without. As in tragedy and comedy, parable and allegory, naturalism and romance, it was to reproach life with the incompleteness and imperfection of its form, was to suggest that on its own scale it couldn't suffice the human mind and imagination. The art of the dramatist, however, was something else again. By stressing the relatedness of all things, it demonstrated the unity of being and meaning, life and art, and so affirmed the wholeness and perfection of existence, its capacity to satisfy the human mind and imagination. By virtue of its power "to make even the most hideous object beautiful" (Joyce), by virtue of its power "to find beauty, grace, charm in the bitterness of truth" (Conrad), the dramatic work of art placed itself and the world it imitated beyond the pale of criticism. Drama, Joyce said, is "of so unswayed, so unchallengeable a nature that in its highest forms it all but transcends criticism." It "has so much in common with a natural process," as Virginia Woolf said of George Eliot's art, "that it leaves us with little consciousness that there is anything to criticize." It wasn't Joyce alone, however, who defined the dramatic art of the novelist as "the art of satisfaction." So, too, did his antagonist, Lawrence. When, Lawrence said, the novelist transcended his metaphysic, when, that is, he dramatized the conflict between that metaphysic and its opposite, he gave us "that supreme equilibrium wherein we know satisfaction." If the modern novelist made so much, then, of the internal coherence and completeness of the work of art, it was to justify not the creator but the creation, not the artist himself but the natural world he imitated. Since the formal harmony and wholeness he sought reflected the formal harmony and wholeness that existed in nature itself, he produced not the illegitimate satisfaction of aesthetic form but the legitimate satisfaction of natural form. He awoke in the reader a satisfaction that was the objective correlative of a satisfaction with the world itself. That art was improper, Joyce accordingly declared, which "not sufficient in itself . . . urges us to seek something beyond itself." The novelist's object, said Mrs. Woolf, was to create "a satisfaction which turns our minds back upon what we have just read" instead of urging us "as the last page is finished to start in search of something that contrasts and completes."

Lawrence of course dissented. Such a formal purity and perfection had no more authority in nature, he charged, than the ideological formulas of Christian moralists and Platonic tragedians. Like the idealism of the Russian novelists, it revealed not a generous satisfaction with the form of life but a mean dissatisfaction with it, not a passionate surrender to experience but a fastidious revulsion against it. Admittedly, there was much in the language of James and Mrs. Woolf to justify his angry suspicions. As "the struggling, floundering cause," life, they seemed to say, had no power to redeem itself. It could only be redeemed in or by or through the work of art. "The consolation, the dignity, the joy of life," said James, "are that discouragements and lapses . . . come to one only as one stands *without* . . . the luminous paradise of art." "To live *in* the world of creation," he went on to say, "to get into it and stay in it . . . to woo combinations and inspirations into being . . . this is the only thing." For Virginia Woolf, too, it was the only thing. To be at all the artist in the novel, she said, "one must get out of life." "I insubstantise, wilfully to some extent," she confessed, "distrusting reality—its cheapness." For her as for James, it would seem, art was an escape from experience rather than a commitment to it, a reformation rather than a revelation of it. On occasion, however, they did feel powerful Laurentian misgivings. That deep disgust or despair of life with which Lawrence had identified Flaubert's craving for form Virginia Woolf would identify with James's craving for form. For the sake of symmetry, she said, James had reduced "the interest and importance of his subject," but, she added, "a writer of greater depth or natural spirits would have taken the risk which his material imposes . . . and so, perhaps achieved symmetry . . . all the same." She accordingly vowed "to go for the central things" and not to sacrifice them to the needs of form or style. To be perfectly fair, however, James himself made the same avowal. "A truce to all subjects that are not superior!" he cried. He would devote his art, he decided in a moment of fervor, only to "the fine, the large, the human, the natural, the fundamental, the passionate things." At the very last, however, he made the same claims for his form that Lawrence made for his. Insofar as it was dramatic, insofar as it defined things in all their subtle interrelatedness, it was an attribute not of the creator *himself* but of the creation *itself* and so acted to affirm Nature, not deny it. "The terrible law of the artist . . . by which everything is grist to his mill" was also the law, James said, "of the acceptance of all experience, of all suffering, of *all* life." "When I practice it . . ." he reported elsewhere, "I feel again the multitudinous presence of all human situations and pictures, the surge and pressure of *life*." By imitating the form rather than the substance of things, James proposed, no less than Lawrence, to foster a faith in life, a satisfaction with its fundamental form and process.

As representation the novel wasn't only a form of faith
in life, however. As representation, it was also a form of
sympathy. The same law, the same universal form or
grammar, that united in a single and continuing communion all things in time and space also united in a single and
continuing communion all human creatures in time and
space both with each other and with the things around
them. Insofar, then, as he represented life, insofar as he
imitated its central form or grammar, the novelist aroused
a reverence for life, a sympathy and solidarity with its aims
and ends. The task of the novelist, said Lawrence, was "to
bring us into sympathy with as many men, as many
objects, as many phenomena as possible." It was to feel
and foster, Conrad said, that "solidarity in dreams, in joy,
in sorrow, in aspirations . . . which binds together all
humanity." Hence the emphasis on particularity, on
"solidity of specification." It wasn't only that the particular was an essential condition of a just understanding of
the real. It was also that it was an essential condition of a
sympathetic appreciation of it. To generalize or simplify
things was to judge or prejudge them, was to paralyze the
power of feeling with or for them. It was to rob life,
Conrad said, "of all its necessary and sympathetic reservations and qualifications which give it its fair form, its just
proportions, its semblance of human fellowship." But to
particularize life, to acknowledge its multiplicity and
complexity, was to enable writer and reader to "enlarge
[their] sympathies by patient and loving observation."
Hauptmann the dramatist "deals with life . . . so
broadly," Joyce could say, "that my personal conscience is
seldom touched."

If the form of satire was repellent to the novelist, then,
it wasn't only because its simplification of reality didn't
consist with representation. It was also because it didn't
consist with sympathy. The novel existed neither to

condone nor condemn, Conrad said, but "to look with a large forgiveness at men's ideas and prejudices." "The more complex a vision," as Virginia Woolf put it, "the less it lends itself to satire: the more it understands the less it is able to sum up and make linear." The novelist rejected, for this same reason, the form of tragedy. Insofar as it reduced to simplicity a world that was defined by multiplicity, it failed at once the value of representation and the value of sympathy. It betrayed, said Conrad and Lawrence with equal force, not a solidarity with the human condition but a heartless superiority to it. "The world," said Lawrence, "is *not* a stage . . . And art, especially novels, are not little theatres where the reader sits aloft and watches—like a god with a twenty-lira ticket—and sighs, commiserates, condones and smiles." For Conrad as well, this world was *not* a stage: the merit of Galsworthy, he said, was that he made "no room for tragedy," was that his "sympathy with mankind [was] too genuine to allow him the smallest gratification of his vanity at the cost of his fellow creatures."

As Lawrence saw it, however, there was more than one form of authorial vanity. The distance and detachment of the Flaubertian novelist seemed to him no less culpable than the distance and detachment of the tragic dramatist. The whole cult of impersonal form was, he decided, a species of "French showing-off," was just "another apotheosis of personal conceit," that united the reader with the will of the artist rather than with the will of the world itself. Indeed, it awoke in Virginia Woolf the same uneasiness. "The danger is the damned egotistical self; which ruins Joyce and Richardson to my mind," she noted: ". . . is one pliant and rich enough to provide a wall for the book from oneself without its becoming, as in Joyce and Richardson, narrowing and restricting?" As Joyce and Conrad viewed it, however, there was no necessary incom-

patibility between artistic detachment and moral sympathy. On the contrary, they saw the one as indispensable to
the other. To be the omniscient author, to bring upon
things the pressure of a personality or point of view, was to
formalize the split between subject and object, between
the seer and the thing seen. It was to exercise judgment,
multiply distinctions and so set limits on the range of
one's affections. But to be the dramatic author, to
disappear in and become one with the objects represented,
was to formalize the unity of subject and object, seer and
thing seen. It was to practice that Keatsian denial of self or
ego, that negative capability, that empowered the artist to
become one in sympathy with all that he beheld in the
outer world of men and things. That sympathy was not
less sympathetic, Joyce suggested, because it was an
"indifferent sympathy." "He is not insensible," Conrad
insisted, "who pays [human affairs] the undemonstrative
tribute of a sigh which is not a sob, and of a smile which is
not a grin."

The novelist indeed conceived himself as the democrat,
the humanitarian, of life and letters. If, like Wordsworth,
he presented himself as an ordinary man addressing other
ordinary men, it wasn't only because it was the condition
of his power to represent life, of his power to see and feel
the same irreducible reality that all men saw and felt. It
was also because it was the condition of his sympathy with
life, of his power to feel with it and for it. Poets were
poets, were tempted to exaggerate the life and nature
about them, Joyce believed, because they led "haughty
and elaborate lives." But novelists were novelists, were in
close and sympathetic contact with that surrounding life
and nature, because their lives were continuous with and
indistinguishable from the lives of the millions living and
dead. It was "on the other side [of the street] . . ." as
James elaborately phrased it, "where we mostly see the

poets elegantly walk," but it was "on *our* side . . . that I
rather see our encounter with the novelists taking place;
we being . . . more mixed with them, or they at least, by
their desire and necessity, more mixed with us." "A
novelist who would think himself of a superior essence to
other men," said Conrad more succinctly, "would miss the
first condition of his calling." Writers as various as Conrad
and Joyce and Lawrence could accordingly scorn the
whole mystique of Genius, the magical or miraculous view
of the literary artist that set him apart from his fellowmen.
Joyce didn't believe in genius, his brother reported. "He
said it was a fake of vanity. He believed in talent, work,
and what he called 'throwing himself into what he tried to
do.' " The novelist's virtue, said Conrad to the same effect,
was that "he never posed as a scientist or as a seer," never
propounded "a theory for the purpose of giving a tremendous significance to his art." Reality wasn't after all the
creation of the individual genius of the artist; it was the
creation of the common genius of the race, of generation
after generation of anonymous human temperaments, and
was therefore most available to the man who approached
it with none of the special apparatus that set him apart
from other men. "The road to these distant regions," as
Conrad put it, "does not lie through the domain of Art or
the domain of Science . . . it is a path of toilsome silence
upon which travel men simple and unknown." "I can't
understand you when you think so much of books and
genius," Lawrence wrote in the same spirit. ". . . there is
the bread and butter first, the ordinary human contact."
Hence once again the novelist's emphasis on what Lawrence called unconscious writing, on what Conrad called
temperamental writing. Thus to write wasn't only to
represent reality, wasn't only to establish a naked and
therefore truthful connection with the primary reality that
all men inherited in common. It was also to establish a

naked and therefore sympathetic connection
was to write from a level of being that united t
sympathy with his fellowmen and that united
men in sympathy with each other. It was to v
Lawrence, not from the mere "smartness of the
from the novelist's "naked self," from his "most palpitant,
sensitive self," and thus awaken "the gentle flow of
affection" between writer and reader, between world and
man. It was to express in the author and inspire in the
reader, Conrad said, "that mysterious fellowship which
unites in a community of hopes and fears all the dwellers
on this earth."

Every true novelist had, then, as James phrased it, "a
democratic strain in his composition." If he embraced the
lives of perfectly ordinary men and women, it wasn't only
because he hoped, as realist, to achieve a large and
exquisite correspondence with life. It was also because he
hoped, as moralist, to bring into being a sympathy with
life in its simplest and most elemental states. By writers as
apparently poles apart as Joyce and Mrs. Woolf, Meredith
could thus be praised and blamed for the same reasons,
praised for reinstating the poet and philosopher in fiction,
but blamed for trying to reinstate the aristocratic hero in
fiction. For them as for Lawrence, the business of the
novelist was to make "common things beautiful," was to
see "the mystery and magnificence that envelops us even
when we work menially." It was indeed an aspect of his
faith in life that in the ordinary was contained the
extraordinary, that no detail, no thing, no creature, was
too minor and too mean to be, in the crucible of his art,
triumphantly convertible to beauty and importance. His
aim was to celebrate, Joyce had said, the significance of
trivial things. It was to show, said Mrs. Woolf, that life
didn't exist "more fully in what is commonly thought big
than in what is commonly thought small." Hence the

novelist's disdain for the heroic life of epic and romance. It wasn't only that it no longer reflected the human experience itself. It was also that it didn't consort with the humane and humanitarian ethic, the ethic of tolerance and sympathy, that it was the novel's mission to disseminate. Not James alone deplored the "romantic life" with its indifference to the human sociabilities, to the human sympathies and affections. "I am sure . . ." Joyce said, even more forcibly, "that the whole structure of heroism is, and always was, a damned lie and that there cannot be any substitute for the individual passion as the motive power of everything." For all his hunger for the heroic, even Lawrence came out on the same side. "You are Brontë-bitten in your taste in heroes . . ." he wrote at an early stage. "Strong stern men bore and irritate me; their strength lies in their insusceptibility to half the influences that deflect mortality." "The hero is obsolete," he decided at the very end, "and the leader of men is a back number . . . the new relationship will be some sort of tenderness, sensitive, between men and men and men and women."

There came with the novel, then, a powerful moral evangelism, a moral evangelism that was indistinguishable in the end from a social evangelism. "The Poet," Wordsworth said, "binds together by passion and knowledge the vast empire of human society." The novelist claimed for himself no less a purpose and power. By bringing to light the underlying moral unity and community of the human kind, he would hurry into being its social unity and community. By representing reality, by offering the novel as a form of science or history, he would extend the range of man's knowledge and understanding beyond the limits of his immediate observation and experience and so bring home to his business and bosom the reality of human brotherhood. Appealing to our eagerness to live vicariously, "to live the life of others," the novel worked, James said, to increase "our knowledge of ourselves" and of each other. Since it was, as Conrad described it, "the great way open to all sorts of undiscovered countries," it worked, he said, "for the edification of mankind, pinned down by the conditions of its existence to the earnest consideration of the most insignificant tides of reality." In this context solidity of specification was more than a representational necessity. It was a moral and social necessity too. There was, that is, a correspondence between *solidity* and *solidarity*, between the novel's solidity of form and the novelist's solidarity of feeling. Only through a fully particularized and fully presentational account of other lives and conditions could writer relay and reader receive a truly felt knowledge of lives and conditions other than their own and thus transcend those limitations, those isolations and segregations, that arrested the flow of sympathy between man and man.

The novelist indeed conceived his civilizing mission in terms even more comprehensive and ambitious. It wasn't only to transmit a knowledge outside the range of the individual's immediate knowledge. More specifically, it was to transmit the spirit of the age, the essential or moral reality than underlay its surface appearances. Like Words-worth's, Carlyle's, Arnold's, poet as priest or prophet, the novelist proposed to stand as mediator between the reader and the world he occupied. As the modern novelist in fact perceived it, the poet had long ceased to perform the heroic task that the great Victorians had set for him, had long ceased to mediate between humanity and the chaos of the world. "The music-hall, not poetry," as the young Joyce had stated it, "was a criticism of life." "The conservatism or the timidity of poets," Virginia Woolf observed, "still leaves the chief spoils of modern life to the novelist." If the novelist was exhorted to address the reality of his own time and place, then, it wasn't only on the epistemological grounds that such a reality was the only reality available to him. It was also on the moral and social grounds that he was under a special obligation to lay bare, as its only priest or prophet, the heart and inner meaning of it. The novelist, not the poet, said Lawrence in effect, must "reveal the relation between man and his circumambient universe." The novelist, not the poet, as Joyce had said in effect, must "forge in the smithy of [his] soul the uncreated conscience of [his] race." Indeed, for the somber Conrad no less than for Joyce and Lawrence, the novel functioned not just to create reality but to recreate it. It was, he said, like the sea itself, "a scene of great endeavour and of great achievements changing the face of the world."

No wonder, then, that the modern novelist could insist on taking himself and his work and his world so seriously, that he could refuse with Conrad "la plaisanterie en matière d'art," that he could revile with Joyce and Lawrence alike "a literature of entertainment." The novel didn't exist to astonish the world, to "amaze, move, amuse" it. That was for tragedy and comedy, for epic and romance, and for the debased fictions that imitated them. Like the Bible with which Lawrence compared the novel, like the epic with which Joyce would compare it, it existed to justify the ways of God to Man or, in the absence of God himself, to justify the ways of life and nature. It existed to display and diffuse a faith in, a sympathy and solidarity with, the essential form and process of the world itself. "One has to be so terribly religious," Lawrence had said, "to be an artist." But so too, in effect, had James and Conrad, Joyce and Mrs. Woolf. "A man who puts forth the secret of his imagination to the world," Conrad wrote, "accomplishes, as it were, a religious rite." He was, to repeat what Joyce had called him, "a priest of the eternal imagination, transmuting the daily bread of experience into the radiant body of everliving life." If the novel claimed to take a more sober and more somber view of life than the traditional fiction it had displaced, it wasn't only because it was a form of science and so expressed a genuine understanding and knowledge of life. It was also because it was a form of religion and so expressed a sympathetic and reverential feeling for it. To be true-to-life in the representational sense was to be true to it in the moral sense. To be faithful-to-life in the representational sense was to be faithful to it in the moral sense. So much and no less was the novel's gospel, its good news.

Chapter Notes

1. Henry James: The Romance of the Real

page, line

3, 10   *of history*, F. O. Matthiessen, *Henry James, The Major Phase* (New York, 1944), p. 40.

4, 21   *convention."* James, *Partial Portraits* (London, 1919), p. 398. (Referred to hereafter as *PP*.)

4, 23   *the real."* James, "The Lesson of Balzac" in *The Question of Our Speech* (Boston, 1905), p. 78. (Referred to hereafter as *LB*.)

4, 28   *representation." LB*, p. 93.

4, 28   *[to life]." PP*, p. 397.

5, 4   *we feel."* James, *Notes on Novelists* (New York, 1914), p. 131. (Referred to hereafter as *NN*.)

5, 7   *subservient." NN*, p. 136.

5, 10   *any kind."* James, *Hawthorne* (London, 1879), p. 27.

5, 29   *the others." LB*, pp. 71–72.

6, 1   *nature whatever."* James, *Views and Reviews* (Boston, 1908), p. 155.

6, 3   *its own," PP*, p. 102.

6, 5   *powerful imagination." PP*, p. 104.

6, 15   *spirit."* Leon Edel and Gordon N. Ray, eds., *Henry James and H. G. Wells, A Record of their Friendship, their Debate on the Art of Fiction and their Quarrel* (London, 1959), p. 105.

6, 23   *a novel." PP*, p. 390.

6, 26   *the craft." NN*, p. 145.

6, 29   *visible reality."* Percy Lubbock, ed., *The Letters of Henry James*, Vol. I (New York, 1920), p. 219. (Referred to hereafter as *Letters* I.)

7, 2   *other." NN*, p. 113.

7, 10   *the parts." NN*, pp. 132–133.

7, 25   *really is." LB*, pp. 109, 111.

7,   28   *that spell."* Leon Edel, ed., *The Selected Letters of Henry James* (New York, 1960), p. 190.

7,   35   *of things."* PP, p. 246.

8,   5   *every spot."* Leon Edel, ed., *Henry James, The Future of the Novel, Essays on the Art of Fiction* (New York, 1956), p. 76. (Referred to hereafter as *FN.*)

8,   8   *or time."* Leon Edel, "Henry James and Sir Sydney Waterlow, The Unpublished Diary of a British Diplomat," *The Times Literary Supplement,* Thursday, August 8, 1968, p. 844.

8,   10   *prose fiction."* NN, p. 400.

8,   24   *and colleges."* NN, p. 10.

8,   33   *social creatures."* James, *The Art of the Novel, Critical Prefaces* (New York, 1934), pp. 64–65. (Referred to hereafter as *CP.*)

9,   2   *gregarious side."* NN, p. 264.

9,   8   *his time,* NN, p. 136.

9,   11   *[had] seen."* NN, p. 112.

9,   18   *naturally resides."* NN, p. 151.

9,   20   *thinly-composed society"* James, *Hawthorne,* p. 45.

9,   32   *represent."* Letters I, p. 72.

10, 12   *intimate."* Edel, *Selected Letters of Henry James,* p. 199.

10, 19   *restrictions,"* FN, p. 36.

10, 24   *certain fashion."* PP, p. 246.

10, 26   *continuing prosperity.* See especially *FN,* pp. 28–29, 37 ff.

10, 30   *and condition."* FN, p. 40.

10, 35   *and adventures,* See *FN,* pp. 22 ff; *PP,* pp. 399 ff.

11,   5   *for wear."* FN, p. 40.

11, 27   *with life."* PP, p. 402.

12,   3   *of things."* NN, p. 309.

12, 13   *these ideas."* LB, p. 86.

12, 18   *at once."* PP, p. 117.

12, 19   *nefarious name,"* CP, p. 42.

12, 27   *thing,"* PP, p. 402.

12, 32   *imposed itself."* PP, pp. 278, 279.

13,   4   *and hers."* LB, p. 106.

13,   9   *novelists."* NN, p. 136.

13, 16 *that emergence."* CP, pp. 127–128.

13, 22 *creatures unidentified."* LB, p. 105.

13, 24 *[was] concerned,"* LB, p. 103.

13, 28 *attempt."* NN, pp. 149–150.

14, 7 *Spanish Main."* PP, p. 403.

14, 11 *he does."* CP, p. 66.

14, 14 *upon motives.' "* PP, p. 256.

14, 18 *minds."* CP, p. 70.

14, 25 *and escapes."* Albert Mordell, ed., *Literary Reviews and Essays by Henry James* (New Haven, 1957), p. 191. (Referred to hereafter as R & E.)

15, 1 *irresponsible 'authorship,' "* CP, p. 328.

15, 7 *with it."* loc. cit.

15, 16 *clearly intends."* NN, p. 87. James found the same failure in Flaubert's Emma: "We feel her less illustrational than she might have been not only if the world had offered her more points of contact, but if she had had more of these to give it." (NN, p. 84)

15, 21 *the intimate."* FN, p. 229.

15, 33 *'middling' sort,"* NN, p. 157.

16, 1 *whole detail."* NN, p. 159.

16, 8 *life,"* F. O. Matthiessen and Kenneth B. Murdock, eds., *The Notebooks of Henry James* (New York, 1961), p. 135. (Referred to hereafter as *Notebooks.*)

16, 12 *be bewildered."* CP, p. 63.

16, 15 *normal agent.* CP, pp. 56–57.

16, 25 *a heavy."* CP, p. 129.

17, 12 *last word?"* NN, p. 311.

17, 18 *of life,"* PP, p. 390.

17, 20 *evoked."* CP, p. 332.

17, 24 *his pleasure."* PP, p. 116.

17, 27 *historian."* PP, pp. 379–380.

17, 34 par excellence. PP, pp. 116–117.

18, 7 *confusion."* CP, p. 120.

18, 8 *floundering cause."* LB, p. 65.

18, 15 *producing it."* CP, p. 45.

18, 31 *over him."* NN, p. 124.

19, 4 *clear."* James, *French Poets and Novelists* (London, 1878), p. 67.

19, 7 *James declared.* NN, p. 145.

19, 10 *instinct." FN*, p. 88.

19, 13 *its part."* Henry James and H. G. Wells, p. 128.

19, 23 *impure." FN*, p. 93.

19, 32 *escape?"* CP, p. 223.

20, 2 *our desire."* CP, pp. 31–32.

20, 6 *that life."* Cited in *Notebooks*, p. 224. See also CP, p. 168, where James made the same case for his invention in "The Aspern Papers" of an American Byron.

20, 15 *invention." R & E*, p. 150.

20, 20 *of things." R & E*, pp. 188–189.

20, 23 *surprisingly genial." R & E*, p. 185.

20, 29 *contended.* PP, p. 124.

20, 32 *Parisian quatrièmes."* PP, p. 122.

21, 9 *private door."* NN, p. 121.

21, 17 *individual."* NN, p. 57.

21, 20 *personal will."* NN, p. 252.

21, 24 *the soul." FN*, p. 96.

21, 30 *of man."* PP, p. 258.

21, 32 *psychological side." R & E*, p. 191.

22, 8 *cultivated consciousness."* NN, p. 157.

22, 14 *it so."* NN, p. 292.

22, 20 *them."* CP, p. 62.

22, 33 *new centers." Letters* I, p. 327.

23, 3 *of pressure."* CP, p. 128.

23, 11 *built himself."* NN, p. 140.

23, 27 *riotous living." R & E*, p. 162.

24, 6 *flaring gas?"* NN, pp. 312, 313.

25, 1 *the marble."* NN, p. 111.

25, 3 *whole branch."* NN, p. 393.

25, 7 *standing off."* CP, p. 27.

25, 11 *outer air."* CP, p. 39.

25, 23 *action." Notebooks*, p. 197.

25, 29 *contain."* Henry James and H. G. Wells, p. 188.

27,   4   *thrown up.*" LB, p. 86.
27,   20   *less scenic.*" CP, p. 325.
27,   23   *him "dramatically,*" NN, p. 264.
27,   25   *of drama.*" NN, p. 136.
27,   29   *"unarrested drama.*" Notebooks, p. 251.
28,   3   *first order.*" LB, p. 100.
28,   13   *has operated.*" Henry James and H. G. Wells, p. 128.
28,   20   *at large.*" LB, p. 101.
28,   22   *than theirs.*" Henry James and H. G. Wells, p. 167.
28,   28   *and objectively.*" CP, p. 67.
29,   2   *to himself,*" Notebooks, p. 101.
29,   15   *the picture.*" Letters I, p. 333.
29,   24   *visible reality.*" Letters I, p. 219.
29,   28   *for what?*" NN, p. 93.
29,   35   *other organism,*" PP, p. 392.
30,   2   *each other.*" LB, p. 106.
30,   14   *"secret harmonies"* Henry James and H. G. Wells, p. 171.
30,   26   *"the actual.*" FN, p. 29.
31,   17   *as well.*" NN, p. 113.
31,   35   *objects represented.*" CP, p. 144.
32,   10   *value intrinsic.*" CP, p. 329.
32,   29   *ideal.*" NN, p. 396.
33,   1   *taken place.*" CP, p. 31.
33,   5   *and imagination.* NN, pp. 94 ff.
33,   10   *touches.*" R & E, p. 196.
33,   12   *the real.*" Edel, Selected Letters, p. 162.
33,   24   *its nature.*" NN, p. 58.
33,   31   *things big.*" NN, p. 91.
34,   13   *the difference.*" NN, p. 140.
34,   21   *degree considerable.* CP, pp. 33 ff.
35,   23   *different story,*" Hawthorne, p. 63.
36,   4   *of humanity.*" Views and Reviews, pp. 159–160.
36,   6   *greatest novelists.*" Ibid., p. 159.
36,   20   *d'esprit.*" FN, p. 94.
36,   21   *to know,*" loc. cit.

36, 22 *of experience" FN*, p. 33.

36, 23 *the world." Views and Reviews*, p. 160.

36, 26 *character," Ibid.*, p. 159.

36, 31 *distinction." Ibid.*, p. 157.

37, 1 *and dreariness." R & E*, p. 157.

37, 3 *"intense pessimists." Letters* I, p. 103.

37, 19 *developments." NN*, p. 261.

37, 21 *of experience." NN*, p. 310.

37, 22 *expanding consciousness" CP*, p. 142.

37, 24 *improved state." CP*, p. 141.

38, 2 *human nature." Hawthorne*, pp. 46–47.

38, 14 *sweepingly sacrificed." NN*, p. 11.

38, 18 *understands life"; NN*, p. 207.

38, 20 *and sociabilities." NN*, p. 309.

38, 26 *of life." PP*, p. 101.

39, 3 *given us?" NN*, p. 300.

2. Thomas Hardy: The Faithful Imagination

page, line

40, 10 *prose fiction"* Florence Emily Hardy, *The Life of Thomas Hardy* (Hamden, Connecticut, 1970), p. 49. (Referred to hereafter as *Life*.)

40, 14 *downward step."* Vere H. Collins, *Talks with Thomas Hardy at Max Gate 1920–1922* (New York, 1928), p. 52.

41, 1 *business altogether.* William Tinsley, *Random Recollections of an Old Publisher* (London, 1900), p. 128.

41, 5 *a serial." Life*, p. 100.

41, 11 *my existence."* See Ernest Brennecke, Jr., *The Life of Thomas Hardy* (New York, 1925), p. 9.

41, 30 *world's history."* Harold Orel, ed., *Thomas Hardy's Personal Writings, Prefaces, Literary Opinions, Reminiscences* (Lawrence, Kansas, 1966), p. 114. (Referred to hereafter as *PW*.)

42, 2 *the past." loc. cit.*

42, 4 *infancy," PW*, p. 116.

42,   14   *art." Life,* pp. 170–171.

42,   28   *he said. PW,* p. 49.

42,   31   *the Restoration." Life,* p. 439.

42,   34   *of Shakespeare" Life,* p. 108.

43,   2   *Jonson's comedy.* Joseph Warren Beach, *The Technique of Thomas Hardy* (Chicago, 1922), p. 115.

43,   6   *and place, Life,* p. 422.

43,   8   *Sophoclean dimensions,* Hardy, *The Woodlanders* (London, 1912), p. 4.

43,   12   *much larger." PW,* p. 45.

43,   15   *of tragedy. PW,* p. 32.

43,   17   *the tale," PW,* p. 34.

43,   21   *therein." loc. cit.*

43,   30   *Elizabethan dramatists." PW,* pp. 126–127.

44,   2   *be heard." PW,* p. 129.

44,   6   *in iniquity." PW,* p. 131. (Italics mine.)

44,   12   *and James.* See Cyril Clemens, *My Chat with Thomas Hardy* (London, 1944), p. 27.

44,   19   *warmest praise. PW,* pp. 121–122.

44,   23   *to Fielding." Life,* p. 273.

45,   7   *signified." PW,* pp. 42–43.

45,   13   *own experience." Life,* p. 310.

45,   20   *change." PW,* p. 39.

45,   25   *of Tess. PW,* p. 27.

45,   28   *that novel. PW,* pp. 32–33.

45,   31   *the age." Life,* p. 375.

46,   6   *plausibility." PW,* p. 40.

46,   17   *dogmatic opinions." PW,* p. 118.

46,   20   *the edification." Life,* p. 225.

46,   27   *was dramatic. PW,* p. 115.

47,   10   *Shakespeare." PW,* p. 114.

47,   17   *of humanity." PW,* p. 118.

47,   25   *of life." Life,* p. 185.

47,   28   *of things." PW,* p. 139.

47,   31   *vital qualities." PW,* p. 137.

48,   4   *better things." PW,* p. 119.

48,   17   *observances." Life,* p. 104.

48,   20   *only." loc. cit.*

48,   25   *would allow," Life,* p. 291.

48,   28   *really universal." PW,* p. 46.

48,   34   *ago." PW,* p. 4.

49,   1   *vanishing life." PW,* p. 46.

49,   5   *materials. PW,* p. 6.

49,   8   *and supplementary. PW,* p. 46.

49,   9   *he said; PW,* p. 23.

49,   11   *manners. PW,* p. 46.

49,   17   *manners," Life,* p. 291.

49,   31   *and woman." Life,* p. 252.

50,   12   *give reality. Life,* p. 150.

50,   18   *as new." Life,* p. 225.

50,   19   *the familiar,"* Evelyn Hardy, ed., *Thomas Hardy's Notebooks* (London, 1955), p. 100.

50,   27   *such thing." Life,* p. 362. "Howells and those of his school forget," he said, "that a story *must* be striking enough to be worth telling" (*Life,* p. 239).

51,   4   *obliterated." PW,* p. 124.

51,   12   *and habits." Life,* p. 149. (Italics mine.)

51,   15   *of character."* See Edmund Blunden, *Thomas Hardy* (London, 1942), p. 78.

51,   28   *same level." PW,* p. 124.

52,   14   *a Mystery." Life,* p. 185.

52,   20   *unconscious Nature," Life,* p. 116.

52,   28   *indubitable spectre."* William Archer, *Real Conversations* (London, 1904), p. 37.

52,   32   *etc., etc." Life,* pp. 369–370.

53,   4   *expatiate in."* Archer, p. 45.

53,   20   *centuries." Ibid.,* p. 33.

53,   22   *Norman colonists,* Blunden, *Thomas Hardy,* p. 78.

54,   7   *these volumes." PW,* pp. 9–10.

54,   13   *chief characters." PW,* p. 120.

54,   15   *as narratives." PW,* p. 121.

54,   24   *the characters." Life,* p. 150.

54, 34 *make her."* See Carl J. Weber, *Hardy and the Lady from Madison Square* (Waterville, Maine, 1952), p. 89.

55, 10 *of events."* PW, p. 45.

55, 15 *the incidents."* PW, p. 11.

55, 29 *be depicted. Life,* p. 204.

56,   7 *own." Life,* p. 210.

56, 20 *considered unattractive. PW,* p. 124.

56, 32 *time's fool."* PW, p. 46.

57, 10 *and emotions."* PW, p. 139.

57, 30 *Mrs. Radcliffe,"* PW, p. 135.

58,   2 *of Ingenuity,"* PW, pp. 44–45.

58, 13 *vividly visible." Life,* p. 177.

58, 20 *to observe." Life,* p. 153.

58, 29 *the day."* Collins, *Talks with Thomas Hardy,* p. 18.

59,   3 *external observation."* PW, p. 137.

59,   8 *scientific game." Life,* p. 104.

59, 14 *that sort." Life,* p. 291.

59, 28 *and transform."* PW, p. 119.

59, 34 *closest observation."* PW, pp. 135–136.

60,   4 *of life." Thomas Hardy's Notebooks,* p. 54.

60, 14 *not Art." Life,* p. 229.

60, 22 *by fiction."* PW, p. 122.

61,   9 *poor puppet's." Life,* p. 272.

61, 13 *"low art." Life,* p. 228.

62, 14 *of falsity." Life,* p. 152.

62, 20 *as late." Life,* p. 232.

62, 26 *was offered."* PW, p. 11.

63,   4 *eludes him."* PW, p. 117.

63, 17 *of it. Life,* p. 153.

63, 21 *the All." Life,* p. 185.

63, 23 *"faithful imagination,"* PW, p. 116.

63, 35 *imaginative reason.' " Life,* p. 147.

64, 12 *think of." Life,* p. 211.

64, 15 *one." Life,* p. 310.

64, 19 *its shape."* PW, p. 80.

64, 23 *regards substance."* PW, p. 122.

64,   34   *describing them." Life,* p. 99.

65,   9   *called Casterbridge." PW,* p. 18.

65,   22   *thing signified." PW,* p. 96.

65,   27   *Hardy said. PW,* p. 115.

66,   3   *and there." Life,* p. 105.

66,   21   *unperceived beauty." Life,* p. 114.

66,   23   *poet." Life,* p. 213.

3. Joseph Conrad: To Make You See

page,   line

69,   5   *to verse."* Gérard Jean-Aubry, *Joseph Conrad, Life and Letters,* Vol. I (London, 1927), p. 273. (Referred to hereafter as *Letters* I.)

69,   7   *dramatic gift." Letters* I, p. 228.

69,   13   *ever written."* Edward Garnett, ed., *Letters from Joseph Conrad, 1895–1924* (Indianapolis, 1962), p. 193. (Referred to hereafter as *Garnett.*)

69,   17   *even epic."* Joseph Conrad, *Last Essays* (London, 1955), p. 126. (Referred to hereafter as *Last.*)

70,   5   *purely spectacular."* Joseph Conrad, *A Personal Record* (London, 1946), p. 92. (Referred to hereafter as *PR.*)

70,   8   *in itself." PR,* p. 93.

70,   15   *obvious meaning."* Joseph Conrad, *Notes on Life and Letters* (London, 1949), p. 21. (Referred to hereafter as *Notes.*)

70,   18   *is." PR,* p. xix.

70,   27   *existence." Conrad's Prefaces to His Works* (London, 1937), p. 49. (Referred to hereafter as *CP.*)

71,   5   *many ages" Last,* p. 142.

71,   9   *had it." Garnett,* p. 193.

71,   11   *philosophical intention."* Jean-Aubry, *Joseph Conrad, Life and Letters,* Vol. II, p. 38. (Referred to hereafter as *Letters* II.)

71,   19   *of life." Garnett,* p. 258.

71,   24   *prehistoric ages." Garnett,* p. 240.

71,   27   Kreutzer Sonata. H. V. Marrot, *The Life and Letters of John Galsworthy* (New York, 1936), p. 229.

71,   32   to me." *Letters* II, p. 289.

71,   34   too closely," *Letters* I, p. 302.

71,   35   the world." *Letters* II, p. 242.

72,   5   naturalistic creed," *Notes*, p. 8.

72,   11   conception." *Notes*, p. 10.

72,   12   vanishing creed" *Notes*, p. 21.

72,   14   of art." *Notes*, p. 45.

72,   20   and people." *Letters* II, p. 185.

72,   30   appear sublime." Joseph Conrad, *Chance* (London, 1949), p. 328.

73,   1   every step." *Letters* II, p. 217.

73,   10   over it." *Notes*, p. 22.

73,   12   and tears," *PR*, p. xix.

73,   31   vain appearances." *Notes*, p. 28.

73,   35   national novel." *Last*, p. 134.

74,   3   an observer." *Last*, p. 127.

74,   5   he observes." *Last*, p. 130.

74,   8   and observation," *Last*, p. 133.

74,   10   observed facts. *Notes*, p. 27.

74,   19   you see." *CP*, p. 52.

74,   29   too summarily." *Garnett*, p. 218.

74,   33   fully." *Letters* II, p. 116.

75,   3   detail." *CP*, p. 37.

75,   11   of art?" William Blackburn, ed., *Joseph Conrad, Letters to William Blackwood and David S. Meldrum* (Durham, North Carolina, 1958), p. 155. (Referred to hereafter as *Blackwood and Meldrum*.)

75,   20   other delusion." *Letters* I, p. 174.

75,   22   demolishes theories." *CP*, p. 50.

75,   34   second-hand impression." *Notes*, p. 17.

76,   8   own life." *Last*, p. 145.

76,   14   outside." *Garnett*, p. 15.

76,   19   valuable details." *CP*, p. 85.

76,   25   roman dessus." *Letters* I, p. 315.

77,   5   [his] imagination." *CP*, pp. 153, 154.

77,   25   *people's making."* *Letters* I, p. 184.

77,   29   *one's individuality."* Richard Curle, ed., *Conrad to a Friend* (New York, 1928), p. 88.

77,   32   *world."* Joseph Conrad, *Nostromo* (New York, 1904), p. 255.

77,   34   *Conrad declared.* PR, p. 95.

78,   13   *or men."* Notes, p. 30.

78,   16   *be imitated."* *Letters* II, p. 54.

78,   29   *am free."* *Letters* II, p. 204.

79,   3   *innermost beliefs."* Notes, p. 7.

79,   11   *human emotions."* CP, p. 80.

79,   15   *this world"* CP, p. 174.

79,   20   *tangible world."* CP, p. 173.

79,   25   *its humanity."* *Letters* I, p. 259.

79,   30   *our mark."* Conrad, *Chance,* p. 23.

79,   35   *of ages."* Notes, p. 16.

80,   2   *his time* Notes, p. 54.

80,   4   *commonplace way."* Notes, p. 23.

80,   9   *produce.* *Letters* I, pp. 212–213.

80,   11   *imaginative freedom,"* CP, p. 153.

80,   14   *subject matter.* CP, p. 154.

80,   17   *the forests."* CP, p. 38.

80,   24   *of story.* *Letters* I, pp. 212–213.

80,   28   *nothing happens."* Garnett, p. 80.

80,   30   *in individuals."* Notes, p. 9.

80,   34   *of malevolence."* loc. cit.

81,   5   *their professions."* loc. cit.

81,   8   *faithful record."* Notes, pp. 6–7.

81,   24   *inevitably emerge.* CP, p. 52. (Italics mine.)

81,   29   *of life,"* *Letters* I, p. 200.

82,   7   *all suggestiveness."* *Letters* II, p. 128.

82,   11   *inexplicable character."* *Letters* II, p. 291.

82,   14   *a definition."* Garnett, p. 273.

82,   18   *nor life."* CP, p. 157.

82,   21   *[its] characters."* *Letters* I, p. 184.

82,   29   *and marriage."* Notes, p. 55.

82,   32   *appear false.*" *Letters* I, 183.

83,   6   *death.*" *Notes,* p. 18.

83,   10   *going on.*" *Notes,* p. 19.

83,   27   *of senses.*" *CP,* p. 167.

83,   35   *definite statement.*" *Last,* p. 95.

84,   2   Agent. *Letters* II, p. 38.

84,   6   *with that.*" *Letters* II, p. 205.

84,   18   *proceeding.*" *loc. cit.*

84,   25   *symbolic character.*" *loc. cit.*

84,   26   *of style*" *Garnett,* p. 135.

84,   32   *of reality,*" Joseph Conrad, *Under Western Eyes* (London, 1947), p. 3.

85,   2   *your readers.*" *Letters* I, p. 280.

85,   7   *of words*" *CP,* p. 51.

85,   14   *pages* Conrad, *The Nigger of the "Narcissus"* (London, 1950), p. 6.

85,   15   *style.*" *Letters* II, p. 147.

85,   17   *its cleverness.*" *Last,* pp. 130, 125.

86,   7   *consciousness.*" *PR,* p. 92.

86,   19   *interesting.*" *Letters* I, p. 183.

86,   23   *tale.*" *CP,* p. 79.

87,   1   *poetical feeling.*" *Notes,* p. 56.

87,   4   *this earth.*" *Notes,* p. 50.

87,   10   *revealing life.*" *Garnett,* p. 172.

87,   16   *picturesque men.*" *Notes,* p. 50.

87,   20   *the men.*" John A. Gee and Paul J. Sturm, eds., *Letters of Joseph Conrad to Marguerite Poradowska, 1890–1920* (New Haven, 1940), p. 116.

87,   30   *or reveals.*" *Garnett,* p. 240.

87,   35   *this T.*" *Garnett,* p. 184.

88,   5   *living universe,*" *PR,* p. 92.

88,   15   *embraced.*" *Last,* p. 126.

88,   22   *imaginative freedom.*" *CP,* p. 153.

88,   25   *at all. CP,* p. 59.

88,   26   Bleak House *PR,* p. 124.

88,   27   *Fenimore Cooper Notes,* p. 57.

89,   2   *their strictures.*" PR, pp. 36–37.

89,   15   *the mirror.*" Marrot, *Life and Letters of John Galsworthy,*
            p. 188.

89,   20   *air.*" *Letters* I, p. 255.

89,   25   *the idea.*" *Garnett,* p. 111.

90,   9   *of life.*" *Garnett,* p. 46.

90,   15   *of folly.*" *Letters* II, p. 12.

90,   18   *for deductions.*" *Notes,* p. 30.

90,   22   *own sensations.*" CP, p. 79.

90,   31   *sensations,*" Conrad, *Nostromo,* p. 254.

91,   5   *all faded.*" *Garnett,* p. 59.

91,   24   *and time.*" CP, p. 51.

91,   27   *up imitators.*" *Letters* II, p. 54.

91,   33   *large public.*" *Letters* II, p. 147.

92,   6   *own exaggeration.*" PR, pp. xvii–xviii.

92,   9   *his voice,*" PR, p. 93.

92,   18   *good service.*" PR, pp. xvi–xvii.

92,   23   *fine frenzy.*" PR, p. 69.

92,   31   *charmed.*" CP, p. 52.

92,   34   *artistic virtue. Garnett,* p. 184.

93,   4   *humoristic writer.*" PR, p. 98.

93,   8   *probity.*" *Notes,* p. 26.

93,   11   *sublime spectacle,*" PR, p. 92.

93,   14   *of truth.*" *Letters* I, p. 301.

93,   19   *it up.*" *Garnett,* p. 292.

93,   29   *own sensations.*" CP, p. 154.

93,   34   *great novelist.*" Curle, ed., *Conrad to a Friend,* p. 147.

94,   6   *Edward Garnett. Garnett,* p. 273.

94,   10   *can help.*" *Letters* I, p. 321.

94,   16   *steady mind.*" *Last,* p. 132.

94,   18   *am doing*" *Blackwood and Meldrum,* p. 154.

94,   26   *business enterprise.*" *Blackwood and Meldrum,* p. 155.

94,   31   *their style.*" *Last,* p. 139.

95,   5   *unreliable master.*" *Blackwood and Meldrum,* p. 27.

95,   11   *Pure luck.*" *Garnett,* p. 243.

95,   14   *is disclosed.*" *Garnett,* p. 66.

95,	21	*itself written." Garnett*, pp. 41–42.
95,	28	*world." PR*, p. 98.
96,	1	*make believe." CP*, p. 110.
96,	6	*the characters." Blackwood and Meldrum*, p. 192.
96,	24	*literary minds."* Marrot, *Life and Letters of John Galsworthy*, p. 188.
96,	27	*said. Notes*, p. 9.
96,	31	*of expression."* Marrot, *Life and Letters of John Galsworthy*, p. 213.
97,	1	*is disputable." Letters* I, pp. 302–303.
97,	10	*of myself." Blackwood and Meldrum*, pp. 153–154.
97,	24	*human mind." Notes*, p. 7.
97,	26	*the toiler," Notes*, p. 20.
97,	33	*even now." Letters* II, p. 235.
98,	30	*this earth." Notes*, p. 8.
98,	32	*our earth." Notes*, p. 31.
99,	4	*of tales." PR*, p. 25.
99,	14	*others."* Conrad, *Chance*, p. 328.
99,	23	*terrible ocean!" Notes*, p. 22.
99,	28	*us believe." Notes*, pp. 21–22.
99,	34	*it is." PR*, p. xv.
100,	1	*intelligence," Garnett*, p. 258.
100,	4	*large forgiveness." Notes*, p. 9.
100,	7	*the disagreeable." Last*, p. 133.
100,	11	*truth." loc. cit.*
100,	18	*in me." Letters* I, p. 206.
100,	26	*his handling." Letters* I, p. 271.
100,	33	*such detachment." CP*, p. 148.
101,	9	*the living." CP*, p. 173.
101,	11	*it is." loc. cit.*
101,	17	*mystical contradictions." Notes*, pp. 47, 48.
101,	27	*and misery."* Conrad, *Chance*, p. 217.
101,	32	*of romance." CP*, p. 153.
102,	14	*women." Notes*, pp. 14–15.
102,	28	*one's work?" PR*, p. xviii.
102,	32	*Conrad said. Garnett*, p. 214.

102,   35   du coeur." *PR*, p. xv.

103,   8   *the spectacle.*" *Letters* II, pp. 83–84.

103,   14   *compassionate heart.*" *Notes*, p. 29.

103,   28   *things.*" *Last*, p. 142.

104,   3   *many eyes.*" *Letters* II, p. 214.

104,   6   *common reader.*" *Letters* II, p. 68.

104,   9   *not matter.*" *Letters* II, p. 151.

104,   13   *than myself.*" *Letters* II, p. 10.

104,   19   *all mankind.*" *CP*, pp. 148–149.

104,   29   *visible world.*" *CP*, p. 52.

104,   30   *and places, CP*, p. 37.

104,   34   *things credible*" *CP*, p. 154.

104,   35   *far away.*" *CP*, p. 38.

105,   3   *than reality?*" *PR*, p. 15.

105,   11   *recorded before.*" *Letters* II, p. 291.

105,   22   *to care.*" *Notes*, p. 23.

106,   4   *my writing.*" *PR*, pp. 18–19.

106,   10   *the novelist.*" *Notes*, p. 6.

4. James Joyce: It's All Won

page, line

107,   8   *form.*" Stanislaus Joyce, "Early Memories of James
                Joyce," *The Listener*, XLI (May 26, 1949), p. 897.

107,   13   *out.*" Ellsworth Mason and Richard Ellmann, eds., *The
                Critical Writings of James Joyce* (New York, 1959), p.
                39. (Referred to hereafter as *CW*.)

107,   18   *literary curios.*" *CW*, p. 40.

108,   9   *literary models.* See Richard Ellmann, *James Joyce* (New
                York, 1959), p. 330. (Referred to hereafter as *Ellmann.*)

108,   19   *and love.*" Joyce, *A Portrait of the Artist as a Young Man*
                (New York, 1916), p. 173. (Referred to hereafter as
                PAYM.)

108,   23   *everything else.*" John J. Slocum and Herbert Cahoon,
                eds., *Stephen Hero by James Joyce* (New York, 1955),
                p. 186. (Referred to hereafter as *SH*.)

108,   27   *and directed."* SH, p. 174.

109,   7   *age."* CW, p. 45.

109,   13   *unintended.* J. Mitchell Morse, *The Sympathetic Alien, James Joyce and Catholicism* (New York, 1959), p. 129.

109,   18   *patience enough."* SH, p. 36.

109,   19   *from life."* Stuart Gilbert, ed., *Letters of James Joyce,* Vol. I (New York, 1957), p. 52. (Referred to hereafter as *Letters* I.)

109,   23   *with God."* CW, p. 134.

109,   32   *of day."* SH, p. 186.

110,   11   *scornfully observed.* Frank Budgen, *James Joyce and the Making of Ulysses* (Bloomington, 1960), p. 180. (Referred to hereafter as *Budgen.*)

110,   14   *meeting.* See *Ellmann,* p. 106.

110,   17   *reactionary."* Richard Ellmann, ed., *Letters of James Joyce,* Vol. II (New York, 1966), p. 217. (Referred to hereafter as *Letters* II.)

110,   22   *esthetic purpose."* SH, p. 79.

110,   23   *Dedalus said.* SH, p. 96.

110,   26   *a poet."* CW, p. 100.

110,   29   *about patriotism."* See *Ellmann,* p. 673.

110,   35   *theologian."* *Letters* II, p. 110.

111,   8   *and care."* CW, p. 21.

111,   17   *to him."* CW, p. 101.

111,   20   *Ezra Pound;* *Letters* I, p. 101. See also p. 113, letter to Harriet Weaver: "I fear I have little imagination."

111,   26   *truth."* CW, pp. 43–44.

111,   30   *"angelic dispassionateness."* CW, p. 65.

111,   33   *of indifference."* *Letters* II, p. 217.

112,   3   *novelists."* See Herbert Gorman, *James Joyce* (New York, 1939), p. 181.

112,   4   *écrivains français."* *Letters* I, p. 118.

112,   10   *solid bodies."* SH, p. 78.

112,   11   *present things."* loc. cit.

112,   18   *private contracts?"* *Letters* II, p. 109.

112,   23   *episode.* *Letters* I, p. 136.

112,   25   *these people."* *Letters* I, p. 174.

112,   35   *words."* See *Ellmann,* p. 529.

113,   3   *my book." Budgen*, pp. 67–68.

113,   16   *they knew."* Stanislaus Joyce, *My Brother's Keeper* (London, 1958), p. 105. (Referred to hereafter as *MBK*.)

113,   17   *to date MBK*, p. 154.

113,   21   *for people."* Stanislaus Joyce, *Recollections of James Joyce* (New York, 1950), p. 8. "No writer in English since Sterne," Stanislaus believed, "has exploited the minute, unpromising material of his immediate experience so thoroughly as my brother did" (*MBK*, p. 52).

113,   30   *write them." Letters* II, p. 205.

114,   2   *and letters.* Stanislaus Joyce, "The Background to 'Dubliners'," *The Listener*, LI (March 25, 1954), p. 527.

114,   27   *patrimony." CW*, p. 184.

114,   31   *than folklore."* See *Ellmann*, p. 107.

114,   35   Music." *Letters* II, p. 217.

115,   18   *truly." CW*, p. 41.

115,   19   *or program.* See *Budgen*, pp. 193–194: "The multiplicity of technical devices in *Ulysses* is proof that Joyce subscribed to no limiting aesthetic creed. . . . It was hardly likely that, having denied all religious dogma, and having carefully avoided all political doctrine, he would submit to artistic limitations. There are hints of all practices in *Ulysses* . . . and this is the clearest proof that he was attached to none. . . . When an artist believes in no creed he is the more likely to believe in himself, in what he sees, hears, experiences."

116,   13   *artistic power." CW*, p. 215.

116,   22   *is drama." CW*, p. 36.

116,   24   *human,"* Stanislaus Joyce, *Recollections*, p. 16.

116,   26   *Faust."* See *Ellmann*, p. 430. See also p. 450.

117,   4   *roystering!" CW*, p. 45.

117,   8   *heroic." CW*, p. 100.

117,   10   *monstruous" [sic]. SH*, p. 97.

117,   10   *classical writer,"* loc. cit.

117,   16   *uncompromising truth." CW*, p. 63.

117,   25   *liberally purveyed." CW*, p. 116.

117,   31   *emotions."* Stanislaus Joyce, "Early Memories of James Joyce," *The Listener*, XLI (May 26, 1949), p. 896.

118,   1   *called it*, Richard Ellmann, ed., *Letters of James Joyce*,
           Vol. III (New York, 1966), p. 146.

118,   4   *literary interest."* MBK, p. 106.

118,   8   *his characters."* CW, p. 100.

118, 15   *passionate conflict."* Budgen, pp. 15–16.

118, 25   *poetry,"* CW, p. 75.

118, 28   *of societies."* SH, p. 78.

118, 32   *them out."* CW, p. 40.

119,   2   *defining circumstances."* SH, p. 78.

119, 12   *other thing."* PAYM, p. 250.

119, 14   *Aquinas' "quidditas,"* SH, p. 211.

119, 16   *thing*, SH, p. 213.

119, 21   *local writer.* See *Ellmann*, p. 520.

119, 26   *father's asses."* See Gorman, *James Joyce*, p. 136.

119, 30   *the universal."* See *Ellmann*, p. 520.

119, 35   *to another,"* SH, p. 78.

120,   9   Madame Bovary *Ellmann*, p. 78.

120, 12   *of D'Annunzio.* CW, p. 71.

120, 17   *literary manners."* Letters II, p. 99.

120, 25   *been apprehended"* CW, p. 147.

120, 31   *his dreams."* SH, p. 77.

120, 35   *the public."* SH, p. 86.

121,   1   *artistic faculty"* CW, p. 221.

121,   9   *remarriage.* SH, p. 40.

121, 22   *universal import."* CW, p. 45.

121, 26   *"the sensible"* PAYM, p. 248.

121, 31   *of onions."* SH, p. 95.

122,   1   *itself."* SH, p. 211.

122,   2   *us radiant."* SH, p. 213.

122,   7   *or heroic."* CW, p. 100.

122, 12   *everliving life."* PAYM, p. 260.

122, 18   *extraordinary.* It's been said of the novel's Homeric
           parallelism (most famously by T. S. Eliot) that it
           exposes the unheroic present by *contrasting* it with the
           heroic past, that its elaborate structural ironies are all in
           favor of the past and all at the expense of the present.

But if it does contrast the past and the present, it also *compares* them, identifies them with each other, and to this extent asserts, with perfect "seriousness," the heroic basis of modern life. It asserts in effect that Leopold Bloom is just as heroic in his way as his Homeric original. For Joyce as for James and Conrad after all, heroism was not less heroism because it was moral rather than physical, because it expressed itself in acts of moral self-renunciation rather than in acts of moral aggression. Not the "legitimate hero" whom he despised but the moral hero whom he honored, Bloom expresses Joyce's confidence that the heroic and the unheroic, the extraordinary and the ordinary, were no longer separable and perhaps never were.

122,	31	*actors." CW*, p. 63.
123,	7	*caste." Budgen*, p. 171.
123,	17	*emotion."* See *Ellmann*, p. 150.
123,	20	*presumably posthuman." Letters* I, p. 180.
123,	27	*is doubtful."* See *Ellmann*, p. 709.
124,	1	*eternity." Letters* I, p. 160.
124,	5	*prayer, death."* See Eugene Jolas, "My Friend James Joyce" in Seon Givens, ed., *James Joyce: Two Decades of Criticism* (New York, 1963), p. 12.
124,	20	*forget them." CW*, p. 75.
124,	27	*universal philosophy." CW*, p. 220.
124,	30	*his experience SH*, p. 40.
125,	4	*with observation." Letters* II, p. 24.
125,	6	*it*, Italo Svevo, *James Joyce, A Lecture Delivered in Milan in 1927* (Milan, 1950), no page numbers.
125,	10	*so little.* See *Ellmann*, p. 673, n.
125,	21	*their eyes." CW*, p. 21.
125,	27	*his dreams." SH*, p. 77.
126,	5	*of God." CW*, p. 42.
126,	10	*the work." CW*, p. 75.
126,	17	*called it.* See *Ellmann*, p. 275.
126,	19	*produced me." PAYM*, p. 237.
126,	32	*(or drama?)."* Gorman, *James Joyce*, p. 96. (Italics mine.)
126,	35	*Joyce declared. CW*, p. 43.
127,	24	*his fingernails." PAYM*, p. 252.

128,   1   *its scene."* CW, p. 41.
128,   10   *unuttered."* SH, p. 78.
128,   12   *direct statement,"* Budgen, p. 21.
128,   16   *woe."* CW, p. 42.
128,   24   *natural process"* CW, p. 145.
128,   25   *natural process,"* SH, p. 171.
128,   33   *or conventional."* CW, p. 41.
129,   2   *natural phenomenon."* SH, p. 41.
129,   6   *in time.* Walton Litz, "The Making of *Finnegans Wake,"* in Marvin Magalaner, ed., *A James Joyce Miscellany, Second Series* (Carbondale, 1959), p. 211.
129,   13   *the text."* Jolas, "My Friend James Joyce" in Givens, *Two Decades of Criticism,* p. 7.
129,   20   *the design."* Letters I, p. 253.
129,   24   *boasted.* Gorman, *James Joyce,* p. 138.
129,   32   *in advance."* SH, pp. 32–33.
130,   1   *as possible."* See *Ellmann,* p. 275.
130,   7   *and peace."* SH, p. 78.
130,   14   *loathing."* PAYM, p. 240.
130,   17   *or loathing.* PAYM, p. 239.
130,   21   *something."* CW, p. 144.
130,   35   *its own,"* MBK, p. 116.
131,   3   *matter:* PAYM, p. 242.
131,   20   *intention,"* SH, p. 92.
131,   21   *missionary result.* CW, p. 43.
131,   31   *wilful energy."* CW, p. 41.
132,   3   *obtuse."* Letters II, p. 99.
133,   3   *and fidelity."* CW, p. 129.
133,   13   *soul's malady."* CW, p. 134.
133,   16   *it is."* CW, p. 133.
133,   20   *the gift."* SH, p. 79.
133,   32   *and sympathy."* CW, p. 65.
134,   2   *joyful spirit."* SH, p. 78.
134,   15   *own humanity":* SH, p. 142.
134,   20   *calm,"* CW, p. 48.
134,   26   *answer."* SH, p. 41.

135,   5   *and sympathy."* CW, p. 65.
135,   9   *the street."* CW, p. 127.
135, 25   *and lived."* CW, p. 67.
136,   5   *Budgen observed;* Budgen, p. 151.
136,   7   *any empire."* loc. cit.
136, 15   *Bersirk freedom."* CW, p. 22.
136, 18   *their heads."* Stanislaus Joyce, *Recollections*, p. 16.
136, 23   *truly virile."* loc. cit.
136, 25   *for virility."* CW, p. 116.
136, 31   *madness."* Budgen, p. 16.
136, 33   *the war."* Georges Borach, "Conversations with James Joyce," *College English*, XV (March, 1954), p. 325.
137,   7   *his flower."* Letters II, p. 99.
137, 10   *and Disraeli."* Letters II, p. 108.
137, 12   *wrote about."* MBK, p. 205.
137, 16   *in literature."* Budgen, p. 75.
137, 24   *father."* Letters II, p. 106.
138,   4   *his stories."* Stanislaus Joyce, *Recollections*, p. 18.
138,   6   *Russian fiction.* Letters II, p. 106.
138,   9   *unreal murder."* Budgen, p. 180.
138, 16   *shall be."* Budgen, p. 17 (Italics mine.)
138, 23   *and Dickens.* Wyndham Lewis, *Time and Western Man* (Boston, 1957), pp. 76, 105.
139,   2   *with compassion."* MBK, p. 206.
139,   7   *read me."* Stanislaus Joyce, "Early Memories of James Joyce," *The Listener*, XLI (May 26, 1949), p. 897.
139, 10   *to live."* See Ellmann, p. 551.
139, 19   *would enrich."* SH, pp. 146–147.
139, 27   *[his] race,"* PAYM, p. 299.
139, 32   *liberation."* Letters I, pp. 62–63.
139, 35   *polished looking-glass."* Letters I, p. 64.
140,   3   *my race."* Letters II, p. 248.
140,   6   *wretched race."* Letters II, p. 311.
140, 22   *their own."* PAYM, p. 280.
141,   5   *of life."* MBK, p. 110.
141,   6   *and whole."* CW, p. 65.

141,   12   *to live."* SH, p. 80.

141,   19   *usurpers."* MBK, p. 120.

141,   22   *everliving life,"* PAYM, p. 260.

141,   31   *taste."* Letters II, p. 115.

141,   35   *sympathy, too."* MBK, p. 53.

142,   9   *entertainers?"* Letters II, p. 99.

5. D. H. Lawrence: The One Bright Book of Life

page,   line

143,   11   *her children.* See Richard Aldington, *D. H. Lawrence,
            Portrait of a Genius But* . . . (New York, 1950), p.
            150.

143,   12   *told her.* See Mark Schorer, *D. H. Lawrence* (New York,
            1968), p. 3.

144,   7   *freshening."* D. H. Lawrence, *Lady Chatterley's Lover*
            (New York, 1959), pp. 117–118.

144,   10   *conscious."* D. H. Lawrence, *Assorted Articles* (London,
            1930), p. 98.

144,   26   Dorian Gray, E. T. [Jessica Chambers], *D. H. Lawrence,
            A Personal Record* (London, 1935), p. 110. (Referred to
            hereafter as *E. T.*)

144,   28   *upset you")* E. T., p. 102.

144,   30   *Maupassant").* E. T., p. 107.

144,   31   *corrupt feelings."* Lady Chatterley's Lover, p. 118.

144,   34   *present generation."* Edward D. McDonald, ed., *Phoenix,
            The Posthumous Papers of D. H. Lawrence* (New
            York, 1936), p. 532. (Referred to hereafter as *Phoenix.*)

145,   5   *detached understanding."* Harry T. Moore, ed., *The
            Collected Letters of D. H. Lawrence,* Vol. I (New
            York, 1962), p. 508. (Referred to hereafter as *CL* I.)

145,   13   *and recoils,"* Lady Chatterley's Lover, p. 118.

145,   16   *gone dead."* Ibid., p. 117.

145,   30   *read him."* Harry T. Moore, *The Collected Letters of D.
            H. Lawrence,* Vol. II (New York, 1962), p. 846.
            (Referred to hereafter as *CL* II.)

146,   12   *myself famous."* Lawrence, *Assorted Articles,* p. 146.

146, 17 *religious experience."* CL I, p. 273.

146, 27 *of sympathy."* Ada Lawrence and G. Stuart Gelder, *Early Life of D. H. Lawrence* (London, 1932), p. 206. (Referred to hereafter as *Ada Lawrence*.)

146, 28 *vastly sympathetic";* CL I, p. 40.

146, 30 *artist."* CL I, p. 51.

147, 1 *don't like."* See Catherine Carswell, *The Savage Pilgrimage, A Narrative of D. H. Lawrence* (London, 1932), p. 137.

147, 4 *discriminative sympathy."* Lady Chatterley's Lover, p. 117.

147, 6 *and jeering."* CL I, p. 273.

147, 10 *[came] instead." loc. cit.*

147, 13 *in praise."* CL I, p. 304.

147, 18 *of Life."* CL I, p. 47.

147, 21 *sanguinity."* CL I, p. 94.

147, 25 *and despair."* CL I, p. 150.

147, 30 *lose interest."* Phoenix, p. 367.

147, 33 *on life." Ibid.,* p. 369.

148, 7 *the artist."* CL II, p. 1,083.

148, 10 *the sinner."* CL I, pp. 300–301.

148, 12 *the gladness."* CL I, p. 304.

148, 22 *the Resurrection."* CL I, p. 301.

148, 25 *in 1926. Ada Lawrence,* p. 117.

148, 27 *nor anti!"* CL II, p. 1,051.

149, 7 *to feel."* Phoenix, p. 752.

149, 10 *and women,"* CL I, p. 200.

149, 12 *physical realities,"* CL II, p. 1,111.

149, 25 *to pass."* D. H. Lawrence, *Studies in Classic American Literature* (New York, 1964), p. 65. (Referred to hereafter as *SCAL*.)

149, 29 *repulsion"* CL II, p. 1,123.

149, 32 *headsman."* CL II, p. 811.

150, 1 *new world."* Phoenix, p. 185.

150, 3 *world too."* CL I, p. 482.

150, 4 *of urge."* Aldous Huxley, ed., *The Letters of D. H. Lawrence* (New York, 1932), p. 721.

150,   10   *brutal."* CL I, p. 77.

150,   16   *way somewhere."* CL I, p. 32.

150,   20   *new country").* E. T., p. 120.

150,   26   *of existence."* Phoenix, p. 224.

150,   29   *marvellously beautiful."* SCAL, p. 55.

150,   33   *almost prophetic."* SCAL, p. 51.

151,   7   *of life."* Phoenix, p. 750.

151,   8   *"unrelenting."* CL I, p. 35.

151,   12   *festering sore."* CL I, p. 36.

151,   24   *stuff is."* Huxley, *Letters,* pp. 387–388.

152,   5   *world."* CL I, p. 488.

152,   26   *the universe."* CL II, p. 994.

153,   7   *not heroic."* Phoenix, p. 226.

153,   13   *in triumph."* Ibid., pp. 436–437.

153,   24   *commonplace people."* Ibid., p. 227.

154,   2   *save Homer."* Ibid., p. 228.

154,   10   *heroine—* Lawrence, *The Plumed Serpent* (New York, 1926), p. 135.

154,   29   *beyond humanity."* Huxley, *Letters,* p. 407.

154,   31   *of man."* Lawrence, *Kangaroo* (London, 1923), p. 386.

154,   33   *he insisted.* CL II, p. 993.

155,   3   *people."* CL I, p. 514.

155,   8   *ad nauseam,"* CL II, p. 799.

155,   9   *is non-human"* SCAL, p. 134.

155,   12   *upon it."* Phoenix, p. 419.

155,   18   *than ours."* Lawrence, *St. Mawr* (London, 1925), p. 34.

155,   20   *human activity,"* SCAL, p. 156.

155,   22   *men do."* SCAL, p. 146.

155,   24   *[could] grasp,"* Phoenix, p. 419.

155,   28   *man."* Ibid., p. 415.

156,   1   *an indifference."* Lawrence, *Aaron's Rod* (London, 1922), p. 212.

156,   12   *himself."* Phoenix, p. 719.

156,   28   *physical cliché."* Ibid., p. 579.

156,   35   *human conception."* CL I, pp. 281–282.

157,   17   *of character."* See John Middleton Murry, *Reminiscences of D. H. Lawrence* (London, 1933), p. 48.

157,   19   *human people."* CL I, p. 566.

157,   29   *to offer!"* CL II, p. 711.

158,   1   *to man."* Phoenix, p. 722.

158,   6   *real being."* CL I, p. 226.

158,   10   *and convention."* Phoenix, p. 410.

158,   19   *really life."* CL II, p. 717.

158,   23   *around it."* CL I, p. 180.

158,   28   *one's soul."* Huxley, Letters, p. 351.

158,   32   *veering round."* Lawrence, *Fantasia of the Unconscious* (New York, 1922), p. 14.

159,   1   *and effect."* SCAL, p. 65.

159,   4   *chronological sequence."* Phoenix, p. 249.

159,   7   *all explosive."* Ibid., p. 410.

159,   17   *inside oneself."* Witter Bynner, *Journey with Genius, Recollections and Reflections Concerning the D. H. Lawrences* (New York, 1951), p. 311.

159,   23   *presentation."* CL I, p. 259.

159,   25   *of them."* CL I, p. 263.

159,   32   *bit visualised."* CL I, p. 193.

160,   4   *ashamed of."* D. H. Lawrence, *Reflections on the Death of a Porcupine and Other Essays* (Philadelphia, 1925), p. 108.

160,   30   *universe";* CL II, p. 994.

161,   4   *and change."* Phoenix, p. 536.

161,   13   *the universe,"* Lawrence, *Fantasia*, p. 14.

161,   21   *simplicity."* Ibid., p. 216.

161,   27   *flowers do."* Lawrence, *Kangaroo*, p. 122.

162,   1   *the universe."* Lawrence, *Fantasia*, p. 218.

162,   4   *many gods."* SCAL, p. 18.

162,   7   *me differences."* CL II, p. 652.

162,   12   *for likenesses."* Phoenix, p. 565.

162,   16   *the object."* CL I, p. 308.

162,   21   *to life."* Phoenix, p. 577.

162,   25   *far attained,"* Lawrence, *Reflections*, pp. 103–104.

162,   30   *the novel."* Phoenix, p. 537.

162, 33 *of being."* Ibid., p. 480.
163,   3 *old, dead."* CL I, p. 281.
163,   8 *it up."* SCAL, p. 146.
163, 17 *bosh today."* SCAL, p. 2.
163, 21 *his day."* loc. cit.
163, 32 *he announced.* CL I, p. 182.
163, 34 *other novels."* CL I, p. 399.
164,   9 *year ago."* Phoenix, p. 536.
164, 12 *their hour."* CL I, p. 264.
164, 21 *awful feeling."* CL I, p. 189.
165,   5 *of solidity."* Phoenix, p. 563.
165, 13 *nor impure."* loc. cit.
165, 17 *and sensual."* Phoenix, p. 565.
165, 20 *lumpy body."* Ibid., p. 564.
166,   4 *of art."* Lawrence, *Women in Love* (London, 1921), p. 453.
166,   9 *Gustave Flaubert."* Phoenix, p. 308.
166, 23 *he said.* Ibid., p. 561.
166, 33 *abstract words."* Ibid., p. 346.
167,   3 *human character."* CL II, p. 1,047.
167,   9 *in men."* CL I, p. 5.
167, 12 *Henry Wilton."* CL I, p. 258.
167, 23 *social being."* Phoenix, p. 540.
167, 31 *inconceivable."* Lawrence, *Psychoanalysis and the Unconscious* (London, 1923), p. 41.
168,   5 *the unconscious,"* Ibid., p. 45.
168,   7 *electricity."* Ibid., p. 38.
168,   9 *unaccountable evolutions."* Ibid., pp. 43–44.
168, 10 *or habits."* Ibid., p. 45.
168, 21 *the universe."* Phoenix, p. 708.
168, 27 *the parents."* Lawrence, *Psychoanalysis,* p. 39.
169,   2 *human being."* Phoenix, p. 243.
169, 11 *human beings."* CL I, p. 282.
169, 24 *else."* Phoenix, p. 227.
169, 32 *rolled together."* CL I, p. 474.
170, 10 *a week."* SCAL, p. 60.

170, 13 *the real. loc. cit.*

170, 18 *actuality. SCAL*, p. 76.

170, 20 *known world." Phoenix*, p. 255.

171, 10 *novel, no." Ibid.*, p. 528.

171, 20 *has discovered." loc. cit.*

171, 32 *of Man." CL* I, p. 302.

172, 3 *was." CL* II, p. 1,194.

172, 7 *not symbols." Phoenix*, p. 296.

172, 13 *their own." Ibid.*, p. 295.

172, 23 *out clean." CL* I, p. 264.

172, 27 *form."* Lawrence, *Kangaroo*, p. 105.

172, 30 *form willy-nilly." Phoenix*, p. 252.

173, 7 *no finality." Ibid.*, pp. 218–219.

173, 13 *arranged developments." Ibid.*, p. 313.

173, 17 *as blood." CL* I, p. 160.

173, 30 *mere impertinence." Phoenix*, p. 539.

174, 6 *of life" CL* I, p. 258.

174, 10 *always true." CL* I, p. 180.

174, 14 *of them. Phoenix*, p. 480.

174, 18 *aim." Ibid.*, p. 479.

174, 25 *conscious intention. SCAL*, p. 2.

174, 27 *dribbling liar."* Lawrence, *Reflections*, p. 123.

175, 4 *one page" Phoenix*, p. 309.

175, 6 *every word." loc. cit.*

175, 9 *I cannot." CL* I, p. 176.

175, 20 *the novels.* Lawrence, *Fantasia*, p. xiv.

175, 31 *of reality."* F. R. Leavis, *D. H. Lawrence: Novelist* (New York, 1956), p. 52.

176, 1 *them over."* Lawrence, *Reflections*, p. 104.

176, 13 *in everything." CL* II, p. 881.

176, 16 *not warrant." CL* I, p. 68.

176, 21 *thought out." CL* II, p. 761.

177, 1 *to life." CL* II, p. 959.

177, 12 *English bathos." CL* I, pp. 35–36.

177, 19 *I don't." CL* II, p. 827.

177, 30 *universe itself." CL* II, p. 994.

177,   32   can't alter." CL I, p. 491.
177,   34   of nature." Phoenix, p. 419.
178,   8   of life." Ibid., p. 246.
178,   18   of life." CL I, p. 485.
178,   25   a leprosy." Phoenix, p. 312.
178,   30   may be." loc. cit.
178,   32   accepted appearances," Ibid., p. 566.
179,   6   or heaven." CL II, p. 975.
179,   18   all mysticism." CL I, p. 51.
180,   3   the scrimmage." CL II, p. 827.
180,   7   self-importance." Phoenix, p. 566.
180,   10   life revealed." Ibid., p. 312.
180,   15   admire." CL II, p. 827.
180,   15   and genius" CL I, p. 258.
180,   20   the elect." Phoenix, p. 565.
180,   35   fellow-men." CL II, p. 827.
181,   9   Hugo's self-effusion." Phoenix, pp. 247–248.
181,   20   of life." Ibid., p. 313.
181,   30   of parturition." Lawrence, Assorted Articles, p. 149.
182,   13   is lost." Ibid., p. 152.
182,   16   and woman." Ibid., p. 102.
182,   24   among them." Phoenix, p. 542.
183,   5   life." Ibid., p. 535.

6. Virginia Woolf: Fire in the Mist

page, line
185,   9   imaginative literature." Virginia Woolf, Granite and
              Rainbow (London, 1958), p. 141. (Referred to hereafter
              as Granite.)
185,   17   we perish," Virginia Woolf, The Common Reader (New
              York, 1925), p. 93. (Referred to hereafter as CR.)
185,   20   of values." Virginia Woolf, The Common Reader, Sec-
              ond Series (London, 1932), p. 80. (Referred to hereafter
              as CRSS.)

185, 24 *most perfect."* CRSS, p. 234.

185, 31 *his genius,"* Granite, p. 113.

186, 6 *the world."* CR, p. 235.

186, 14 *woven together."* CR, p. 80.

186, 19 *of Dickens.* Leonard Woolf, ed., *A Writer's Diary, Being Extracts from the Diary of Virginia Woolf* (New York, 1953), p. 301. (Referred to hereafter as *Diary.*)

186, 23 *the next."* Granite, p. 52.

187, 1 *before it?"* CRSS, p. 49.

187, 8 *a poet."* Granite, pp. 78–79.

187, 15 *gills." Ibid.*, p. 41.

187, 18 *of touch."* CR, p. 328.

187, 33 *not solitude."* CR, p. 316.

188, 6 *Mr. Bennett."* Virginia Woolf, *The Moment and Other Essays* (New York, 1948), pp. 121–122. (Referred to hereafter as *Moment.*)

188, 11 *know it." Moment*, p. 151.

188, 15 *modern life" Ibid.*, p. 157.

188, 17 *observe, particularize.* CRSS, p. 209.

188, 24 *freedom lavishly."* Granite, p. 108.

188, 29 *poetic Hardy."* Virginia Woolf, *The Death of the Moth and Other Essays* (London, 1942), p. 105. (Referred to hereafter as *Moth.*)

189, 10 *we provide."* CR, p. 211.

189, 18 *two ago."* Virginia Woolf, *Contemporary Writers* (London, 1965), p. 67. (Referred to hereafter as *CW.*)

189, 21 *and seeing." Moth*, p. 103.

189, 27 *be impeded." Diary*, p. 206.

190, 3 *sovereignty assured."* CR, p. 218.

190, 13 *facts."* Granite, p. 33.

190, 17 *the particular."* CR, p. 81.

190, 21 *the* Electra." CR, p. 44.

190, 26 *in them."* Granite, p. 52.

190, 31 *the poetry,"* CRSS, p. 51.

191, 1 *of fact"* Granite, p. 20.

191, 2 *never reach."* CR, p. 68.

191, 9 *of language."* Granite, p. 136.

191,   16   *"execrable" style. Moment*, p. 63.

191,   27   *tragic.'* " *CR*, p. 216.

191,   32   *quality apiece."* Virginia Woolf, *The Captain's Death Bed* (London, 1950), p. 15. (Referred to hereafter as CDB.)

191,   34   *names suggest," loc. cit.*

192,   3   *the moral." CDB*, p. 13.

192,   13   *life itself. CR*, p. 328 ff.

192,   16   *cannot generalise." CR*, pp. 329–330.

192,   19   *trace."* Virginia Woolf, *The Waves* (New York, 1931), p. 239.

192,   21   *to reality." CRSS*, p. 256.

192,   29   *held together." CR*, p. 249.

192,   34   *been evolved." CDB*, p. 97.

193,   2   *adventures" CR*, p. 129.

193,   4   *of events." CDB*, p. 58.

193,   10   *or pamphleteers." CDB*, p. 98.

193,   16   *abstract." CRSS*, p. 232.

193,   20   *human being." CDB*, p. 13.

193,   27   *temperament." CR*, p. 79

193,   30   *in fiction." Moment*, p. 32.

193,   35   *of time" Granite*, p. 143.

194,   1   *living change." Moment*, p. 133.

194,   8   *their surroundings." Moth*, p. 105.

194,   20   *observe it." Granite*, p. 120.

194,   27   *to give." Ibid.*, p. 22.

194,   33   *writer himself." Ibid.*, p. 120.

195,   6   *possess." CR*, pp. 312–313.

195,   10   *aloof world." Granite*, p. 121.

195,   18   *humdrum lives." CRSS*, p. 51.

195,   21   *heroic conflict." CRSS*, p. 28.

195,   27   *by individuals." Granite*, p. 16.

195,   33   *pneumonia"; CR*, p. 74.

195,   35   *in Genoa." CR*, p. 75.

196,   4   *Cross Road." Granite*, pp. 14–15.

196,   7   *its companions," Moment*, p. 165.

196, 14 *human life?" CRSS,* p. 49.
196, 19 *a Lord." Granite,* p. 103.
196, 21 *experience." Ibid.,* p. 110.
196, 23 *no heroism" CR,* p. 197.
196, 25 *existence," CR,* p. 202.
196, 28 *by another." CR,* p. 197.
197, 10 *certain quality," CR,* p. 328.
197, 12 *and emotions." CR,* pp. 329–330.
197, 17 *part pain." Granite,* p. 16.
197, 24 *inextricably confused." CR,* p. 251.
197, 28 *shreds now." Diary,* p. 56.
197, 30 *the fragmentary." CDB,* p. 111.
198, 7   *of friendship." CDB,* p. 108.
198, 9   *and fragments." CDB,* p. 110.
198, 12 *chaotic condition," loc. cit.*
198, 19 *on Dostoevski." CR,* p. 252.
198, 31 *live there." CDB,* p. 106.
198, 35 *live in." loc. cit.*
199, 17 *as possible." CR,* pp. 212–213.
199, 26 *familiar place. CR,* pp. 328–329; *Granite,* p. 95.
199, 28 *psyche CR,* p. 252.
199, 30 *inextricably confused." CR,* p. 251.
200, 17 *an inventory?" Granite,* p. 145.
200, 23 *infantile realisms." CW,* p. 62.
200, 26 *paint?" loc. cit.*
201, 5   *called them." Moment,* p. 77.
201, 11 *so much." Granite,* p. 132.
201, 14 *the novel." Ibid.,* p. 136.
201, 16 *she said. Ibid.,* p. 22.
201, 18 *the detail," Ibid.,* p. 18.
201, 21 *life." Ibid.,* p. 83.
201, 28 *of fiction." Ibid.,* p. 18.
201, 31 *the unessential" Diary,* p. 203.
202, 6   *will develop." Granite,* pp. 50–51.
202, 15 *imaginative power." Ibid.,* p. 44.

202,   17   *deal with."* Moth, p. 112.

202,   19   *facts,"* CR, p. 227.

202,   21   *life itself."* CRSS, p. 257.

202,   28   *on Defoe.* CR, p. 127.

202,   32   *transcend reality."* CR, p. 227.

202,   35   *and heightened."* CRSS, p. 257.

203,   6   *the mist."* Diary, p. 22.

203,   15   *the world."* CRSS, p. 225.

203,   20   *human nature."* CR, p. 135.

203,   23   *of bitterness."* Granite, p. 99.

203,   28   *of imagination."* Ibid., p. 142.

203,   33   *and bedtime."* Moment, p. 156.

204,   6   *from it."* CR, p. 75.

204,   9   *Austen."* CRSS, p. 228.

204,   17   *seemed limitless."* Virginia Woolf, To The Lighthouse (New York, 1955), p. 96.

204,   19   *in us."* CR, p. 70.

204,   26   *want fantasy,"* Diary, p. 134.

204,   28   *the novel.* Diary, p. 122.

205,   6   *manners."* CDB, p. 120.

205,   13   *general ideas."* Granite, pp. 18–19.

205,   15   *outside themselves;"* CDB, p. 58.

205,   18   *our aims."* CR, p. 255.

205,   23   *the conception."* CR, p. 211.

205,   25   *in solitude,"* Granite, p. 19.

205,   31   *its dreams."* Ibid., p. 34.

206,   8   *of outline."* Ibid., p. 140.

206,   19   *of psychology."* Ibid., p. 23.

206,   30   *in prose."* CRSS, p. 211.

206,   34   *cannot rival."* CRSS, pp. 212–213.

207,   4   *a phrase,"* Diary, p. 260.

207,   5   *person's character."* Ibid., p. 153.

207,   13   *and women."* CDB, p. 57.

207,   16   *other arts,"* Moment, p. 110.

207,   18   *resentment 'artificial.' "* Granite, p. 122.

207,   26   *human character."* Diary, p. 51.

207, 28 *have none."* *Ibid.,* p. 170.

208, 4 *our hands."* *Granite,* p. 142.

208, 12 *value whatever."* *Ibid.,* p. 46.

208, 15 *perish."* *Moment,* p. 111.

208, 17 *and ordered."* *Granite,* p. 22.

208, 27 *for himself."* CDB, pp. 99–100.

208, 34 *have written."* *Moment,* p. 153.

209, 2 *the past."* *Ibid.,* p. 97.

209, 7 *times over."* *Ibid.,* pp. 111–112.

209, 11 *breathless anguish."* See Aileen Pippett, *The Moth and the Star, A Biography of Virginia Woolf* (New York, 1957), p. 288.

209, 20 *copper coins."* CR, p. 330.

209, 28 *pug dog."* *Moment,* p. 111.

209, 33 *"perfunctory fast-recording."* *Granite,* p. 103.

210, 8 *extinguished."* CRSS, pp. 133, 134.

210, 11 *plain prose."* *Diary,* p. 269.

210, 15 *the novel."* *Granite,* p. 140.

210, 21 *summary."* *Ibid.,* p. 139.

210, 25 *it again."* *Diary,* p. 126.

210, 28 *what? Elegy?"* *Ibid.,* p. 78.

211, 10 *of life."* *Granite,* p. 19.

211, 18 *from reality."* CR, p. 75.

211, 21 *advantage."* *loc. cit.*

211, 23 The Waves. *The Waves,* p. 242.

211, 32 *or sky."* *Diary,* pp. 129–130.

212, 7 *to saturate."* *Ibid.,* p. 136.

212, 11 *them."* *Granite,* p. 33.

212, 16 *the vision."* CDB, p. 56.

212, 21 *and houses."* CR, p. 226.

212, 25 *eternal fires."* *Moth,* p. 108.

212, 31 *resist it."* *Diary,* p. 184.

212, 32 *the vision."* *Ibid.,* p. 191.

213, 8 *his hoard?"* *Moth,* p. 95.

213, 12 *in externality,"* *Diary,* pp. 184–185.

213, 14 *of life. Ibid.,* p. 229.

213,   17   *inner."* *Ibid.*, p. 250.

213,   24   *the extraordinary."* *CW*, p. 124.

213,   29   *the mind."* *CR*, pp. 97–98.

213,   30   *objects beautiful,"* *CRSS*, p. 57.

213,   33   *upholstered furniture."* *CW*, p. 124.

214,   3   *to life."* *CW*, p. 22.

214,   7   *touch."* *Granite*, p. 137.

214,   12   *humanity."* *Ibid.*, p. 141.

214,   16   *the drama,"* *Ibid.*, p. 22.

214,   24   *prodigious."* *CRSS*, p. 232.

214,   29   *mind."* *CDB*, p. 54.

215,   1   *outwardly trivial."* *CR*, p. 197.

215,   12   *then another."* *CRSS*, p. 247.

215,   18   *things. Granite*, p. 51.

215,   22   *the novel."* *Ibid.*, p. 137.

215,   26   *real life."* *Diary*, p. 48.

215,   27   *"less lyrical."* *Ibid.*, p. 61.

216,   3   *the other."* *Granite*, pp. 143–144.

216,   10   *spacious."* *Diary*, p. 27.

216,   15   *into collision."* *Granite*, p. 117.

216,   19   *interest."* *loc. cit.*

216,   27   *thing"* *Moth*, p. 108.

216,   28   *the symbolical."* *Ibid.*, p. 109.

216,   30   *something else."* *Ibid.*, p. 108.

217,   1   *the others."* *CDB*, p. 57.

217,   10   *suggest."* *Diary*, p. 165.

217,   14   *slight touches."* *CR*, p. 50.

217,   23   *daily life."* *Granite*, p. 22.

217,   31   *incongruous."* *Ibid.*, p. 33.

217,   34   *into poetry."* *Ibid.*, p. 21.

217,   35   *a patch."* *Ibid.*, p. 20.

218,   8   *you feel."* *Moment*, p. 160.

218,   11   *come first."* *Ibid.*, p. 161.

218,   13   *the crisis."* *Diary*, p. 39.

218,   16   *get it."* Pippett, *The Moth and the Star*, p. 225.

218,   18   *the emotion.*" *Moth*, p. 104.
218,   22   *I do?*" *Diary*, p. 56.
218,   33   *can create.*" *Moment*, p. 134.
219,   3   *fables.*" *Granite*, p. 69.
219,   19   *our knowledge,*" CW, p. 67.
219,   24   *and recognized.*" *Granite*, p. 144.
219,   27   *entire being.*" *Ibid.*, p. 95.
219,   31   *street below.*" *loc. cit.*
220,   9   *vanity.*" CR, p. 249.
220,   14   *up children.*" *Diary*, p. 26.
220,   24   *day returns.*" *Moment*, p. 67.
221,   18   *set free.*" CR, pp. 214–215.
221,   26   *is revived.*" CR, p. 235.
221,   34   *be manipulated.*" *Granite*, p. 49.
222,   12   *the dungfly.*" *Ibid.*, p. 51.
222,   24   *writer's mind.*" CR, p. 214.
222,   27   *deeply human,*" CR, p. 236.
222,   29   *compassionate.*" CR, p. 217.
223,   7   *shut out.*" *Diary*, p. 183.
223,   15   *to feel.*" *Granite*, p. 125.
223,   20   *judgment.*" *loc. cit.*
223,   30   *and despicable.*" CR, p. 251.
224,   8   *human life.*" *Diary*, pp. 180–181.
224,   14   *the mind.*" CR, pp. 214–215.
224,   19   *discriminations,*" CDB, p. 15.
224,   23   *ignore them.*" CR, p. 328.
224,   29   *was accomplished.*" *Granite*, p. 51.
225,   1   *found him.*" *loc. cit.*
225,   15   *slighter shades.*" CRSS, p. 9.
225,   20   *beautiful.*" CRSS, p. 57.
225,   32   *three.*" *Granite*, p. 51.
225,   34   *of tolerance,*" CR, p. 234.
226,   1   *of sympathy.*" CR, p. 236.
226,   12   *plain.*" Virginia Woolf, *Jacob's Room* (London, 1960), p. 163.
226,   30   *compassion.*" CR, p. 252.

226, 33   *of others.*" CR, pp. 252–253.
227,   2   *of man.*" CRSS, p. 216.
227, 18   *soul.*" CR, p. 209.
227, 21   *hired lodging,*" CR, p. 250.
227, 22   *[their] fiction.*" CR, p. 249.
227, 25   *human spirit.*" CR, p. 217.
227, 30   *innermost flame.*" CR, p. 214.
228, 26   *with . . . life.*" Moth, p. 136.
229,   1   *to poetry.*" Granite, pp. 17, 18.
229,   5   *modern life.*" Ibid., p. 145.

7. Epilegomena: The Single Vision

page, line
230, 10   *for style.*" See Mrs. Hardy, *Life of Thomas Hardy*, p. 246.
230, 13   *infinite sentences.*" See F. W. Dupee, *Henry James, His Life and Writings* (New York, 1956), p. 139.
230, 19   *itself.*" Letters I, p. 309.
231,   3   *davvero!*" Collected Letters II, p. 1,076.
231,   6   *press,*" Leonard Woolf and James Strachey, eds., *Virginia Woolf & Lytton Strachey Letters* (New York, 1956), p. 76.
231,   8   *nauseating.*" Writer's Diary, p. 46.
231, 27   *represent life.*" James, *Partial Portraits*, p. 378.
232,   2   *for facts,*" James, *Notes on Novelists*, p. 146.
232,   4   *visible world,*" Notes on Life and Letters, p. 28.
232,   5   *before him.*" "The Lesson of Balzac" in *The Question of Our Speech*, p. 86.
232, 10   *verification.*" Notes on Novelists, pp. 151–152.
232, 19   *heaven.*" A Personal Record, p. 95.
232, 20   *after him.* Kangaroo, p. 164.
232, 22   *circumstance.*" Phoenix, p. 528.
232, 35   *[his] time.*" The Moment and Other Essays, p. 130.
233,   9   *of saying.* Jean-Aubry, *Conrad, Life and Letters* II, p. 182.
233, 13   *the case.*" Conrad's Prefaces, p. 73.

233,   24   *life-situations.* Ellmann, *James Joyce,* p. 452.

234,   9   *divinity."* Collected Letters I, p. 432.

234,   16   *Lawrence's letters. Writer's Diary,* p. 182.

234,   20   *the reverse." Fantasia of the Unconscious,* p. xiv.

234,   23   *consistent philosophy." Personal Writings,* p. 48.

235,   3   *Conrad's Marlow) Chance,* p. 310.

235,   5   *unabashed tears."* loc. cit.

235,   7   *one thing." Writer's Diary,* p. 130.

235,   21   *lives."* Stanislaus Joyce, *My Brother's Keeper,* pp. 106–107.

235,   30   *called him. Last Essays,* p. 126.

235,   32   *fanciful invention,"* loc. cit.

236,   5   *in literature)." Letters to William Blackwood and David S. Meldrum,* p. 156.

236,   7   *and heard."* Gorman, *James Joyce,* p. 150.

236,   12   *of seeing."* Lubbock, ed., *Letters of Henry James,* I, p. 176.

236,   18   *and salvation." Life and Letters* I, p. 301.

236,   22   *this earth." Notes on Life and Letters,* p. 10.

236,   31   *without shame." A Personal Record,* pp. 111–112.

237,   2   *in ecstasy." Collected Letters* I, p. 300.

237,   17   *from others." Partial Portraits,* p. 384.

237,   23   *of fiction." A Personal Record,* p. 108.

237,   32   *own head?"* See Ellmann, *James Joyce,* p. 275.

237,   35   *with emphasis. Life and Letters* II, p. 68.

238,   2   *their authority." Collected Letters* I, p. 182.

238,   10   *or think." Writer's Diary,* p. 213.

238,   18   *after him.* Cf. above, pp. 90–91, 125–126, 164.

238,   27   *a novelist." Notes on Life and Letters,* p. 7.

238,   29   *forbidden." Common Reader,* p. 218.

239,   8   *novelist's art." Notes on Novelists,* p. 145.

239,   9   *detail." Letters to Blackwood and Meldrum,* p. 40.

239,   26   *the eye"* Garnett, *Letters from Joseph Conrad,* p. 32.

239,   33   *too much."* James, *Critical Prefaces,* p. 43.

240,   2   *surround us." Partial Portraits,* p. 397.

240,   3   *of life." Ibid.,* p. 398.

240,   11   *a fiction." Hawthorne*, p. 64.

240,   12   *not allegory," Collected Letters* II, p. 1,205.

240,   15   Progress." *Collected Letters* I, p. 432.

240,   27   *ranging," The Moment*, p. 95.

240,   30   *to him." Granite and Rainbow*, p. 123.

241,   10   *room." Writer's Diary*, p. 93.

241,   19   *novel." The Moment*, p. 96.

241,   22   *in itself." Captain's Death Bed*, p. 92.

241,   28   *in character." Partial Portraits*, p. 104.

241,   31   *with events." Collected Letters* II, p. 1,047.

242,   3   *simply is."* Garnett, *Letters from Joseph Conrad*, p. 258.

242,   6   *the years."* Virginia Woolf, *The Death of the Moth and Other Essays*, p. 104.

242,   10   *and universality,"* Joyce, *Portrait*, p. 173.

242,   22   *is nothing." Notes on Life and Letters*, p. 17.

242,   29   volume." *Collected Letters* I, p. 44. Cf. Conrad above, p. 86.

243,   3   *Joyce observed. Critical Writings*, p. 23.

243,   5   Mrs. Woolf. *Granite and Rainbow*, p. 16.

243,   7   *not heroic." A Personal Record*, p. xii.

243,   19   *as failures." Literary Reviews and Essays*, p. 192.

243,   27   *outwardly acknowledged." Under Western Eyes*, p. 54.

243,   29   *the journalist."* See Ellmann, *James Joyce*, p. 470.

243,   34   *his purpose." A Personal Record*, p. xviii.

244,   2   *art." Conrad's Prefaces*, p. 124.

244,   9   *with literature." My Brother's Keeper*, p. 121.

244,   12   a Tower." *Phoenix*, p. 731.

244,   19   *even epic." Last Essays*, p. 126.

245,   12   *accidents only." Life and Letters* I, p. 183.

245,   15   *of things."* Edel, *Selected Letters of Henry James*, p. 203.

245,   21   *surface." Notes on Life and Letters*, p. 22.

245,   25   *outer life." Collected Letters* I, p. 453.

245,   34   *General himself." Common Reader*, p. 252.

246,   15   *their index." Personal Writings*, p. 124.

246,   23   *themselves." Common Reader*, p. 252.

246,   26   *social individuals." Phoenix*, p. 763.

247,   2   *any more." Collected Letters* II, p. 940.

247,   11   *personal relations." Granite and Rainbow*, p. 19.

247,   15   *have it." Common Reader*, p. 214.

248,   9   *outside." Collected Letters* II, p. 905.

248,   11   *beneath it." Contemporary Writers*, p. 122.

248,   24   *said Joyce. Critical Writings*, p. 41.

248,   26   *universe itself." Collected Letters* II, p. 994.

248,   33   *of Dante." Critical Writings*, p. 101.

249,   3   *the novel." Phoenix*, p. 520.

249,   20   *of actuality."* Huxley, ed., *Letters of D. H. Lawrence*, p. 407.

249,   24   *of environment." Granite and Rainbow*, p. 18.

250,   1   *the thing." Critical Prefaces*, p. 67.

250,   8   *instinct" Phoenix*, p. 264.

250,   11   *of life." Collected Letters* I, p. 291.

250,   16   *a thought-adventure." Kangaroo*, p. 313.

250,   31   *these appearances." Contemporary Writers*, p. 122.

251,   9   *paste." Views and Reviews*, p. 234.

251,   13   *and brutality." Orlando*, p. 31.

251,   15   *nor magnanimous," Common Reader*, p. 215.

251,   17   *the ideal." Literary Reviews and Essays*, p. 146.

251,   24   *call life." Collected Letters* II, p. 851.

251,   28   *of creating," Studies in Classic American Literature*, p. 65.

251,   35   *Razumov?" Collected Letters* I, p. 155.

252,   2   *written."* See Witter Bynner, *Journey with Genius*, p. 274.

252,   5   *way through." Phoenix*, p. 520.

252,   13   *to contain, Letters* I, p. 167.

252,   15   *to contain. My Brother's Keeper*, p. 137.

253,   3   *the world." Portrait*, p. 297.

253,   30   *have seen." Letters* I, p. 30.

253,   33   *of us." Granite and Rainbow*, p. 44.

254,   4   *a 'purpose.' " Literary Reviews and Essays*, p. 147.

254,   7   *purpose." Reflections on the Death of a Porcupine*, p. 104.

254,   21   *the world." Critical Writings*, p. 89.

254,   24   *powerful imagination.*" *Common Reader, Second Series,*
             p. 257.

254,   35   *of* appreciation." *Critical Prefaces,* p. 65.

255,   4   *upon.*" *Collected Letters* I, p. 180.

255,   6   *the thing.*" *Personal Writings,* p. 124.

255,   8   *to observe.*" *Life,* p. 153.

255,   17   *and Dostoevski, Letters* II, p. 237.

255,   34   *facts.*" *Henry James and H. G. Wells,* p. 196.

255,   35   *of bricks.*" Brennecke, *Life of Thomas Hardy,* p. 6.

256,   14   *or belief.*" *Collected Letters* I, p. 395.

256,   17   *for poetry.*" *Granite and Rainbow,* p. 19.

256,   23   *his personages.*" *Life and Letters* I, p. 301.

256,   28   *characters.* See above, p. 122.

256,   31   *rhythmic form.*" *Collected Letters* I, p. 282.

257,   17   *"allotropic states,"* loc. cit.

257,   23   *or dies.*" *Collected Letters* I, p. 429.

257,   33   *of it.* See Givens, ed., *James Joyce: Two Decades of
             Criticism,* pp. 11–12.

258,   3   *want 'she.'* " *Writer's Diary,* p. 140.

258,   23   *invariably powerful.*" *Critical Writings,* p. 65.

258,   35   *human consciousness.*" *Phoenix,* p. 419.

259,   8   *human thought,*" *Writer's Diary,* p. 107.

260,   2   *of life. Common Reader, Second Series,* pp. 220 ff.

260,   9   *great abundance.*" See Pippett, *The Moth and the Star,*
             p. 254.

260,   27   *fighting spunk?*" *Collected Letters* II, p. 1,083.

261,   7   *of life.*" *Collected Letters* I, p. 291.

261,   14   *men . . .*" *Notes on Life and Letters,* p. 55.

261,   17   *human life.*" *Collected Letters* I, p. 411.

261,   33   *strangest adventures.*" *To the Lighthouse,* p. 96.

262,   3   *wrote indignantly. Phoenix,* p. 517.

262,   19   *the conscious?*" See Ellmann, *Joyce,* p. 450.

262,   28   *sham psychology.*" *Writer's Diary,* p. 41.

263,   10   *of conception.*" Huxley, *Letters of D. H. Lawrence,* p.
             407.

263,   16   *Picasso.*" *The Moment and Other Essays,* p. 173.

263, 26   *are many." The Plumed Serpent*, p. 359.

263, 28   *seven colours."* Gorman, *James Joyce*, p. 137.

264,   1   *meaning." Partial Portraits*, p. 390.

264,   4   *their existence." Conrad's Prefaces*, p. 49.

264, 19   *of things." Phoenix*, p. 220.

264, 21   *of life." Notes on Novelists*, p. 292.

264, 24   *with it." Phoenix*, p. 525.

264, 30   *other parts." Partial Portraits*, p. 392.

264, 32   *at all." Reflections on the Death of a Porcupine*, p. 104.

265, 33   *a haze." Heart of Darkness* in *Three Stories* (London, 1946), p. 48.

266,   4   *conscious aim." Phoenix*, p. 479.

266,   9   *the balance." Phoenix*, p. 529.

266, 15   *synthetically." Critical Prefaces*, pp. 87–88.

266, 27   *symbol." Portrait*, pp. 249, 250.

266, 30   *the artist.* See above, pp. 84, 171–172.

266, 32   *[were] symbolic,"* See Gérard Jean-Aubry, *The Sea-Dreamer: A Definitive Biography of Joseph Conrad* (New York, 1957), p. 275.

266, 33   *fond symbolic," Collected Letters* II, p. 1,194.

267, 22   *faintly encouraging." Conrad's Prefaces*, p. 53.

268,   2   *remained "unuttered."* See above, p. 128.

268,   5   *inner life,"* See Marrot, *The Life and Letters of John Galsworthy*, p. 509.

268,   7   *veiled greatness." Life and Letters* II, p. 292.

268, 27   *to another"* Stephen Hero, p. 40.

269,   2   *of existence." Conrad's Prefaces*, pp. 153–154.

269,   5   *own person." Granite and Rainbow*, p. 66.

269,   9   *triumphantly convertible." Notes on Novelists*, pp. 184–185.

269, 12   *be beautiful." Critical Writings*, p. 147.

269, 17   *of reality." Classic American Literature*, p. 55.

269, 20   *the fact." Notes on Novelists*, p. 76.

269, 25   *a wrinkle."* Edel, *Henry James, The Future of the Novel*, p. 232.

269, 29   *same scene." Captain's Death Bed*, p. 56.

270,   2   *at Meredith." Life*, p. 370.

270,   28   *and strange.* James, *Literary Reviews and Essays*, p. 213.
270,   31   *small things."* Notes on Novelists, p. 272.
270,   35   *of literature."* Hawthorne, p. 107.
271,   2   *its own."* Stanislaus Joyce, *My Brother's Keeper*, p. 116.
271,   8   *entire expression."* Critical Prefaces, p. 144.
271,   10   *of satisfaction."* Stephen Hero, p. 97.
271,   13   *extension."* Notes on Novelists, p. 94.
271,   16   *of Othello."* Budgen, *James Joyce and The Making of Ulysses*, p. 179.
271,   20   *people."* Phoenix, p. 227.
271,   27   *or other."* Collected Letters I, p. 51.
271,   34   *grandest things."* Life, p. 171.
272,   1   *things credible."* Conrad's Prefaces, p. 154.
272,   3   *things human.* See William York Tindall, *A Reader's Guide to James Joyce* (New York, 1959), p. 223.
272,   21   *James wrote.* Letters I, p. 30.
272,   23   *imagination."* Phoenix, p. 559.
272,   26   *glow."* Conrad's Prefaces, pp. 153–154.
272,   31   *current combination."* Notes on Novelists, p. 113.
272,   35   *fact."* Captain's Death Bed, p. 56.
273,   25   *vision."* Death of the Moth, pp. 106–107.
273,   28   *moral sense."* Ibid., p. 106.
273,   35   *perfect measure."* Notes on Life and Letters, p. 48.
274,   10   *whole hog."* Phoenix, p. 535.
274,   23   *artist himself."* Notes on Life and Letters, p. 16.
274,   26   *them all."* Reflections on the Death of a Porcupine, p. 109.
274,   35   *inextricably mixed."* Death of the Moth, p. 101.
275,   12   *was reestablished.* Phoenix, p. 761.
275,   18   *Lawrence said.* Jessica Chambers, *D. H. Lawrence, A Personal Record*, p. 105.
275,   24   *internal."* Writer's Diary, p. 229.
275,   27   *the others."* Ibid., p. 248.
276,   9   *in nature."* Notes on Life and Letters, p. 30.
276,   14   *of time."* Phoenix, p. 527.
276,   28   *secret harmonies."* Henry James and H. G. Wells, p. 171.

276,   30   presence." *A Personal Record*, p. xiii.
277,   10   and taste." Edel, ed., *James, The Future of the Novel*, p. 41.
277,   11   and intensity" "The Lesson of Balzac," pp. 77–78.
277,   12   "studied compactness." *Literary Reviews and Essays*, p. 215.
277,   17   immense intensity." *Writer's Diary*, p. 191.
277,   25   be themselves." *Granite and Rainbow*, p. 138.
277,   34   human being." *Phoenix*, p. 243.
278,   4   life." See Ellmann, *James Joyce*, p. 524.
278,   6   of Cézanne. *Phoenix*, p. 570.
278,   9   to facts." *Virginia Woolf & Lytton Strachey Letters*, p. 146.
279,   8   intention." *Life and Letters* II, p. 96.
279,   14   these functions." *Critical Writings*, p. 43.
279,   21   prime sensibility." James, *Critical Prefaces*, p. 45.
280,   23   and thanks," *Stephen Hero*, pp. 78–79.
280,   26   its ideals" *Ibid.*, p. 78.
280,   31   life arose." Harry T. Moore, ed., *D. H. Lawrence, Sex, Literature and Censorship* (New York, 1953), p. 116.
280,   35   for us." *Ibid.*, p. 117.
281,   5   and colour." *Conrad's Prefaces*, p. 54.
281,   18   of things." *Collected Letters* I, p. 51.
281,   19   giving in" *Collected Letters* I, p. 152.
281,   25   pessimistic intention." *Conrad to a Friend*, p. 114.
281,   27   for despair." *Personal Record*, p. 92.
281,   31   of pessimisms." *Stephen Hero*, p. 40.
281,   34   ignoble meaning." *My Brother's Keeper*, p. 121.
282,   24   transcends criticism." *Critical Writings*, p. 42.
282,   27   to criticize." *Common Reader*, p. 235.
282,   34   satisfaction." *Phoenix*, p. 477.
283,   11   beyond itself." *Critical Writings*, p. 144.
283,   15   and completes." *Granite and Rainbow*, p. 116.
283,   31   of art." *Notebooks*, p. 111.
283,   33   only thing." *Ibid.*, p. 112.
283,   35   of life." *Writer's Diary*, p. 47.

284,   2   *its cheapness." Ibid.,* p. 56.

284,   14   *the same." Granite and Rainbow,* p. 123.

284,   16   *style. Writer's Diary,* p. 57.

284,   18   *he cried. Notebooks,* p. 135.

284,   21   *things." Ibid.,* p. 166.

284,   29   *all life." Ibid.,* p. 111.

284,   32   *of life." Ibid.,* p. 135.

285,   13   *as possible."* Ada Lawrence, *Early Life of D. H. Lawrence,* p. 209.

285,   16   *humanity." Conrad's Prefaces,* p. 50.

285,   25   *human fellowship." Ibid.,* p. 157.

285,   28   *loving observation." Notes on Life and Letters,* p. 10.

285,   31   *seldom touched." Letters* II, p. 173.

286,   2   *and prejudices." Notes on Life and Letters,* p. 9.

286,   5   *make linear." Writer's Diary,* pp. 238–239.

286,   15   *and smiles." Collected Letters* II, p. 827.

286,   17   *for tragedy," Last Essays,* p. 129.

286,   20   *fellow creatures." Ibid.,* p. 130.

286,   26   *showing-off," Collected Letters* I, p. 264.

286,   27   *personal conceit," Phoenix,* p. 566.

286,   34   *and restricting?" Writer's Diary,* p. 22.

287,   16   *"indifferent sympathy." Critical Writings,* p. 127.

287,   19   *a grin." A Personal Record,* p. xix.

288,   4   *with us." Notes on Novelists,* p. 399.

288,   7   *his calling." Notes on Life and Letters,* p. 9.

288,   14   *do.' " My Brother's Keeper,* p. 131.

288,   17   *his art." Notes on Life and Letters,* p. 21.

288,   26   *and unknown." Ibid.,* p. 22.

288,   29   *human contact." Collected Letters* I, p. 258.

289,   5   *the ego" Collected Letters* II, p. 852.

289,   7   *sensitive self," Collected Letters* I, p. 94.

289,   8   *affection" Collected Letters* II, p. 1,140.

289,   12   *this earth." A Personal Record,* p. 9.

289,   24   *fiction.* See above, pp. 137, 225.

289,   27   *work menially."* Lawrence, *The White Peacock* (London, 1911), pp. 42–43.

289, 35 *thought small."* Common Reader, p. 213.

290,   8 *and affections.* See above, p. 38.

290, 12 *of everything."* Letters II, p. 81.

290, 17 *deflect mortality."* Collected Letters I, p. 34.

290, 20 *and women."* Collected Letters II, p. 1,045.

290, 35 *of others,"* Edel, ed., *James, The Future of the Novel,* p. 33.

291,   1 *of ourselves" Ibid.,* p. 96.

291,   3 *undiscovered countries,"* A Personal Record, p. 108.

291,   6 *of reality."* Notes on Life and Letters, p. 13.

291, 34 *novelist."* Common Reader, Second Series, p. 213.

292,   7 *circumambient universe."* Phoenix, p. 527.

292, 14 *the world."* A Personal Record, p. 108.

292, 18 *matière d'art,"* See Jean-Aubry, *The Sea-Dreamer,* p. 236.

292, 33 *religious rite."* Life and Letters II, p. 89.

Index

Aaron's Rod, 135, 175
Aeschylus, 47, 117
Almayer's Folly, 75
Ambassadors, The, 7
American, The, 25
Anna of the Five Towns, 147
Antigone, 190
Aquinas, Saint Thomas, 110, 119, 120, 121, 269
Arcadia, 186
Aristotle, 120, 128
Arnold, Matthew, 291; Hardy on, 63; Joyce on, 140–141; Woolf on, 228
Augustine, Saint, 109, 267
Aurora Leigh, 206
Austen, Jane, James on, 24; Woolf on, 187, 192, 194, 196, 197, 199, 204, 208, 213, 216, 224
Awkward Age, The, 29

Balzac, Honoré de, James on, 5, 7, 9, 12, 13, 15–16, 18–19, 21, 22, 24–25, 31, 32, 34, 272, 277; Joyce on, 110, 248; Lawrence on, 146, 151, 177, 254
Barnes, William, 64, 65
Bennett, Arnold, 96–97; James on, 25, 255; Conrad on, 96, 104;

Lawrence on, 147, 163, 250; Woolf on, 188–189, 198, 201, 208, 213, 227, 245, 250, 255
Besant, Sir Walter, 10–11
Bible, 42, 46, 292
Blake, William, 116, 120–121, 144
Bleak House, 88
Bouvard et Pécuchet, 33
Braque, Georges, 278
Brecht, Bertolt, 62
Brontë, Emily, Joyce on, 125; Lawrence on, 144; Woolf on, 202, 212, 213, 215, 216, 277
Brothers Karamazov, The, 87
Browne, Sir Thomas, 204
Browning, Robert, 32, 206, 228
Bruno, Giordano, 109, 133
Budgen, Frank, 123, 136, 138
Bulwer-Lytton, Edward George Earle, 1st Baron Lytton, 85, 137
Bunyan, John, 12, 144, 240, 265
Butler, Samuel, 150

Carlyle, Thomas, 260, 291
Catilina, 110
Cervantes, Miguel de, 216
Cézanne, Paul, 123, 258, 263; Lawrence on, 156, 162, 278
Chamber Music, 114

Chance, 104
Chaucer, Geoffrey, 228
Chekhov, Anton Pavlovich, 191, 192, 241
Christmas Carol, A, 150
Congreve, William, 193
Conrad, Joseph, x–xi, 107, 108, 115, 132, 142, 143, 146, 163, 184, 228, 230–293; and Edward Garnett, 69, 76, 90–91, 94, 95; on The Secret Agent, 71, 83–84, 87, 95–96; on Dostoevski, 71, 87, 101, 233–234; on Tolstoi, 71, 233–234; H. L. Mencken on, 71; on Daudet, 72, 80, 97; on English novels, 73, 74, 92–93, 94, 95, 100; on French novels, 73, 74, 92–93, 94, 95; on Green Mansions, 73; on Galsworthy, 74, 85, 96, 100, 268, 286; on Dickens, 74, 88, 100; on Thackeray, 74, 93, 100; on Flaubert, 74; on Maupassant, 74, 90, 93, 98, 103, 276; on Almayer's Folly, 74–75, 104; on Scott, 75; on George Eliot, 75; on "Youth," 76; on "Heart of Darkness," 76, 233; on "The End of the Tether," 76, 87, 92; on Nostromo, 76; on Wells, 79, 90, 94; on The Shadow-Line, 79, 100; on James, 79, 82–83, 100, 102, 230; on Marryat, 80, 82; on The Nigger of the "Narcissus," 80, 83, 100; on Cooper, 82, 88, 261; on Edward Noble, 82, 86; on Bulwer-Lytton, 85; on Stevenson, 85, 91; on "Falk," 86; on Crane, 87; on Lord Jim, 87; on The Brothers Karamazov, 87; on Bleak House, 88; on Don Quixote, 88; on The Man of Property, 89, 96; on The Rescue, 89; on Shaw, 90; and Wordsworth, 91, 101; on "The Secret Sharer," 95; on The Outcast, 95; on Under Western Eyes, 96; on Strife, 96; on Bennett, 96, 104; on Turgenev, 101, 273; and Richardson, 101; and Defoe, 101; on Chance, 104; on Within the

Tides, 104; on Proust, 105, 268; Woolf on, 195; Lawrence on, 163, 251–252, 281; on To Let, 268; on the Russian novel, 280
Cooper, James Fenimore, Conrad on, 82, 88, 261; Lawrence on, 150, 151–152, 170, 269
Crabbe, George, 133
Crane, Stephen, 87

D'Annunzio, Gabriele, James on, 11, 21, 22, 23, 37, 270; Joyce on, 110, 113
Dante Alighieri, 116
Daudet, Alphonse, 245; James on, 20; Conrad on, 72, 80, 97
David Copperfield, 28
Death of Ivan Ilyich, The, 71
Deerslayer, The, 151, 170
Defoe, Daniel, 239, 244, 265; and Conrad, 101; Joyce on, 108; Woolf on, 192–193, 199, 201, 203, 209, 213, 219
De Quincey, Thomas, 210
Derain, André, 263
Dickens, Charles, 143; James on, 5–6, 9, 20, 36; Conrad on, 74, 88, 100; Lawrence on, 145–146, 150; Woolf on, 185–186, 195, 201
Disraeli, Benjamin, 137
Don Quixote, 88, 116, 220
Dostoevski, Fyodor, Conrad on, 71, 87, 101, 233–234; Joyce on, 138; Lawrence on, 145, 147, 151, 162–163, 173, 176, 234, 240; Woolf on, 197–198, 201, 218, 222, 245
Dreiser, Theodore, 255
Dubliners, Joyce on, 112, 114, 120, 138, 139, 141, 252
Dumas, Alexandre (père), 57
Dynasts, The, 46

Éducation sentimentale, L', 15
Einstein, Albert, 158, 161, 171
Electra, 190
Eliot, George, James on, 8, 14, 19; Conrad on, 75; Lawrence on, 150, 175; Woolf on, 185, 186, 194, 195, 221, 222, 225, 282

Elle et Lui, 38
"End of the Tether, The," 76
Enemy of the People, An, 117
Erewhon, 150
Eugénie Grandet, 177

"Falk," 86
Far from the Madding Crowd, 64
Faust, 116
Fielding, Henry, Hardy on, 44, 62; Lawrence on, 275
Finnegans Wake, 252, 259; Joyce on, 123–124, 129, 138, 257
Flaubert, Gustave, xii, 143; James on, 15, 20, 29, 33, 254, 269, 271; Conrad on, 74; Joyce on, 120, 138; Lawrence on, 145, 147, 148, 149, 152, 153, 166, 173, 174, 175, 177, 178, 180, 181, 240, 281, 284; Woolf on, 209, 218
Forster, E. M., 149; Lawrence on, 155, 166; Woolf on, 188, 194, 201, 208, 212, 216
France, Anatole, 180
Freud, Sigmund, 167, 262
Fuoco, Il, 113

Galsworthy, John, Conrad on, 74, 85, 96, 100, 268, 286; Lawrence on, 163, 182, 248; Woolf on, 198, 201, 208, 213, 227
Garnett, Edward, and Conrad, 69, 76, 90–91, 94, 95; and Lawrence, 156, 159, 173, 175
Ghosts, 121
Golden Bowl, The, 32
Goldsmith, Oliver, Joyce on, 120, 132–133, 137, 138, 142; Woolf on, 191
Green Mansions, 73

Hamlet, 16, 22, 116
Hand of Ethelberta, The, 42, 55
Hardy, Thomas, ix–xi, 69, 107, 184, 230–293; on *Marmion*, 40; on Tennyson, 40; on the Bible, 42, 46; on Meredith, 42, 270; on *The Hand of Ethelberta*, 42, 55, 62; on *The Return of the Native*,

43; on *The Woodlanders*, 43, 54; on *Jude the Obscure*, 43, 44, 45, 49, 61; and Poe, 44; and Melville, 44; and Howells, 44, 302n; on James, 44, 64, 230, 269–270; on Scott, 44; on Fielding, 44, 62; on Zola, 44, 57; on *Tess of the d'Urbervilles*, 45; on *The Dynasts*, 46; on *Under the Greenwood Tree*, 48–49; on Dumas père, 57; on Radcliffe, 57; on Sir Henry Irving, 62; and Thackeray, 62; and Trollope, 62; and Brecht, 62; and Matthew Arnold, 63; on Richardson, 64; on *Far from the Madding Crowd*, 64; on Barnes, 64, 65; on *The Mayor of Casterbridge*, 65; Lawrence on, 148, 149, 152, 153, 155, 158, 160, 174, 177, 230; Woolf on, 185, 188, 201, 213, 215, 216, 230, 254; James on, 230; on Aldous Huxley, 241; on the French novel, 253; on Dreiser, 255
Hauptmann, Gerhart, 285
Hawthorne, Nathaniel, 5, 38
"Heart of Darkness," 76
Homer, 8, 116, 122
Howells, William Dean, 9, 44, 302n
Hudson, W. H., 73
Hugo, Victor, 180
Huxley, Aldous, 149, 241

Ibsen, Henrik, Joyce on, 110, 111, 116, 121, 122, 124, 128, 131, 133–135, 256, 268, 271; Lawrence on, 163, 280; Woolf on, 213, 216
Iliad, 136
Invisible Man, The, 79
Irving, Sir Henry, 62
Italo Svevo, 125

Jacob's Room, 207, 215, 278
James, Henry, ix–xi, 40, 107, 108, 115, 132, 142, 143, 146, 184, 228, 230–293; on Zola, 5, 20, 21, 32, 33, 37, 281; on Balzac, 5, 7,

9, 12, 13, 15–16, 18–19, 21, 22, 24–25, 31, 32, 34, 272, 277; on Hawthorne, 38; on Scott, 5, 32; on Thackeray, 5, 28; on Dickens, 5–6, 9, 20, 36; on Sand, 5, 38, 269; on Trollope, 6, 12, 17, 20; on Wells, 6, 28; on Meredith, 6, 8, 29; on Stevenson, 6, 8, 10–11, 38; on Turgenev, 8, 14, 15, 21, 29, 33, 243, 269; on George Eliot, 8, 14, 19; on the English novel, 8–9, 20, 25; on the French novel, 8–9, 20, 21, 23; on the American novel, 9; on Howells, 9, 33, 253, 277; and Jewett, 10; and Besant, 10–11; on Maupassant, 10, 12, 14, 21; on Stendhal, 11, 36–37; on D'Annunzio, 11, 21, 22, 23, 37, 270; on Flaubert, 15, 20, 29, 33, 254, 269, 271; on The Spoils of Poynton, 16, 27; on Serao, 17, 37, 38; on Daudet, 20; on Tolstoi, 22, 255; on Austen, 24; on Bennett, 25, 255; on Jane Eyre, 28; on David Copperfield, 28; on Robinson Crusoe, 28; on Lord Ormont, 29; on What Maisie Knew, 31, 37; on The Golden Bowl, 32; on Browning, 32; on Elle et Lui, 38; Hardy on, 44, 64, 230, 269; Conrad on, 79, 82–83, 100, 102, 230; Woolf on, 195, 207, 218–219, 230, 240, 284; on Tess of the d'Urbervilles, 230; on Dostoevski, 255; on Salammbô, 269; on La Tentation de Saint-Antoine, 269; Lawrence on, 283

Jane Eyre, 28, 221
Jewett, Sarah Orne, 10
Jolas, Eugene, 129
Jonson, Ben, 43
Joyce, James, ix–xi, 143, 146, 184, 228, 230–293; on Defoe, 108; and Saint Augustine, 109, 267; and Bruno, 109, 133; on Balzac, 110, 248; and Yeats, 110, 114, 252–253; and Saint Thomas Aquinas, 110, 119, 120, 121, 269; and Ibsen, 110, 111, 116, 121, 122, 124, 128, 131, 133–135,

256, 268, 271; on Kipling, 110, 113, 125; on Tolstoi, 110, 119, 137; on D'Annunzio, 110, 113; on Renan, 110; on Newman, 110; and Pound, 111; on the English novel, 111–112, 137–138; on the French novel, 111–112, 252; on Dubliners, 112, 114, 120, 138, 139, 141, 252; on Ulysses, 112, 123–124, 138–139, 140, 257; and Wyndham Lewis, 112; on Mangan, 114; and Chamber Music, 114; on Blake, 116, 120–121; on Homer, 116, 122; on Hamlet, 116; on Don Quixote, 116; on Dante, 116; on Faust, 116; on Aeschylus, 117; on An Enemy of the People, 117; on Shakespeare, 107, 118; on Turgenev, 119; on Flaubert, 120, 138; and Aristotle, 120, 128; on The Vicar of Wakefield, 120, 137, 142; on Ghosts, 121; and Budgen, 123, 136, 138; on Finnegans Wake, 123–124, 129, 138, 257; on Stephen Hero, 123, 131; on French literature, 125; and Italo Svevo, 125; on Emily Brontë, 125; and Eugene Jolas, 129; and James Stephens, 129; on Maupassant, 131–132; on Goldsmith, 132–133, 137, 138; on Crabbe, 133; on the Odyssey, 136; on the Iliad, 136; and brother Stanislaus, 137, 138–139, 141; on Meredith, 137, 289; on Bulwer-Lytton, 137; on Disraeli, 137; on the Russian novel, 137, 138, 252; on Dostoevski, 138; on Jean Jacques Rousseau, 138; and A Portrait of the Artist as a Young Man, 138, 141; and Spenser, 140; and Milton, 140; and Matthew Arnold, 140–141; Woolf on, 221, 224, 227, 231, 247, 250, 251, 286; on Lady Chatterley's Lover, 230; Lawrence on, 230–231, 250, 252, 262, 281; on When We Dead Awaken, 271; on Proust, 278

Joyce, Stanislaus, 137, 138–139, 141

Jude the Obscure, 62; Hardy on, 43, 44, 45, 49, 60–61; Lawrence on, 159

Kangaroo, 161, 172, 175, 250
King Lear, 22
Kipling, Rudyard, 110, 113, 125
Kreutzer Sonata, The, 71

Lady Chatterley's Lover, Joyce on, 230; Lawrence on, 148, 149, 150, 171–172; Woolf on, 251
Lawrence, D. H., x–xi, 142, 184, 228, 230–293; on *The Picture of Dorian Gray*, 144; on *Wuthering Heights*, 144; on Maupassant, 144, 151–152, 180; on Dostoevski, 145, 147, 151, 162–163, 173, 176, 234, 240; on Flaubert, 145, 147, 148, 149, 152, 153, 166, 173, 174, 175, 177, 178, 180, 181, 240, 281, 284; on Dickens, 145–146; on Balzac, 146, 151, 177, 254; on Wells, 146, 179, 246, 250, 271, 281; on *The Rainbow*, 147, 149, 158, 172, 175; on Bennett, 147, 163, 250; on *Anna of the Five Towns*, 147; on the Russian novel, 147, 151–152, 162–163, 172–173, 179, 280, 283; on Rozanov, 147; on Tolstoi, 147, 151, 162–163, 173, 174, 177; on Hardy, 148, 149, 152, 153, 155, 158, 160, 174, 177, 230; on *Lady Chatterley's Lover*, 148, 149, 150, 171–172; on Wilde, 149; on Poe, 149, 158; on Aldous Huxley, 149; on *A Passage to India*, 149, 155; on Forster, 149, 155, 166; on *Women in Love*, 150, 158, 159, 164, 166, 175; on *The White Peacock*, 150, 181; on Scott, 150; on Stevenson, 150; on Butler, 150; on *A Christmas Carol*, 150; on *Silas Marner*, 150; on Cooper, 150, 151–152, 269; on *The Pioneers*, 150; on the French novel, 151–152, 172–173, 174–175, 177, 178, 179, 181; on Zola, 151, 168; on *The Deer-*

slayer, 151, 170; on Turgenev, 151, 162–163; on the Anglo-American novel, 151–152, 177; on Verga, 153, 154, 159, 168–169, 277; and Yeats, 153; and Synge, 153, 180; and *The Plumed Serpent*, 154, 175; and Murry, 155, 157; on Melville, 155; on *St. Mawr*, 155; on *Aaron's Rod*, 135, 175; and Cézanne, 156, 162, 278; and Garnett, 156, 159, 173, 175; and Einstein, 158, 161, 171; on *Sons and Lovers*, 159, 175; on *Jude the Obscure*, 159; on *Kangaroo*, 161, 172, 175, 250; on Conrad, 163, 251–252, 281; on Plato, 163, 280; on Galsworthy, 163, 182, 246; on Ibsen, 163, 281; on Strindberg, 163; on Van Gogh, 165, 276; on Post-Impressionists, 165; on *The World of William Clissold*, 166; on Whitman, 167, 174; on Freud, 167; on Swinburne, 169; on Mann, 175, 176, 178, 181; F. R. Leavis on, 175; on *Eugénie*, 177; on *The Man Who Died*, 179; and Carlo Linati, 179; on Anatole France, 180; on Sophocles, 180; on Hugo, 180; Woolf on, 208–209, 223, 231, 240, 241, 251; Joyce on, 230; on Joyce, 230–231, 250, 252, 262, 281; on *The Pickwick Papers*, 244; on *Two on a Tower*, 244; on Proust, 250, 262; on Dorothy Richardson, 262; on *Tono-Bungay*, 271; on George Eliot, 275; on Fielding, 275; on Matisse, 278; on Braque, 278; on the Bible, 292
Leavis, F. R., 44, 175
Lewis, Sinclair, 188
Lewis, Wyndham, 112
Linati, Carlo, 179
Lord Jim, 87
Lord Ormont, 29
Lubbock, Percy, 218

Madame Bovary, 120
Man from the North, The, 96

Mangan, James Clarence, 114
Mann, Thomas, 175, 176, 178, 181
Man of Property, The, 89
Man Who Died, The, 179
Marmion, 40
Marryat, Frederick, 80, 82
Matisse, Henri, 263, 278
Maupassant, Guy de, 143; James on, 10, 12, 14, 21; Conrad on, 74, 90, 93, 98, 103, 276; Joyce on, 131–132; Lawrence on, 144, 151–152, 180; Woolf on, 203, 209, 219
Mayor of Casterbridge, The, 53, 65
Melville, Herman, Hardy on, 44; Lawrence on, 155; Woolf on, 213, 215, 216, 277
Mencken, H. L., 71
Meredith, George, 284; James on, 8, 29; Hardy on, 42, 270; Joyce on, 137, 289; Woolf on, 185, 186, 188, 190, 193, 201, 204, 210, 214, 215, 222, 224–225, 289
Milton, John, 16
Moby Dick, 213
Montaigne, Michel Eyquem de, 213
Moore, George, 189, 218
Mrs. Dalloway, 204, 215
Murry, John Middleton, 155, 157

Newman, John Henry, Cardinal, 110
Nigger of the "Narcissus," The, 80, 83, 100
Noble, Edward, 82, 86
Nostromo, 76

Odyssey, 136
Orlando, 204, 210, 213
Othello, 271
Our Mutual Friend, 5–6
Outcast of the Islands, The, 95

Passage to India, A, 149, 155
Pater, Walter, 267
Peacock, Thomas Love, 201, 204, 210, 262
Picasso, Pablo, 123, 263
Pickwick Papers, The, 244

Picture of Dorian Gray, The, 144
Pilgrim's Progress, The, 240
Pioneers, The, 150
Plato, 163, 280
Plumed Serpent, The, 154, 175
Poe, Edgar Allan, 44, 149, 158, 240
Portrait of the Artist as a Young Man, A, 141, 238
Pound, Ezra, 111
Proust, Marcel, 82, 262; Conrad on, 105, 268; Lawrence on, 250, 262; Woolf on, 190, 220, 223, 250, 263; Joyce on, 278

Radcliffe, Ann, 57, 188
Rainbow, The, Lawrence on, 147, 149, 158, 172, 175; Woolf on, 231
Renan, Joseph Ernest, 110
Rescue, The, 89
Return of the Native, The, 43
Reverberator, The, 64
Richardson, Dorothy, Woolf on, 250, 286; Lawrence on, 262
Richardson, Samuel, 44, 244; Hardy on, 64
Robinson Crusoe, 28
Rousseau, Jean Jacques, 138
Rozanov, Vasiliy, 147

St. Mawr, 155
Salammbô, 269
Sand, George, 5, 38, 269
Scott, Sir Walter, James on, 5, 32; Hardy on, 44; Conrad on, 75; Lawrence on, 150; Woolf on, 187, 191, 192, 196, 197, 199, 220, 224
Secret Agent, The, 71
"Secret Sharer, The," 95
Serao, Matilde, 17, 37, 38
Shadow-Line, The, 79
Shakespeare, William, 46, 47, 184; Joyce on, 107, 118; Woolf on, 228
Shaw, George Bernard, 90
Sidney, Sir Philip, 186, 196
Silas Marner, 150

Smollett, Tobias, 239, 244
Sons and Lovers, 159, 175
Sophocles, 180, 184
Spenser, Edmund, 140
Spoils of Poynton, The, 16, 27
Stendhal (Marie Henri Beyle), 11, 36–37
Stephen Hero, 123, 131
Stephens, James, 129
Sterne, Laurence, Woolf on, 185, 191, 201, 204, 208, 210
Stevenson, Robert Louis, 53; James on, 6, 8, 10–11, 38; Conrad on, 55, 91; Woolf on, 196
Strife, 96
Strindberg, August, 163
Swinburne, Algernon Charles, 169
Synge, John Millington, 153, 180

Taine, Hippolyte Adolphe, 59
Tennyson, Alfred, Lord, 40
Tentation de Saint Antoine, La, 120, 269
Tess of the d'Urbervilles, 45, 62, 230
Thackeray, William Makepeace, 62; James on, 5, 28; Conrad on, 74, 93, 100
To Let, 268
Tolstoi, Count Leo, James on, 22, 255; Conrad on, 71, 233–234; Joyce on, 110, 119, 137; Lawrence on, 147, 151, 162–163, 173, 174, 177; Woolf on, 205, 209, 215, 220, 222, 245
Tono-Bungay, 271
Tory Lover, The, 10
To the Lighthouse, 204, 210
Tristram Shandy, 217
Trollope, Anthony, 62; James on, 6, 12, 17, 20; Woolf on, 204, 209, 219
Trumpet Major, The, 43, 53
Turgenev, Ivan Sergeyevich, James on, 8, 14, 15, 21, 29, 33, 243, 269; Conrad on, 101, 273; Joyce on, 119; Lawrence on, 151, 162–163; Woolf on, 193, 201, 205, 207, 213, 216–217, 272
Two on a Tower, 244

Ulysses, Joyce on, 112, 123–124, 138–139, 140, 257; Woolf on, 221, 231, 251
Under the Greenwood Tree, 48–49, 53
Under Western Eyes, 96

Van Gogh, Vincent, 165, 276
Verga, Giovanni, Lawrence on, 153, 154, 159, 168–169, 277
Vicar of Wakefield, The, 120, 137, 142, 191
Vie, Une, 12

War and Peace, 209
Waves, The, Woolf on, 207, 211, 212, 217, 257–258, 275
Wells, H. G., 143; James on, 6, 28; Conrad on, 79, 90, 94; Lawrence on, 146, 179, 246, 250, 271, 281; Woolf on, 188, 198, 201, 208, 213, 227, 245, 250, 255
What Maisie Knew, 31
When We Dead Awaken, 271
White Peacock, The, 150, 181
Whitman, Walt, 167
Wilde, Oscar, 149
Wings of the Dove, The, 218
Within the Tides, 104
Women in Love, Lawrence on, 150, 158, 159, 164, 166, 175
Woodlanders, The, 43, 54
Woolf, Virginia, ix–xi, 230–293; on Sterne, 185, 191, 201, 204, 208, 210; on George Eliot, 185, 186, 194, 195, 221, 222, 225, 282; on Meredith, 185, 186, 188, 190, 193, 201, 204, 210, 213, 215, 222, 224–225, 289; on Hardy, 185, 188, 201, 213, 215, 216, 230, 254; on Dickens, 185–186, 195, 201; on Arcadia, 186; on Scott, 187, 192, 196, 197, 199, 220, 224; on Austen, 187, 192, 194, 196, 197, 199, 204, 208, 213, 216, 224; on the English novel, 187–188, 197–198, 199, 209, 221–222, 224, 226–227, 246; on Sinclair Lewis, 188; on Wells,

188, 198, 201, 208, 213, 227, 245, 250, 255; on Bennett, 188–189, 198, 201, 208, 213, 227, 245, 250, 255; on Radcliffe, 188; on Forster, 188, 194, 201, 208, 212, 216; on George Moore, 189, 218; on *Electra*, 190; on *Antigone*, 190; on Proust, 190, 220, 223, 250, 263; on Chekhov, 191, 192, 241; on Goldsmith, 191; on *The Vicar of Wakefield*, 191; on Defoe, 192–193, 199, 201, 203, 209, 213, 219; on Turgenev, 193, 201, 205, 207, 213, 216–217, 272; on Congreve, 193; on Conrad, 195; on James, 195, 207, 213, 218–219, 230, 240, 284; on Stevenson, 196; on Dostoevski, 197–198, 201, 218, 222, 245; on the Russian novel, 197–198, 199, 209, 221–222, 224, 226–227; on Galsworthy, 198, 201, 208, 213, 227; on Peacock, 201, 204, 210; on Emily Brontë, 202, 212, 213, 215, 216, 277; on Maupassant, 203, 209, 219; on Trollope, 204, 209, 219; on Sir Thomas Browne, 204; on *Mrs. Dalloway*, 204, 215; on *To the Lighthouse*, 204, 210; on *Orlando*, 204, 210, 213; on Tolstoi, 205, 215, 220, 222, 245; on *Aurora Leigh*, 206; on *The Waves*, 207, 211, 212, 217, 257–258, 275; on *The Years*, 207, 212, 213, 224, 275; on *Jacob's Room*, 207, 215, 278; on Lawrence, 208–209, 223, 240, 241, 251; on the French novel, 209, 216; on Flaubert, 209, 218; on *War and Peace*, 209; on De Quincey, 210; on Ibsen, 213, 216; on Montaigne, 213; on Melville, 213, 215, 216, 277; on *Moby Dick*, 213; on *Wuthering Heights*, 213; on Cervantes, 216; on *Tristram Shandy*, 217; on *The Wings of the Dove*, 218; on Lubbock, 218; on Wordsworth, 218, 228; on *Don Quixote*, 220; on Stendhal, 220; on *Ulysses*, 221, 231, 251; on Joyce, 221, 224, 227, 231, 247, 250, 251, 286; on Matthew Arnold, 228; on Chaucer, 228; on Shakespeare, 228; on Browning, 228; on *The Rainbow*, 231; on Dorothy Richardson, 250, 286; on *Lady Chatterley's Lover*, 251; on Dreiser, 255

Wordsworth, William, 91, 101, 228, 287, 290, 291; Woolf on, 218

World of William Clissold, The, 166

Wuthering Heights, 144, 213

Years, The, Woolf on, 207, 212, 213, 224, 275

Yeats, William Butler, and Joyce, 110, 114, 252–253; and Lawrence, 153

"Youth," 76

Zola Emile, James on, 5, 20, 21, 32, 33, 37, 281; Hardy on, 44, 57; Lawrence on, 151, 168